BORIS
GODUNOV

RUSLAN G. SKRYNNIKOV

BORIS
GODUNOV

Edited and Translated
by
Hugh F. Graham

Academic International Press

1982

THE RUSSIAN SERIES/Volume 35

Ruslan G. Skrynnikov, *Boris Godunov*
Translation of *Boris Godunov* (Moscow, 1978)

ISBN: O-87569-046-7

Composition by Jayne Berndsen

Title page by King & Queen Press

Illustrations courtesy of the author

Printed in the United States of America

*A list of Academic International Press publications
is found at the end of this volume.*

ACADEMIC INTERNATIONAL PRESS
Box 1111 Gulf Breeze FL 32561

CONTENTS

EDITOR'S INTRODUCTION

Professor Ruslan Grigorevich Skrynnikov has established an enviable reputation as a leading authority on the history of Russia in the six- teenth century, the field he teaches at Leningrad State University. He also has made a commitment to bring serious history to the atten- tion of the general public. To further this aim he lectures to numerous groups and has written scholarly works on early Russian history in a popular format. The present volume, one in his series, sheds new light on an epoch, the treatment of which in the past has been marred by sensationalism. It is appropriate to comment on certain aspects of the narrative.

The first chapter supplies background and discusses the reign of Ivan the Terrible. The tsar had divided Russia into an *oprichnina* (crown lands) which was a sprawling appanage he ruled without con- straint, and a *zemshchina* (the realm) which was the remainder of the realm administered in the traditional way by prominent boyars. The oprichnina had its own court, council, chanceries and army. The suspicious ruler needed new men he felt he could trust to staff them. The Godunov family's fortunes recently had been in decline but the oprichnina revived them. Boris' uncle obtained a high position in the royal retinue and was able to advance his nephew's interests. Boris avoided the capricious tsar's official displeasure, which might mean exile, confiscation of estates, or even death, and took advantage of his court service, which provided him with a valuable political education. Professor Skrynnikov disposes of persistent legends that Boris was of Tatar origin and illiterate.

Professor Skrynnikov emphasizes that a connection with the royal house was a passport to power. Keenly aware of this the Godunov family strove to forge such a link, an effort crowned with success when Boris' sister Irina was married to Fedor, Ivan's second son. The tsar's rash act—killing his elder son—cleared the way for the latter to succeed to the throne, and since Fedor was not in full possession of his faculties and was incapable of ruling chance seemed to have fur- nished Boris a splendid opportunity. However, Professor Skrynnikov points out that in spite of the marriage connection Boris' position was weaker than has often been supposed. He was neither president of a regency council Ivan had decreed should act in Fedor's name nor even a member of it. This explains why Godunov initially proceeded against leading figures like Prince Mstislavskii and the Shuiskii brothers. He wanted to eliminate members of the regency council who barred his way, and he quietly succeeded. He soon established an ascendancy over Fedor and became *de facto* head of the government. Professor Skrynnikov stresses the major role rumor played in shaping the course of events as soon as Godunov's star began to rise. Many unfounded stories and gossip eventually found their way into historical literature, were accepted as fact, and have been repeated over and over again from the seventeenth century to the present.

One of Boris' first accomplishments was to make the Moscow metropolitanate a patriarchal see, as churchmen had long craved. He devised an ingenious stratagem to outwit Jeremiah, the credulous patriarch of Constantinople. This achievement won him popularity and increased support. The chapter on this topic closes with a useful dissection of the theory of Moscow the Third Rome. It was a defensive ideology, designed merely to enhance Russia's status in the Orthodox hierarchy.

Professor Skrynnikov conducts a detailed analysis of the Uglich affair, central to any estimate of Godunov's character, and clearly demonstrates that young Prince Dmitrii, an epileptic, accidentally caused his own death. The Nagoi family was responsible for the riot and lynchings in Uglich and the later arson in Moscow. Boris was not involved in any way; in fact, Dmitrii's death was disadvantageous because rumor inevitably linked him to the deed. If Boris' complicity had been palpable he might well have been driven from office. In this connection Professor Skrynnikov plausibly argues that Boris formed no plans to acquire the throne himself until some six years later. The repressions he carried out in Uglich were motivated by fear, not anger.

A key chapter investigates the involved question of forbidden and fixed years, essential to any inquiry into the root causes of serfdom in Russia. This has been an issue of exceptional importance and concern to historians. Professor Skrynnikov has given a succinct outline of a very complex topic. He is a member of the nonjuridical school that considers circumstance created a particular climate to which government statutes responded by tying peasants to the land, although Koretskii[1] has shown that Soviet historians may hold other views. The primary concern was to shore up the tax base, which was threatened by increasing problems occurring during the two weeks before and after St. George's Day in November when peasants traditionally enjoyed the right (known technically as *departure*) to leave one landlord for another. Historians generally have held that the origin of serfdom should be sought in a rescript abrogating the right of St. George's Day issued by Tsar Ivan in 1581, but Professor Skrynnikov flies in the face of tradition, contending no such rescript ever was promulgated for the simple reason that one has never been found and later references to it are equivocal. This means Boris Godunov, not Tsar Ivan, was primarily responsible for establishing serfdom in Russia, but he was not deliberately scheming to deny peasants freedom of movement in an effort to curry favor with the lesser gentry (with the advancement of whose interests he has been identified); he was anxious merely to solve immediate financial problems. No one foresaw what the long range results of this measure to stabilize government revenues would be nor that temporary, transient expedients would become permanent and legally binding on the majority of the population.

The long chapter describing Boris' successive maneuvers to be elected tsar in the teeth of aristocratic opposition affords ample insights into this dramatic event, showing that Godunov had considerable support among the people, and was a master at organizing and manipulating street demonstrations and other agitational techniques. When these alone proved ineffective he ingeniously contrived the Serpukhov campaign to repel a nonexistent Tatar threat. The land assembly of 1598 that ratified his election was duly constituted and fully representative for its time.

Professor Skrynnikov shows that once Godunov came to power he recognized the futility of trying to rule effectively without the support of the boyars and awarded honors and conciliar rank to many of them. He could not, and so he did not, base his regime exclusively on the gentry. An intriguing question has been why in 1600 Boris moved against Bogdan Belskii and members of the Romanov family, claiming they were practising witchcraft, a serious charge at the time. He believes Boris' chronically poor health was the reason. Godunov was taken ill in 1599 and again the following year; rumor, his nemesis, immediately exaggerated his disability and created an artificial dynastic crisis. His rivals were encouraged to position themselves to struggle for the throne. Boris managed to survive by banishing (not executing) his opponents and was free for a short while to pursue his own policies before disaster overtook him. Professor Skrynnikov applauds Boris' building program, his interest in western technology and culture, and his concern for education, which was ahead of its time. He concludes that on balance Boris was a talented ruler, a fact contemporaries failed to appreciate until after the Time of Troubles.

Analyzing Godunov's debacle, Professor Skrynnikov develops a fundamental thesis—the commons encompassed Boris' ruin. The events of this period, in which Marxists detect evidence of the class struggle, have provided materials that have been enticing to Soviet historians, and Professor Skrynnikov has marshaled an impressive array of facts to buttress his opinion. This approach to Boris' misfortunes has often been ignored; the usual reasons given for his fall are opposition from boyars and princes or from chancery officials, False Dmitrii's cunning, the intrusion of Poland, or Boris' lack of moral qualities. It is stimulating to consider the present concept.

Boris was a victim of sheer bad luck. No sooner had he consolidated his position than Russia was assailed by protracted crop failures that induced hardship and ultimately caused famine and mass starvation. The government did what it could to alleviate suffering, but its relief measures were concentrated in the towns because Boris was trying to stimulate their growth and expand their capacity to pay taxes—his so-called "town edifice." Peasants received comparatively little assistance; the harsh fiscal policy was making their life more difficult, and the bondage statutes encouraged landlords to increase their exactions. Discontent festered in the countryside.

Fearing a mass rising, Boris reinstituted the right of peasant departure at St. George's Day in 1601, but, significantly enough, did not extend the provision to include estates belonging to great nobles and monasteries, crown lands, or the regions around Moscow. This serves as a clear indication that Boris now had become a champion of the upper strata of society, whose wrath he feared, but was not afraid to provoke the lesser gentry. His move failed to achieve its objective. Peasants interpreted his statutes to mean they might depart whenever they pleased, and they refused to render service for or pay imposts and fees either to the crown or their landlords. The latter, faced with ruin, retaliated swiftly with intensified repression. In 1603 the growing confrontation led to an outbreak of large scale violence, headed by a certain Khlopko, which engulfed the central region of the country and spilled over into Moscow. When Khlopko's capture and execution failed to abate the rioting the government realized it could not prevail without help from the lesser gentry. The price Boris had to pay for their support was annulment of the right of departure. Repeal of the statute understandably aroused the peasants further and created an even more volatile situation, especially when it is remembered that the cossacks in the southern borderland were in ferment. Boris constantly harassed them because he knew that their enclaves, which attracted runaway peasants, were a potent force for destabilizing the center. It is against this background that the career of the pretender must be set.

Professor Skrynnikov believes the Muscovite boyars sponsored the pretender. He was unquestionably the Yurii Otrepev the authorities claimed him to be, who had served in the course of his variegated career as a courtier in the Romanov establishment before Boris shattered its power in 1600. Yurii (Grigorii after he became a monk) had fascinating adventures. Using contemporary sources that previously have been largely ignored, Professor Skrynnikov traces Otrepev's activities in detail and shows that he was a man of skill, ability and tenacity, as well as a consummate opportunist, who while intriguing in Poland maintained contact with the cossacks. In desperation they turned to him as a feasible alternative to the hated Godunov; thus, False Dmitrii was given a chance to lead a broad-based peasant revolt, but his temperament made him reluctant to commit himself to such a course and he preferred to negotiate with his Polish patrons. This combination of factors spelled disaster for Boris and ruin for Russia.

Although Otrepev promised the king of Poland lavish awards of Russian territory if he should succeed, the royal council was divided as to the wisdom of backing a pretender and at best he received lukewarm support. The small mercenary army he recruited in Poland was defeated, but Godunov's commanders were slow to follow up their victory. This respite gave peasants and cossacks time to rally to Otrepev, in whom they sensed a leader capable of formulating the goals of their spontaneous movement.

Principal figures in Moscow felt obliged to close ranks around the tsar, but the residue of ill will towards him remained such that resistance to Otrepev's peasant and cossack army was feeble and some officers went over with their men. As the situation deteriorated Boris stepped up repression, further alienating society as denunciations multiplied and his government carried out summary reprisals. Boris withdrew to the Kremlin and gave himself over to the sorcery and divination to which he always had been prone. He died suddenly in April 1605, thereby ensuring False Dmitrii's triumph. The narrative closes with the murder of Godunov's wife and son. His dynasty was extinct and its collapse was the prologue to a massive peasant war that shook Russia to its foundations.

No previous discussion of Boris Godunov has provided such a cohesive explanation of the ramifications of his career. The justice of this observation becomes clear when available literature on the topic is passed in review, with special emphasis upon different authors' attitudes towards the central issue of the death of Dmitrii and the appearance of the pretender.

The historiographical tradition concerning Boris Godunov is complex. Contemporaries and near-contemporaries, coming to grips for the first time in Old-Russian literature with the problem of character delineation,[2] described him as a handsome, eloquent man with great powers of reasoning, pious and charitable, a mighty builder, solicitous of his country's welfare, and author of "many wondrous deeds." At the same time they claimed he dabbled in "black arts." Seduced by what they thought was a remarkable manifestation of God's striking down the wicked who exult, they declared that Boris, consumed with insatiable lust for power, had had the temerity to plot his sovereign's murder and he received the punishment he deserved. In short, contemporaries confessed they were unable to assess the "strange blend of good and evil" they discerned in Boris.[3]

Seldom has the evaluation of a major political figure been so strongly influenced by subsequent historical developments, which in Boris' case created the hostile climate in which he was viewed until quite recently. False Dmitrii received support from the Poles, who thus were inclined to vilify Boris, his opponent. The Jesuits in False Dmitrii's train had an additional motive because they hoped the pretender might help them submit the Orthodox to the Pope. It was advantageous for all these interested parties to claim that Boris was guilty of ordering the abortive murder of Dmitrii, and reports originating in Poland in the seventeenth century and circulated in Europe reflect this attitude and unhesitatingly convict Godunov of this charge. Grevenbruch,[4] who called Irina Godunova a crafty, conniving woman cynically advancing her brother's interests, popularized the story the pretender originally concocted to explain his miraculous survival. A "kindly tutor" substituted another boy in his stead; it was he who was slain by the assassins Boris dispatched to Uglich for that purpose. A few decades later Petreius[5] repeated this tale, adding that Fedor and Irina had had a son whom Boris stole away to clear his own way to the throne. Petreius used these incidents to contrast the splendid Dmitrii with the evil Boris. Twenty years after that an anonymous writer[6] portrayed Boris as an abandoned scoundrel who personally tried to slay the substitute boy and performed other unspeakably wicked acts to advance his own interests.

Vasilii Shuiskii had been in charge of an investigative commission Boris had quickly dispatched to Uglich to examine the events associated with Dmitrii's death, which concluded that the young prince had met with an accidental death. However, when Shuiskii later was anxious to have a pretender drive Godunov from the throne he espoused the latter's version of his amazing escape, and on becoming tsar he found it advantageous to his own interests to declare that Boris had slain the real Dmitrii. The church obligingly canonized the boy and his *Life,* composed in 1606, unequivocally stated that Boris had murdered the martyr. This meant both government and church had placed the full weight of their authority behind this version, so that for at least two centuries, as Shcherbatov's narrative demonstrates,[7] Godunov's guilt was accepted as a matter of course. Now it was easy to attribute every kind of wrongdoing to him: he employed surrogates in an attempt to assassinate Tsar Fedor, murdered Prince Mstislavskii, killed Dmitrii, tampered with the investigation, falsified the record, and had the church, dominated by his creature Iov, supinely whitewash his guilt; burned down Moscow and summoned the Crimean khan to divert popular attention from his crimes, murdered his niece Feodosiia, ruined his benefactor Andrei Shchelkalov, coerced the people into electing him tsar, unleashed a reign of terror against members of the Romanov family, who had a better claim to the throne, and murdered his sister Irina because she refused to give him her blessing as tsar. Everyone in Muscovy hated him and had good reason to do so.[8]

This was the monster the historian and belletrist N.M. Karamzin analyzed in his history of Russia.[9] Karamzin suspected that the tales asserting Boris was responsible for virtually every misfortune that befell Russia were dubious but he did not hesitate to convict Boris of Dmitrii's murder. Again, as in other instances, Karamzin's powerful literary talents rendered his depiction of Godunov extremely influential. Furthermore, the historian directed the attention of Russia's greatest poet to the literary possibilities inherent in the story of Boris' life. Following Karamzin's lead Pushkin accepted Boris' culpability in the death of Dmitrii when he composed his drama[10] about the tragic tsar. His play and Musorgskii's opera have long been regarded by the public in Russia and elsewhere as authoritative sources for Godunov's life and career.

The eminent historians Soloviev and Kliuchevskii display a certain unanimity in their discussions of Godunov. Both their opinions are negative although their emphases differ. Polosin has observed caustically[11] that the clerical background from which the two historians came made them reluctant to challenge an official position sanctified by the church. Be that as it may, Soloviev's treatment of Boris' career[12] is factual, thorough, and capacious. He believes the version of Dmitrii's death put forward by the Nagoi family is intrinsically more probable than that of the commission, which acted dishonestly. In assessing Godunov he comes to the conclusion that although Boris possessed good qualities he was envious of the boyars. His fall was inevitable when he aroused the ranks of officialdom against him. He failed because he was unworthy and unable to rise to the moral level required of a tsar. Soloviev thought the boyars created the pretender, whose activities he described in considerable detail. He was indisputably Grigorii Otrepev.

Kliuchevskii,[13] less interested in Boris than Soloviev, in his brief assessment uses words like "usurper" and "dictator" to describe him. Kliuchevskii also believed that the Uglich commission bungled its task and he was sure Boris must have had something to do with Dmitrii's death. The pretender was an impostor, but not Otrepev, although Kliuchevskii does not elaborate his thesis. He rejects the extreme tales of Boris' villainy, is uncompromising in his statement that Godunov did *not* introduce serfdom into Russia, and grants the ruler a few positive qualities, but in his summary he stated that the skills Boris possessed were more than offset by his failings of "heart and conscience." Boris, "a parvenu converted into a poltroon with the instincts of a constable," was consumed with malice. Kliuchevskii's explanation of Boris' fall is ingenious: insufficiently flexible and innovative, he continued to rule in the old way, thus conjuring up the shade of Ivan IV and the hated oprichnina from which Godunov sprang.

The authority of Soloviev and Kliuchevskii was more than enough to perpetuate the negative image of Boris in the historiography of the late nineteenth and early twentieth centuries. E.A. Belov alone, who in 1873 published an article[14] examining the activity of the Uglich commission, came to the conclusion its findings were valid and that tales of Boris' evil ways were later contrivances, products of rumor, spiteful gossip, and empty speculation. His work attracted little attention at the time and Kostomarov[15] lent his prestige in support of the traditional interpretation.

This was the situation when S.F. Platonov embarked on a major study of the Time of Troubles and events preceding it. He reported on this in specialized monographs and in a careful biography of Boris Godunov,[16] to which Professor Skrynnikov as he acknowledges owes a considerable debt. Platonov's ideas should be examined in detail. He broke decisively with previous historiographical tradition to emerge as Godunov's determined champion. Russia's foreign policy was uniformly successful during Boris' administration, and the ruler, astute enough to recognize it was essential to advance the gentry's corporate interest as a counterpoise to the fractious nobility, proceeded to do so in a number of ways. Addressing the vexed problem of serfdom Platonov followed Kliuchevskii's lead, contending Godunov was not its author, and elaborated the former's theory. As a member of the nonjuridical school Platonov argued that great and small landowners and landholders alike had long employed economic leverage to tie peasants to the land, while the latter had retaliated by fleeing to the periphery to form cossack bands. Their behavior caused severe dislocation at the center, characterized by chronic labor shortages and competition among landlords for peasants that became increasingly fraught with violence until the government felt required to intervene in order to secure the public weal. Platonov formulated an ingenious hypothesis that claimed Boris succored the peasants by preserving them from exploitation by great landowners, and saved the small proprietors as well by guaranteeing them a steady supply of bonded labor. On this showing the decrees establishing forbidden years (the first of which, Platonov is certain, originated with Ivan although the rescript has not survived) benefited peasants, smallholders, and the state. Platonov acknowledges that Boris was hostile to the cossacks, but claims this was due to their refusal to cooperate with the government as it sought to carry out necessary policy.

Russia's problems at that time were so manifold that perhaps no single person could successfully have coped with them but Boris proved himself more capable than anyone else. The quality of life improved substantially during his administration, which was mild and beneficent. He could be ruthless if provoked, but the actions he initiated against his opponents always were designed to foster the interests of the state. Boris was far-sighted, and he was right to champion the lesser service-gentry and tax-paying townspeople, but unfortunately these entities were insufficiently well organized to back him properly when the landed aristocracy and the serfs simultaneously turned against him. This leads Platonov to review what he terms the Tragedy of Boris. It began with the Uglich affair.

Platonov observes that the sanction the church had conferred on Boris' complicity in Dmitrii's death made it perilous to refute the charge. Singling out the commission report for comment, he argues that denigrating or ignoring it has made room for every conceivable story and fable, whereas it should be recognized that the commission's procedures were legal and correct and its findings irreproachable. In contrast to the commission's scientific approach, the tales of Boris' guilt belong to the realm of legend; Platonov examines several works preserving such stories to demonstrate their implausibility and refutes them one by one. He also holds that in 1591 Godunov had nothing to gain and much to lose if he eliminated Dmitrii.

In the matter of Boris' election to the throne Platonov believes the accession of Irina, who had a stronger claim than Dmitrii, was everywhere tacitly accepted; only her poor state of health constrained her abdication. Discussing the difficulties the opposition occasioned for Boris, Platonov states that the Serpukhov campaign was called to counter the genuine threat of a Tatar invasion; it was not a further maneuver in the electoral contest as Professor Skrynnikov considers it to be. Both historians agree that the land assembly of 1598 that ratified Boris' election was duly constituted and expressive of the popular will.

Platonov's conception of the history of this period is consistent. In his biography of Ivan the Terrible[17] he set himself the task of proving the tsar was rational and deliberately had contrived the oprichnina to blunt the power of the old nobility that favored traditional separatist ways. Next he defended Boris Godunov with equal passion, and it should be noted that his efforts to vindicate his new hero involved him in contradictions; he was forced to score Ivan's cruelty and folly in order to demonstrate the soundness of Boris' policies, thus undermining the thesis he originally had propounded. Nevertheless, by presenting Boris in a favorable light Platonov single-handedly reversed previous trends and set the tone that largely has prevailed in Russia until the appearance of Professor Skrynnikov's book. It is instructive to consider representative works on this epoch that have appeared in other countries.

Contemporary foreign sources played a vital role in disseminating information about the period; later historians frequently have cited the works of individuals like Sir Jerome Horsey, Giles Fletcher, Captain Jacques Margeret, Isaac Massa, and Konrad Bussow. Most of these writers were critical of Boris and did much to create the attitude of hostility with which he has subsequently been regarded. After they were gone, interest in Godunov's era waned and did not revive until comparatively recently. The traditional view finds expression, but Platonov's position of late has become influential.

In his famous study of relations in the triangle involving Muscovy, Poland, and the Papacy Paul Pierling, S.J.[18] accepted stories that

Boris was of Tatar origin and barely literate. A parvenu thirsting for power, he attacked the nobility. Pierling berated the Uglich commission for failing to do its duty and declared its findings were unreliable; Boris was unquestionably responsible for the murder of Dmitrii. In this section of his work one derives the impression that Pierling was doing little more than paraphrasing Kliuchevskii. The sprightly stylist Kazimierz Waliszewski developed a different interpretation of the Uglich affair that exonerated Boris for the simple reason that Dmitrii never died. The commission report was accurate as far as it went, but Dmitrii was only wounded by the knife, and the Nagoi family speedily removed him to a distant monastery where he grew up; thus, Waliszewski considered False Dmitrii to be genuine, an idea that has intrigued commentators from time to time. The traditional canards are all repeated in the biography of Boris penned by Stephen Graham:[20] Boris was illiterate, ordered Dmitrii murdered (although the child miraculously survived to become the genuine heir), and egged on Ivan the Terrible to kill his elder son. Boris was a tyrant whose unslakable appetite for power led him to commit every conceivable crime.

It may well have been Kliuchevskii's influence in the west that for some time prevented Platonov's views from obtaining wide currency, but the situation changed in the 1950s. In a slight piece Nikolaieff[21] argued that Boris, an able ruler, was not responsible for Dmitrii's death and George Vernadsky developed Platonov's thesis. In a close analysis of the Uglich affair[22] he found the commission report trustworthy and criticized earlier historians for having failed to utilize it. His general appraisal of Boris' career, made in his last major work,[23] is remarkably favorable. Patriarch Iov, usually dismissed as Boris' toady, appears as a man of sincere faith and high moral qualities, who gave generous alms and conducted inspiring services. The members of the Nagoi family were conspirators; their punishment was richly deserved.

Sounding a theme dear to his own heart, Vernadsky praised Boris for realizing that it was of paramount importance to develop Russia's Eurasian empire. Godunov ascended the throne because virtually everyone wished him to do so, and Vernadsky also is prepared to argue that the Serpukhov campaign was justified because the Crimean khan intended to attack Moscow. He extols Boris for his westernizing propensities and the generosity he displayed during the famine years. There is little discussion of Boris' part in enserfing the peasantry; his statutes that reestablished the right of peasant departure in 1601-1602 receive attention, and Vernadsky is sure Godunov would have granted greater latitude in this direction if the Troubles had not intervened. He has no idea of the identity of False Dmitrii although he considers it doubtful the impostor was Otrepev. The boyar opposition "coached" a young man to assume the part; the Poles played a sinister role by meddling in Moscow's affairs, and Jerzy Mniszech was motivated by a desire to recoup his fortunes. The possibility that Boris was poisoned by his enemies should not be dismissed entirely. In short, Vernadsky, arriving at conclusions directly opposed to the traditional ones, portrayed Boris as a man of exceptional capacity, one of Russia's greatest rulers, who was more sinned against than sinner.

A few other modern studies treat the era of Boris Godunov; they are mostly biographies of uneven merit and quality. A recent essay[24] restates the Platonov-Vernadsky thesis in popular form, as does a second[25] written in journalistic fashion. Another work,[26] composed in a florid, breathless style, but containing a substantial scholarly apparatus, vindicates Boris in a discussion of the Uglich affair and revives the notion that False Dmitrii was "somehow" genuine.

It can be seen that both Russian and western conceptions of Boris have altered radically. He was an evil, crafty, power-mad intriguer who ruthlessly and callously destroyed all obstacles in his path in his single-minded pursuit of the throne. Now he has become one of Russia's greatest rulers, whose fall was due to circumstances beyond his control. Modern historiography is as pro-Boris as earlier historiography was anti-Boris. Professor Skrynnikov has at last removed Godunov from the realm of tendentious apologetics, special pleading, feelings and impressions (from which Platonov's pioneering study is by no means free) in which he has languished for centuries. He has based his work as much as possible on primary sources and has sought to redress the balance and find a middle ground, being fair to his subject and avoiding extremes of partisanship. His conclusions are guarded and cautious, but in a field that heretofore has been long on conclusions and short on evidence he may be excused for having gone in the opposite direction. Professor Skrynnikov has inaugurated a new era in the study of this fascinating and important epoch. His excellent biography will certainly stimulate further serious research.

AUTHOR'S INTRODUCTION

The personality of Boris Godunov, his extraordinary rise and tragic end naturally struck the imagination of contemporaries and has attracted the attention of historians, novelists, poets, artists and musicians. His life was highly unusual. Starting as an ordinary member of the gentry Godunov became regent during the reign of a feeble-minded tsar and ultimately ruler of a large country.

Russia had experienced serious reverses. For a decade severe natural disasters had been sapping its productive forces and a protracted war completed the havoc. The country was in a state of indescribable ruin. For nearly a quarter of a century after conquering Narva Russia had an outlet to the Baltic sea, but after losing the Livonian war it was deprived of the port it needed in order to develop trade with western Europe. The defeat weakened Russia's international position, and the disasters abroad intensified a burgeoning internal crisis, the sources of which lay in the relationship between the two principal estates in feudal society, landowners and peasants. By the end of the sixteenth century the rapacious gentry had won and the yoke of serfdom had been fastened upon millions of Russian peasants.

The turbulent years of the oprichnina had provided opportunities for many lowborn members of the gentry, and Boris Godunov was among them, for his early success was due entirely to the oprichnina. Ivan the Terrible's actions had split the feudal estate into two rival camps and left many hard problems which Godunov had to confront as regent. His life was filled with dramatic events. During his first years as regent Dmitrii, the last member of the dynasty that had ruled Muscovy for three hundred years, died in Uglich, and his mysterious double, the pretender, who brought irretrievable misfortune on Boris and his family, drove the unstable Godunov dynasty from the throne.

The novelist and historian N.M. Karamzin, who believed that only lawful autocrats had the right to hold power, once claimed Godunov might have been hailed as one of the greatest rulers in the world if he had been born to the purple, but since Boris killed the last member of the royal dynasty and usurped power, he ensured his own destruction. The court historiographer's estimate of Godunov is not particularly profound. A.S. Pushkin understood history incomparably better.

He saw the relationship between the people and the government as the source of Godunov's tragedy; he perished because the people turned away from him. The peasants never forgave him for abrogating the ancient right of St. George's Day, which had protected their freedom.

Many historians, from V.N. Tatishchev on, have held the view that Boris was responsible for the system of serfdom. V.O. Kliuchevskii adhered to a different opinion. He wrote that "the idea that Boris Godunov established serfdom is one of our historical fairytales."[1] Kliuchevskii dismissed as slander charges implicating Boris in many brutal crimes. He sketched a vivid portrait of a talented and intelligent man who constantly was suspected of being hypocritical, greedy and callous. To him Boris seemed a strange blend of good and evil. S.F. Platonov's book on Godunov still has value. Platonov similarly rejected the notion that it was Boris who first enserfed the peasantry and insisted that Godunov, who had linked his destiny to the interests of the middle class, designed his policies to safeguard the good of society at large. The innumerable charges brought against Boris have never been proved, but they have compromised him in the eyes of posterity. Platonov suggested that the immediate task of historians was to undertake the rehabilitation of Godunov.

What was Boris Godunov really like? What did his career mean for Russian history? The sources alone can supply answers to these questions. Seeking to assess the known facts, we shall try to examine them again.

Chapter One

THE BEGINNING

Boyar Vasilii Shuiskii, one of the heroes in Pushkin's tragedy,[1] shows his contempt for the lowborn Boris in the devastating phrase "Yesterday a slave, a Tatar, and Maliuta's son-in-law."

Legends that the Godunov family was of Tatar origin are well-known. The founder was thought to be a Tatar, Chet-murza, who purportedly came to Russia in the days of Ivan Kalita.[2] Only one source, the *Tale of Chet,* mentions his existence, and its veracity is suspect. The composers of the Tale were monks of the remote Ipatevskii monastery in Kostroma, where members of the Godunov family were buried. The monks compiled the ancestral story of Chet because they were anxious to demonstrate that Boris' claims to princely origin were justified and also to show that his new dynasty had long been connected with their monastery. The Ipatevskii scribes asserted that Chet, an emir in the Horde,[3] while on his way from Sarai to Moscow, succeeded in founding an Orthodox cloister in Kostroma, etc. The *Tale of Chet* abounds in historical incongruities and deserves no credence whatsoever.[4]

Godunov's ancestors were neither Tatars nor slaves. Natives of Kostroma, they had long been boyars at the Muscovite court. The Saburov family, the senior branch of the line, had been prominent before Ivan the Terrible's time, but then they and the junior lines, the Godunov and Veliaminov families, declined and collapsed. Once boyars in Kostroma, members of the Godunov family eventually became service-tenure landholders[5] in Viazma, and having fallen from the close circle of ruling boyars to become provincial gentry, they ceased to receive appointments at court or major military commands.

Boris Godunov was born in 1552 shortly before the conquest of Kazan. His father, Fedor Ivanovich, was a middle service-tenure landholder. The nickname of "crooked" shows he was physically deformed, but it is impossible to reach any conclusion about his personality. His career was undistinguished: shortly before Boris was born the Muscovite authorities drew up a list of one thousand of their best servitors, which enumerated all the outstanding members of the gentry, but neither Fedor nor his brother, Dmitrii Ivanovich Godunov, were deemed worthy of inclusion in it.

Dmitrii and Fedor were joint proprietors of a small ancestral estate in Kostroma, a circumstance of great importance in Boris' life. After his father died he became part of his uncle's family. Dmitrii Ivanovich was not merely influenced by family ties and the premature death of his own children to become involved in his nephew's affairs; it was vital to prevent division of their sole remaining patrimony.

It might be said that low birth and humble position saved the Godunov family when the menacing oprichnina period burst upon it. The state was divided into an oprichnina (crownlands) and a zemshchina (the realm). Tsar Ivan made Viazma part of the oprichnina and his minions conducted a scrutiny of its inhabitants. Each member of the gentry had to provide a special commission with information about his and his wife's origins and who their friends were. To be related to a boyar, which formerly had been highly valued, could now destroy a serving-man's career. Gentry not of noble birth enrolled in the oprichnina guard received all kinds of privileges, while others were deprived of their lands and removed from the area. The Viazma cadastral books indicate that Dmitrii Godunov survived the ordeal and was placed in the oprichnina guard as soon as it formed.

Anxious to be free of his previous associates, Ivan wanted fresh faces. He threw the court open to them, and the modest Viazma landholder became a courtier. Their uncle's success benefited his niece and nephew. Boris' own chancellery declared that he spent his youth at the court, and his sister Irina grew up in the palace from the age of seven. Irina Godunova was the same age as Ivan's son Fedor, born in 1557. The orphans' entry into the Kremlin coincided with the establishment of the oprichnina.

Boyar Aleksei Basmanov headed the tsar's new council and the armorer, Afanasii Viazemskii, Chamberlain Vasilii Naumov, and Equerry Petr Zaitsev directed the main chanceries in the oprichnina. The founders of the oprichnina believed it was necessary to use unrestrained violence in order to crush the haughty aristocracy, a program they at once proceeded to implement. However, although many princely families were banished to the eastern frontiers during the first months of the oprichnina's existence, its anti-princely animus dissipated in less than a year and Ivan, forced to admit that his policy had failed, decided to restore the majority of the nobles he previously had disgraced. Dmitrii Godunov was not among the founders of the oprichnina, and only chance brought him his first conciliar office when the sudden death of the chamberlain, Naumov, enabled him to become head of the chamberlain's chancery after the oprichnina had become fully operational.

Encouraged by the concessions the tsar had made, boyars began demanding that the oprichnina be abolished, and the feudal leaders voiced their discontent. The throne was in jeopardy, but while Ivan earnestly sought accommodation with the zemshchina, the terrified men who controlled the oprichnina resorted to mass executions for the first time. The terror brought adventurers like Maliuta Skuratov and Vasilii Griaznoi to prominence. Treason trials multiplied daily and, fearing a boyar revolt, Ivan pondered withdrawing to a monastery or fleeing to England with his family, but he remained active in his torture chambers, where he and Skuratov spent long periods of time. On occasion the oprichnina brethren sought quietude in fasting and prayer, and in preparation for his future monastic life Ivan served as their abbot. The armorer was the cellarer. Chamberlain Godunov was assigned a more modest function, but undoubtedly he also wore a black cowl. Although Maliuta Skuratov was one of the minor members of this monastic hierarchy, a sacristan, who spiritedly rang bells, the notoriety of his exploits spread throughout the country.

Skuratov instigated the appalling Novgorod affair,[6] which finally opened his way to power. Those who had founded the oprichnina were its last victims, and Boyar Basmanov, Armorer Viazemskii, and Equerry Zaitsev perished. Chamberlain Godunov alone survived among the higher court dignitaries. Why was he lucky enough to avoid the others' fate? It is inadequate to suggest the personal relationship he enjoyed with Skuratov, for it arose within a specific institution. Their alliance developed inside the chamberlain's chancery.

A distinctive chamberlain's chancery emerged while Aleksei Adashev[7] was reforming the entire state administration, and its head was Ignatii Veshniakov, his close friend and coadjutor. From ancient times chamberlains were responsible for the tsar's chamber, or wardrobe. They were in charge of numerous workshops at court in which tailors, furriers, hatters, bootmakers, and other craftsmen labored. The chancery was concerned with both the physical and spiritual needs of the royal family, and its complement included quite a few lusty singers, who formed a court choir. After the oprichnina was established, the chamberlain's chancery grew enormously. Its senior officials held nearly seven thousand acres of service-tenure land, while the chamberlain controlled large amounts of money. The treasury annually expended as much as one thousand rubles merely to pay the salaries of its servitors and craftsmen.

The chamberlain had to be an efficient, ubiquitous person, who knew how to cushion the royal family in the lap of luxury. Dmitrii Godunov was ideally suited to the task. Tsar Ivan loved luxury and

Boris' Signature

could not do without his services. The chamberlain's chancery supervised the appointments and the daily safety of the first family. During the oprichnina years this second function assumed exceptional importance.[8] The official register of 1573 shows that the chamberlain supervised guards in the bedchamber, other rooms in the palace, the dining hall and distillery, the court furnacemen and the rest of the servants. Only fully reliable and trustworthy individuals were recruited for the palace guard. The chamberlain's chancery was responsible for the royal bedchamber at night. In the evening the chamberlain personally inspected the internal palace watch and then slept in the same room with the tsar.[9] Under normal circumstances the commander of the domestic palace guard would be an insignificant figure, but during a time of conspiracies and executions he inevitably became one of the tsar's closest counsellors, and it is not surprising that Maliuta Skuratov sought the friendship and patronage of the influential chamberlain. Motivated by political calculations, Skuratov married his daughter to Dmitrii Godunov's nephew and thus Boris became the son-in-law of the all-powerful boss of the oprichnina.

The tsar took the advice of his new favorites in all matters. At their instigation he executed boyars, and he arranged his personal life in accordance with their suggestions. In 1571, while Ivan was preparing to marry again and had decided that his son and heir and some courtiers serving in the oprichnina should be married as well, fifteen hundred girls were brought to Aleksandrovskaia Sloboda.[10] Ivan's third wife was Marfa Sobakina, a choice that appeared inexplicable. A host of pretty, healthy girls took part in the bride show, but Sobakina was visibly wasting away. It might be said that Ivan's new bride went straight from church to her grave. Why did the tsar contract such an unfortunate marriage? The murals depicting the event suggest an answer. Maliuta's wife and his daughter, Mariia Godunova, arranged it and Skuratov and his son-in-law stood up for the royal bride. The Skuratov and Godunov families would go to any lengths to become related to the royal family. They were unlucky with Marfa, but did manage to marry the heir to Evdokiia Saburova. The Saburov and Godunov families belonged to the same line.

Kliuchevskii once observed that Boris Godunov was not compromised by his service in the oprichnina and his popularity did not suffer as a result of it, but this is not strictly true. Boris entered the oprichnina as soon as he reached maturity. Serving in his uncle's department, he was soon appointed to his first office as a junior court official, where he discharged the duties of a gentleman-in-waiting.

The murals depicting court functionaries contain this notation: "Whenever the sovereign goes through and arranges his clothing, junior court officials and the chamberlain must pick up and give out the sovereign's clothing." At night junior court officials had to be available in the chamberlain's wing of the Kremlin palace.

The troubled oprichnina years were not a good time for Boris to acquire an education. His young contemporaries considered him completely illiterate. The distinguished crown secretary Ivan Timofeev wrote that from the day he was born to the day he died Boris never "learned his alphabet," and was "the first tsar we have had who has no booklearning."[11] Foreigners had no hesitation in saying that Boris could neither read nor write.[12] However, these contemporaries were mistaken. Boris grew up in a family that valued education. In his later years Dmitrii Ivanovich eagerly donated books from his personal library to monasteries, and at the proper time their uncle and benefactor saw to it that both his nephew Boris and his niece Irina became literate. At approximately the age of twenty, Boris signed a document conveying the ancestral estate to the Ipatevskii monastery in Kostroma.[13] The youthful member of the oprichnina wrote a precise script bordering on calligraphy, but once on the throne Boris permanently abjured writing. Nevertheless, one should not think he had forgotten how to write; the new sovereign merely had no desire to overturn the time-honored tradition which forbade crowned heads to use pen and ink. At any rate, as a youth Boris received no more than an elementary education, and his contemporaries never forgave him because he possessed scant knowledge of holy writ. Church books constituted the indispensable component of any program of study in Old Russia, and so, judged by sixteenth-century standards, Godunov was a poorly educated man.

The Godunov family invariably had benefited from the intrigues at court, but its members still felt insecure. Heads were rolling around them, and uncle and nephew, both of whom were destined to enjoy long lives, prudently took thought for their souls, sending money and deeding land to the family monastery. Kinship with the tsar, on which they had counted so heavily, had not produced the results desired. Evdokiia Saburova had spent less than a year with his son and heir when Ivan packed her off to a nunnery and the tie between the Saburov and Godunov families and the royal house was broken. A few months later a Swedish bullet laid Maliuta Skuratov low before the walls of a small fortress in Livonia. Boris lost his father-in-law, whose support might well have ensured him rapid advancement.

Abolition of the oprichnina and Maliuta's death brought about major changes at court. The members of the Godunov family were prepared for the worst but, displaying rare determination to achieve the goal they desired to reach, again managed to prevail. They had failed to maintain their tie with Ivan, the heir, and so they decided to use Ivan's younger brother, Fedor, in order to consolidate their position at court. Embarking on his fifth marriage, Tsar Ivan had announced he intended to marry off his younger son, and Dmitrii Godunov at once took matters into his own hands and affianced his niece Irina to the new heir. Fedor's appearance displayed marked signs of degeneracy. His sickly body was topped by a disproportionately small head. He was mentally defective and appeared singularly incapable of coping with life, but the chamberlain and his nephew did not consider Fedor's deficiencies important.

Part of the oprichnina guard was disbanded while another part was reorganized as a special court, the institution that took the place of the oprichnina, whose council was headed by Boyar Vasilii Umnoi-Kolychev and Associate Boyar Prince Boris Tulupov. Picked members of the oprichnina, who had survived numerous purges, were coopted into this court. Transferring to its service, Dmitrii Godunov was promoted when the tsar awarded him conciliar rank as an associate boyar. The new government tried to calm the country, shaken by the oprichnina terror but, unable to achieve its aim, collapsed under internal pressure. The Kolychev boyars became involved in a bitter precedence action with the Godunov and Saburov families. Dmitrii Godunov brought suit against Vasilii Umnoi-Kolychev, and Bogdan Saburov caused the death of Boyar Fedor Umnoi-Kolychev. The members of the Godunov family refused to rest until they had destroyed their opponents. Filled with suspicion, Tsar Ivan ordered his most trusted advisors, Vasilii Umnoi and Boris Tulupov, executed and the first post-oprichnina government fell.

The change immediately benefited Boris Godunov; he was awarded the estate of Tulupov, who somehow had dishonored him.[14] The nature of the affront Godunov experienced will never be known, but the man who inflicted it paid the penalty in full; he was impaled on a stake. Boris later sought to divest himself of the estate he had acquired improperly. No sooner had Ivan died than Boris, with Fedor's blessing, conveyed Tulupov's estate to a monastery, telling the monks to pray for the Kolychev brothers, Boris Tulupov, and his mother, Princess Anna, who had died with her son.[15] Boris had performed a pious act, but it served to indicate guilt. His nature was not cruel or bloodthirsty, but he was struggling to reach the summit of power.

After shattering what he believed to be a conspiracy in the court's council, Ivan began organizing a new oprichnina, which acquired the name of his appanage. He ostensibly transferred power to the baptized Tatar khan, Simeon Bekbulatovich, who was proclaimed grand prince of all Russia, leaving himself only the title of appanage prince of Moscow. Unwilling to take former oprichnina gentry into his service, Ivan placed Pskov, Rostov, and Rzhev, which had never formed part of the oprichnina, in his appanage. Local gentry members serving in the zemshchina now entered the appanage army. Assisted by his new praetorians Ivan put down a second conspiracy in Novgorod; this time the victims of the tsar's suspicious nature were Archbishop Leonid who had cooperated with the oprichnina government in Novgorod, the abbot of the Simonov monastery which had been enrolled in the oprichnina, and former oprichnina boyars who were members of the Buturlin and Borisov families. The executions the crown appanage carried out completed Maliuta Skuratov's task. Almost all the surviving members of the original oprichnina leadership had perished and only Dmitrii Godunov and a handful of privy councillors successfully came through the new purge. Afanasii Nagoi, who had not been in the oprichnina, and Bogdan Belskii, who had taken a modest part in it, presided over Ivan's appanage council. Abolition of the crown appanage did not cause a new scrutiny of cadres. To the end of Ivan's days key government positions were in the hands of members of the Belskii, Nagoi and Godunov families, the former appanage rulers.

The court was not dissolved, but the savage executions in Moscow ceased. After the death of Ivan the heir, Tsar Ivan bestowed enormous sums on monasteries to pray for the souls of those he had destroyed. His forgiveness was a guarantee that boyars would no longer be disgraced and persecuted. A royal rescript threatening slaves with harsh punishment for bearing false witness constituted another guarantee. Death awaited anyone who tried to charge boyars with treason unless he had good grounds for doing so.

At the end of his life the tsar named virtually no boyars to either his court or the boyar council, except for members of the Godunov family. Dmitrii Godunov, once a service-tenure landholder in Viazma, was given boyar rank. His long service in the oprichnina, the court, and the appanage received its ultimate reward. Boris, now thirty years old, was not assigned specific duties, but the tsar elevated him to boyar rank as well, and even his relative, Stepan Godunov, became an associate boyar. The Godunov family's success appeared exceptional, but the future still troubled its members. During the oprichnina,

Tsar Ivan had designated his older son Ivan as his successor, and his will had assigned him huge tracts of land. Not wishing to treat his younger son Fedor unfairly, Ivan decided to grant him an appanage duchy larger than many European countries, including the ancient towns of Suzdal, Yaroslavl, and Kostroma, and many estates and villages. Their very condition rendered appanage princes contentious. Throughout the history of Muscovy they almost invariably met with violent deaths, especially when there was a change of rulers. The thought that his sons might become rivals disturbed the tsar, but he hoped the Godunov family's prudence and adroitness would prevent quarrels from arising in the royal family after Fedor's appanage duchy was established. The tsar always had entrusted the care of his younger son to the Godunov family. Whenever he set out on campaign, he left Fedor in a safe place under its members' supervision. Boris' position brought him great honor but confined his activities to the court. He was diligently mastering the secrets of court intrigue while his contemporaries were serving in chanceries and diplomatic bureaux and holding fortresses against the enemy.

At the close of the Livonian war an event occurred in the royal family that decisively altered the Godunov family's fortunes. In November, 1581 the tsar quarreled with his older son and in a fit of rage struck him and his pregnant wife, who suffered a miscarriage. Young Ivan fell ill and soon died from a pronounced nervous disorder induced by the buffeting. The death of his older brother opened the road to the throne for Fedor and greatly benefited the members of his entourage. If the misfortune had occurred later rumor would inevitably have implicated Boris in the tragedy, but Godunov had not yet attracted the boyars' hatred and thus in this first instance managed to avoid slanderous attacks. In fact, subsequent legend interpreted Boris' conduct favorably: the tsar's favorite purportedly tried to intercede on the heir's behalf, was beaten savagely for his efforts, and was taken seriously ill. The source preserving this legend is not particularly trustworthy, but the fact of the matter remains. The royal family's tragedy tarnished the relationship that had existed between Ivan and his favorite, and with good reason. As long as the heir was alive Ivan was comparatively indifferent to Fedor's family circumstances. For many years Fedor had produced no children, and this corresponded with the country's best interests, but when Fedor became heir to the throne the situation changed. His continued marriage to Irina Godunova would inevitably doom the dynasty to extinction. Irina's infertility gave the tsar a useful excuse to arrange for his son's divorce.

Boris Godunov did everything in his power to prevent it, as a divorce
might well put an end to his career, and his obstinacy provoked Ivan
to wrath.

Overcome with grief, the tsar did not venture to treat his younger
son as harshly as he had the elder, and attempts at persuasion were
unavailing. Fedor refused to hear of a separation from his wife, who,
as she was far more intelligent and practical than her husband, had
acquired a strong ascendancy over him during their long marriage.
Nevertheless, Ivan found a way to indicate he disapproved of Fedor's
marriage. Harboring no illusions as to his son's capacity to rule, Ivan
acted as other Muscovite princes had when leaving the throne to
minor successors. He entrusted his son and family to the protection
of a regency council, whose members he enumerated in his will. It is
usually thought that the tsar set Boris Godunov at its head, but critical examination of the sources shows this view to be in error.

A few months after Ivan died, his physician informed the Poles
that the tsar had designated four regents, including Nikita Romanov-
Yurev, Ivan Mstislavskii, and others. The Englishman Horsey,[16] a
witness to events in Moscow, mentioned four boyars on one occasion
and five on another. Horsey intrigued vigorously on behalf of Boris,
and this frequently led him to falsify facts that he knew. Horsey
asserted that Ivan made Boris Godunov chief regent and designated
Ivan Mstislavskii, Ivan Shuiskii, Nikita Romanov, and Bogdan Belskii
to assist him. One of these persons did not appear in the tsar's will.
An informed Muscovite, the author of *A Different Tale*, included
Shuiskii, Mstislavskii and Romanov among the regents, and there is
no question they were all members of the council. It follows that
either Belskii or Godunov must be excluded from the list. Notes made
by the Austrian ambassador, Nicholas Warkoch, help solve the problem. The Austrian court had told him at all costs to ascertain the
content of Ivan's will, and Warkoch was able to learn what his court
desired to know. He wrote: "The late Grand Prince Ivan Vasilevich
drew up a will before he died in which he designated certain lords
as his executors to carry out his wishes, but the aforementioned will
makes no mention of Boris Fedorovich Godunov, brother of the
present grand princess, and assigns him no office, and this has caused
the latter great sorrow."[17]

Circumstances forced Ivan to place representatives of the nobility
he had battled all his life on the regency council. Two of the four,
appanage Prince Ivan Mstislavskii and Boyar Prince Ivan Shuiskii, belonged to the most aristocratic families of Russia. Mstislavskii was a

colorless individual, but Shuiskii was an exceptional person with whose military exploits the entire country was familiar. The defense of Pskov had saved Russia from enemy invasion and utter destruction at the end of the Livonian war, and Shuiskii was its hero. Nikita Romanov-Yurev was Tsar Fedor's uncle and represented the chief ruling boyars. Belskii alone was a lowborn individual who had risen through the oprichnina. Ivan's favorites, Afanasii Nagoi and the Godunov family, were omitted entirely. The former appeared dangerous because he was covertly plotting to acquire the crown for his grandson Dmitrii,[18] and it was undoubtedly the Godunov family that had prevented Fedor from divorcing the childless Irina.

Ivan's testament dealt a deadly blow to the Godunov family's ambitions. As Fedor's closest relatives, they were preparing to assume the mantle of government and needed to make but one more move in order to achieve power until the regency council, mandated by Tsar Ivan's will, appeared as an insurmountable obstacle in their way. While he lived Ivan exercised a decisive influence on events, but on his death the situation altered drastically.

Chapter Two

A TIME OF TESTING

Ivan died in March, 1584. Fearing disturbances, the government tried to hide the truth from the people, proclaiming the sovereign still might recover, while Bogdan Belskii and the leaders of the court council ordered the Kremlin gates closed and locked, fusiliers assigned to the walls, and cannon placed on the ready. In spite of these efforts news of the tsar's death spread throughout the city and provoked unrest. Fear of a potential uprising made the boyars hasten to decide the succession question. In the middle of the night they administered the oath of office to Fedor. Platonov, the distinguished student of the Time of Troubles, has claimed the struggle that broke out after Ivan's death was primarily a court squabble as the tsar's relatives clashed to secure influence, but the facts indicate that the contest revolved around Ivan's political legacy, a much more vital issue than simply acquiring influence at court.

Although it had gone through numerous reorganizations, the court, which resembled the oprichnina and propped up the repressive regime, continued to exist. The zemshchina kept demanding its immediate dissolution and restoration of the pre-oprichnina style of governance. However, the Kremlin guard owed its allegiance to the court, and thus Bogdan Belskii managed to remain in at least partial control of the situation, but he quickly fell foul of the insubordinate nobility, whose members were attempting to employ the institution of precedence to bring the domination of those associated with the court to an end.

Petr Golovin, a zemshchina treasurer, tried to force Belskii to step aside. A courtier's precedence rank was determined primarily by the degree of nobility possessed by his family and his ancestors' service careers and only in the last resort by his personal capacities. Coming from a family deemed unworthy of inclusion in the genealogical registers, Belskii was no match for the noble treasurer, who was supported by Mstislavskii, Romanov and all the zemshchina boyars, whereas Belskii was backed only by the Godunov family and the Shchelkalov brothers, humbly-born crown secretaries. The bickering almost ended in violence. The zemshchina nobles present in the palace assailed Belskii so vigorously that he had to take refuge in the tsar's chambers. The actions of the zemshchina opposition provoked Belskii to extreme measures in a desperate effort to crush the incipient revolt in the zemshchina. Summoning some of the court's fusilier contingents to the Kremlin, the regent secretly promised them large rewards and the privileges they had enjoyed during Ivan's lifetime in an effort to convince them not to fear the boyars and obey his orders alone. Winning them over, Belskii ordered the Kremlin closed and tried to persuade Fedor to retain both the court and the oprichnina.[1] The boyar regents, who had dispersed for supper, soon learned what had happened. Nikita Romanov and Ivan Mstislavskii rushed to the Kremlin with a large band of armed retainers and slaves. The fusiliers refused to open the main gate to them but subsequently admitted a few through a postern gate without their entourages. Their men tried to clear a way by force and the noise attracted people from everywhere. The fusiliers cocked their pieces.

If he had succeeded, Belskii could have abolished the regency council and, relying on force, ruled alone in Fedor's name. The Kremlin was threatened with a new oprichnina, but Belskii and his supporters failed to take one important factor—the people—into consideration. The encounter at the Kremlin gate was a signal for an uprising: "The people all rose without number, with all kinds of weapons."[2] Seizing the cannon in the Red Square, the dissidents turned them against the Frolov gate. In trying to disperse the crowd the fusiliers fired a few salvos and during the exchange some twenty persons were killed and nearly one hundred wounded. Events had taken an ugly turn and the tsar sent boyars to parley in the square. The people demanded to settle accounts with Belskii, who epitomized the harsh governmental regime they hated, with such intensity that Fedor and his advisers had to sacrifice him. When the zemshchina boyars announced Belskii had been banished the disturbance gradually subsided. The favorite's retirement drastically changed the situation.

The popular rising brought attempts to restore the oprichnina to an end and led to the fall of the court's leaders. Three weeks later an assembly was convoked in the Kremlin, at which representatives from the zemshchina were given their first opportunity to air their views about what had occurred. The assembly participants knew that Fedor was genuinely unable to rule independently, but they approved his candidacy, which meant they supported the boyar regime that came to power after Belskii's exile. It is curious that contemporaries interpreted the assembly decision as tantamount to electing Fedor to the throne. On May 31, 1584 Moscow solemnly celebrated the new tsar's coronation. After a private service in the Blagoveshchenskii cathedral Fedor and his retinue repaired to the cathedral of the Archangel, and thence to the cathedral of the Dormition. The road from the palace to the cathedrals was strewn with costly carpets and the route the procession followed was lined with a solid wall of courtiers dressed in golden raiment. Fedor was crowned in the manner of Byzantine emperors, and the lengthy ceremony exhausted him. Without waiting for its conclusion, he handed the Cap of Monomakh[3] to Boyar Prince Mstislavskii and the heavy golden apple (his sceptre) to Boris Godunov. This trifling incident astounded the spectators.

Fedor Ivanovich was not like his father. Witnesses reported that the last sovereign of the dynasty founded by Kalita was sickly and weak, walked clumsily, and wore a constant smile on his face, which was pale like the rest of him. Giles Fletcher,[4] an English envoy, observed: "The tsar is simple and weakminded, hardly capable of formulating policy, and extraordinarily superstitious."[5] The papal nuncio Possevino[6] averred that Fedor's mental incompetence virtually bordered upon idiocy or insanity. Ivan's successor could not rule the country; he had never been trained to do so, and even formal rituals and court ceremonies seemed to him intolerable. The conduct of affairs wearied Fedor, who sought consolation in religion. He prayed at length daily, often rang bells, and once a week made pilgrimages to adjacent monasteries. Russian writers during the Time of Troubles tended to idealize the last legal autocrat and endowed Fedor, whom they saw as a saint on the throne, in Kliuchevskii's neat phrase, with a familiar and beloved mien. Certain enthusiastic apologists assigned him the gift of prophecy, although the people, who were poorly informed, saw little example of it. Those who praised the tsar's remarkable piety avoided mentioning his passion for cruel sports and violent amusements. Fedor loved to watch boxing matches and especially fights involving bears. As he looked on, a hunter armed with a spear would try to fend off a bear as best he could in a circular pit enclosed by a wall from which there was no escape. Such entertainments usually ended in bloodshed. Fedor was unpopular with the nobility, who neither admired nor feared him. The Swedish king said Russians called him a blockhead.

The events transpiring in Moscow after Ivan's death proved that the oprichnina merely had weakened but not destroyed the power and influence of the boyar aristocracy. The nobility raised its head anew under Ivan's weak, insignificant successor. As soon as the menacing Belskii disappeared from the political horizon the boyars ceased to conceal their real feelings about Ivan. Crown Secretary Ivan Timofeev, a close, thoughtful observer, accurately portrayed the atmosphere in the Kremlin at the beginning of Fedor's reign: "The boyars long could not believe that Tsar Ivan was dead, but when they realized it was not a dream and actually had occurred, many of the greatest noblemen, whose careers had been placed in jeopardy, soon annointed their grey locks with sweet-scented myrrh, decked themselves out proudly in finery, and behaved as they wished, like youngsters. Like eagles they for the moment felt rejuvenated, renewed, and changed; scorning Fedor they acted as though the son who had survived the tsar did not exist . . . ."[7] Comparatively few boyars remained in the council at the end of Ivan's life. They had been crowded out by the tsar's non-noble favorites, but in Fedor's time the nobility rushed to fill the council and the number of boyars in it doubled almost instantaneously. On the other hand, the privy councillors were practically decimated. Afanasii Nagoi and Bogdan Belskii were exiled; Mikhail Beznin was sent to a monastery, and Vasilii Ziuzin and Baim Voeikov were deprived of their rank.

These events nearly ruined the Godunov family. The populace risen in revolt had demanded its members' removal from the capital and Boris was humiliated, but he both survived and actually took advantage of these new developments so as to take another major step along the road to power. On the day of his coronation Fedor appointed his brother-in-law Master of Horse, an office Ivan had abolished when he executed its last incumbent. Since the post had from time immemorial been held by representatives of a few of the noblest families, the boyar regime reestablished it. The question of who was to be the new Master provoked a bitter struggle because Boris lacked sufficient patent of nobility to occupy so prominent a position, but the Master ultimately was appointed by those who in fact controlled the government. Boris' designation as Master, accomplished against Ivan's express desires, brought him into the ruling circle.

Godunov's success cannot be explained solely in terms of his kinship with the royal family, for Fedor's influence on the government during the fluid first days of his administration was slight. At thirty-two Boris was aided above all by his political resourcefulness; he lost no time putting distance between himself and Belskii, who had been his associate and protector and was his brother-in-law, as soon as he realized the latter's cause was lost. The patronage of the zemshchina boyars was more important. Until the coronation the group led by the tsar's uncle Nikita Romanov and Crown Secretary Andrei Shchelkalov, who had ruled the zemshchina in Ivan's lifetime, displayed the most strength. Sir Jerome Bowes, the English ambassador, termed them the most influential persons in Moscow. However, the boyar regime proved insecure. Advanced in years, Romanov was seriously ill and everyone expected him to die soon.

Writers during the Time of Troubles kept asserting that the ailing Romanov took the initiative in seeking Godunov's friendship and entrusted his sons, still quite young, to his care. The Troitsa monk Avraamii Palitsyn, who witnessed these events, stated that Godunov promised the regent to watch over his family.[8] The author of the *Tale of Filaret Romanov,* who had access to the Romanov family archives, authoritatively confirmed this statement. The Tale asserts that Boris showed his love for Romanov's children and swore a binding oath always to honor them like brothers,[9] and other contemporaries waxed highly sentimental about this episode. In fact, sober political calculation was what activated an alliance between the Romanov and Godunov factions. The former family's pedigree was far superior to the latter's, but the Shuiskii princes, who traced their descent from Rurik and the Mstislavskii princes, who traced theirs to Gedimin,[10] still considered the Romanov family base-born. The reaction on the part of these aristocrats endangered the Romanov family's prominence, and Nikita had to curry favor among court boyars like the members of the Godunov family. Fedor's relatives needed to close ranks when faced by a common threat. Captain Jacques Margeret, who was one of Boris' bodyguards, flatly stated that Boyar Godunov was brought into the government after rumors began circulating about plans to depose the feebleminded Fedor.[11]

The new ruling group was anxious to bolster Fedor's prestige and win the support of the zemshchina nobility. A general amnesty, proclaimed on the occasion of Fedor's coronation, was a potent device to achieve this purpose. Many noble princes and boyars disgraced during Ivan's reign, including those who had been in prison for twenty years, since the start of the oprichnina, were pardoned, released, and had their estates restored. The zemshchina boyar council obtained clear guarantees against arbitrary disgrace and execution. Decrees once more were promulgated forbidding judges to punish noblemen even for serious crimes that carried the death penalty unless their guilt was palpable.

Witnesses described how the new authorities eliminated the administrative system identified with Ivan. Horsey wrote: "All over the country corrupt officials, judges, commanders and lieutenants were swept away and worthier persons named to their posts, who were ordered under pain of severe punishment to halt the extortion and bribery that had flourished under the former tsar and judge impartially, and to this end the size of their estates and annual salaries were increased."[12] It is hard to say how effective the government's fulminations against bribery and abuse by provincial judges proved to be, but there is no doubt the boyars and judges themselves profited substantially, for they were given more land and larger salaries in order to make them better perform their sworn duties.

Horsey evaluated these innovations positively, but his reports are not always worthy of credence. His account of Fedor's coronation is obviously a piece of apologetics. Since Horsey was Godunov's trusted servitor, he attributed the fresh initiatives to wise Queen Irina and her brother, although there was much to indicate that the Godunov family's influence on events was still marginal. The new course was largely the work of the zemshchina boyar government, and in general the administrative changes were designed specifically to remove former members of the oprichnina and the court from positions of power.

From the outset the new government experienced major financial difficulties. On ascending the throne tsars traditionally had distributed large sums of money to the nobility at their coronations, and the regents' financial policies had caused the treasury considerable loss, but these were not the root of the pressing problems. The boyar government had inherited a country in ruins and finances in utter disarray. To restore order to the financial system obliged the government to face reality.

Popular movements were the chief factors influencing policy. Some scholars, such as P.P. Smirnov, have asserted that the boyars' struggle for power inspired them, while others, like S.V. Bakhrushin, have considered that the revolt of the city poor against the feudatories constituted the driving force behind the uprisings. The facts are conducive to an assumption that gentry joined the city poor and merchants in armed risings against the government. It was they who initiated the revolt that broke out as soon as Ivan died. A chronicler relates that a young lesser boyar galloped about Moscow at that time shouting as loudly as he could: "People! The Godunov faction is murdering boyars." Another chronicler narrates that when the crowd arrived from everywhere to besiege the Kremlin, "many mounted lesser boyars shot arrows at the fortress." Muscovite soldiers participated in the rising, "attacking the fortress in great force with weapons." The rioters were found to include ordinary serving-men and noble provincial gentry from the zemshchina. An investigation showed that the instigators of the revolt were prominent gentry from Riazan, members of the Liapunov family who were to provide eminent activists during the Time of Troubles, members of the Kikin family, and lesser boyars from other towns.

After the townspeople and armed gentry rose, the boyar government was no longer able to resist. On July 20, 1584 the council approved a statute abolishing what were known as immunities, the tax privileges enjoyed by great landowners. Princes of the church and major landowners now were deprived of their exemptions and required to pay the same taxes as all landowners. The government was using this measure in an attempt to ameliorate the economic crisis and win the support of the impoverished petty gentry. In promulgating the law abolishing tax benefits enjoyed by secular and ecclesiastical nobles the authorities were careful to emphasize they were introducing the measure for an unspecified period to help impoverished soldiers until the country recovered, and all such aid was given under the tsar's auspices. Levelling the burden suited the interests of poor soldiers, but the gentry was not the prime beneficiary, for the treasury continued to tax its members heavily.

The attack on boyar privilege fanned noble discontent and the struggle in council assumed a dramatic form. Shortly before it was to discuss immunities, the Polish ambassador in Moscow wrote: "The differences and perpetual squabbles among the Muscovites are unending. Only today I heard that fierce quarrels have broken out among them which have almost led to murder and bloodshed."[13] The authorities were expecting new disturbances and the danger increased in 1584 with the coming of spring, when fires broke out in Moscow. Witnesses reported the capital was infested with bandits, who were responsible for the arson. In fear of the people, that summer the officials literally transformed Moscow into an armed camp. Patrols in the Kremlin were under the command of Prince Ivan Turenin, a relative of the Godunov family, and the outlying districts were supervised by Commander Ivan Kriuk-Kolychev, a supporter of the Shuiskii clan.

Tsar Ivan had not chosen his son's guardians well. While he was alive he had managed to make them obey, and Belskii's banishment did not lead to feuding within the regency council, but Polish envoys communicated that the regents frequently wrangled in Fedor's presence and failed to pay him the least respect. The disagreements inside the boyar regime surfaced with new intensity when it lost its most influential leader after Nikita Romanov suffered a stroke that disabled him for a long time and enabled the Mstislavskii and Shuiskii factions effectively to consolidate their respective positions. These rival groups did not clash over foreign policy or domestic issues; it was the main financial agency, the treasury chancery, that provoked bitter political opposition.

Two persons functioning as checks upon one another usually administered the royal treasury. With boyar support, Petr Golovin, the head treasurer, arranged to have his relative, Vladimir Golovin, appointed deputy treasurer. Generations of this family had been leading financiers to the Muscovite sovereigns for more than a century, but they had never controlled the crown treasury as completely as they were able to do under Fedor, when the treasury chancery became the preserve of Mstislavskii's and Shuiskii's partisans. His personal capacities made Petr Golovin a real leader in the boyar council. A brave man, he had not been afraid to challenge Bogdan Belskii and had procured the powerful favorite's removal. The boyar regime esteemed his services. At the coronation it was he who carried the Cap of Momomakh in front of Fedor. Enjoying Mstislavskii's and Shuiskii's support, Golovin did not hesitate to drive former oprichnina members

out of government and treated Godunov with impudence and dis-
respect. The Golovin family stood far higher on the precedence ladder
than the Godunov family. After winning his precedence suit with
Belskii the noble treasurer was searching for an opportunity to settle
affairs with the latter's brother-in-law. This intrigue of the boyar
party alarmed Boris, who decided to strike first by insisting the council scrutinize treasury personnel. The check turned up peculation so
rapacious that a court composed of boyars was forced to sentence
Golovin to death.

Boris might have had his enemy executed, but he knew such a
cruel act would not be calculated to enhance his popularity, and so
he finally contented himself with a ritual exercise. The condemned
man was led to the place of execution and consigned to the headsman,
who stripped the victim and raised the axe above him. The execution
was cancelled only at the last moment. Golovin was pardoned and
banished to the Kazan region, where Ivan Voeikov, a former oprichnina member and Boris' favorite, was ordered to guard him. When the
treasurer died in captivity it was rumored he had been secretly murdered on Boris' orders. The deputy treasurer, Vladimir Golovin, was
removed from his post, deprived of rank and estates, and sent into
exile. Mikhail Golovin, Petr's brother, fled to Poland. Godunov appointed Demensha Cheremisinov, a former oprichnina member, head
of the treasury chancery. The trial of the Golovin brothers weakened
the boyar party and Romanov's supporters were not slow to take advantage of the situation. The quarrels between Nikita Romanov and
Mstislavskii had attracted widespread attention, and once Godunov
became the ailing Romanov's successor he redoubled the contest with
Mstislavskii, which ended with its most noble member's retirement
from the regency council.

On occasion Tsar Ivan had compelled Mstislavskii, the head of the
boyar council, to perform acts of public contrition. He had acknowledged he was guilty when the Tatars burned down the Russian capital
and the royal regiments suffered defeat in the war with Batory. In
Fedor's reign he was faced with new charges. Moscow was alive with
rumors that Mstislavskii was trying to lure Godunov to his house and
kill him at a party. Boris now had a handy excuse to initiate an important trial, but seeking to avoid unnecessary alarm, he convinced
the elderly regent to retire voluntarily.

I managed to discover a monastery record that constitutes eloquent
testimony to the old guardian's tonsure: "Prince Ivan Fedorovich
Mstislavskii came on a pilgrimage to Solovetskii monastery and gave

twenty rubles to keep two tables."[14] From Solovki he went to the Kirillov monastery in Beloozero, where he was tonsured, taking the name of Elder Iona. The regent did not proceed to his place of confinement like other disgraced traitors; en route he was allowed to stop at the Solovetskii monastery. Mstislavskii's agreement voluntarily to go into exile saved the members of his family from disgrace. His son inherited his father's appanage principality and also became president of the boyar council. Mstislavskii's retirement was preceded by an intense struggle behind the scenes in which a leading role belonged to Andrei Shchelkalov, the chief council secretary. Ivan Timofeev, a writer of the Time of Troubles, called Shchelkalov Boris' mentor, the man who taught him how to prevail over the nobility. Timofeev worked under Shchelkalov and was better informed than most. The head of the chancery bureaucracy had indeed helped Godunov in his clash with Mstislavskii.

Contemporaries described Shchelkalov as a remarkably clever and crafty individual who exhibited an extraordinary capacity for work; resting neither day nor night, he toiled like a mule. The Shchelkalov family had risen from the townspeople. Andrei's grandfather had been a cattle dealer, known as a "little lord of horses." His father had started out as a priest and ended up a secretary, and Andrei, after twenty years in the chanceries, had become a leading figure in the zemshchina. Boris sought his friendship, and in a rush of gratitude went so far as to call the unpedigreed secretary his father. He could not have contrived a better way to denigrate himself, but Godunov had good reasons for cultivating the zemshchina leader.

Early in 1585 Yakov Zaborovskii, an interpreter in the ambassadorial chancellery, when in their country gave the Poles important information about the situation in Moscow. He told them: "The Russians at last have reached agreement amongst themselves and a mere two persons hold the administration of the entire country and the tsardom of Muscovy in their hands. One is called Boris Fedorovich Godunov and the other, a temporary ruler or something like that, is Andrei Shchelkalov." The interpreter thought "Shchelkalov's position is stronger than that of the prince's brother-in-law." The zemshchina could not forgive Godunov his past service in the oprichnina, and the higher he rose the more acutely he felt the insecurity of his position. Many regarded Boris as a mere favorite; Fedor was chronically in poor health and not expected to live long. He was taken seriously ill and almost died during the first year of his reign. Realizing the tsar's death would mean the end of his career, Boris feverishly sought a solution.

Early in 1585 Godunov sent trusted emissaries to Vienna. Their discussions at the Austrian court were shrouded in secrecy, but the Poles soon found out about them, for Interpreter Zaborovskii, a direct participant, supplied them with accurate information. His revelations were sensational. Unable to assume Irina could retain the throne after her husband's death and seeing no other way to keep power, Boris secretly asked Vienna to consider marrying her to an Austrian prince, who subsequently would come to the Muscovite throne,[15] but the negotiations resulted in an unprecedented scandal. Tsar Fedor recovered and the talks became widely known. The Polish ambassador lodged a strong protest about them with the boyar council. Those involved offered clumsy excuses: "We are very surprised that some evildoer and traitor has made such wicked remarks" (about the marriage with a relative of the emperor—R.S.),[16] which convinced nobody. Fedor was mortally affronted and relations between the relatives, heretofore untroubled, grew tense. Later the mild tsar more than once seized his staff to teach his brother-in-law a lesson.

The boyar party fastened on Godunov's debacle in order to obtain revenge. His position looked hopeless and he prepared for the worst. Boris wrote nothing by which to judge his suffering, but like many other men of his time he communicated his feelings not to a diary but to monks. Appeals to the church were sweetened by imposing amounts of money. Anguish can be measured financially in monastery revenue records, and at times these prosaic figures are more useful than rhetorical flourishes in a diary. On November 30, 1585 Godunov gave the Trinity-St. Sergius monastery the amazing sum of one thousand rubles. Even crowned heads only made such sacrifices in rare and exceptional circumstances. To deposit money in a monastery was a sure way to secure a family's future. Disgrace entailed confiscation of estates, but the rule was not applied to money and property conveyed to a monastery. Boris was obviously anxious to provide his family with the support it would need if he should be formally disgraced.

A month before taking this action Godunov had sent Horsey, his agent, on a secret mission to London. Horsey raced to the frontier as though he were being pursued and beat two Russian postboys to death en route. In London the queen's councillors could scarcely believe their ears when Horsey transmitted Godunov's appeal to them: he wanted refuge for himself and his family in England if disaster struck. Horsey's explanation resolved all doubts that Boris was serious. He told the queen that Godunov's treasure was already at the Solovetskii monastery, from where it could easily be conveyed to London at the first suitable opportunity. Queen Elizabeth was astonished and questioned Horsey closely as to why Boris was planning to remove his resources from Russia.

Horsey had another and a delicate commission to execute in London. He consulted the best English physicians about Queen Irina, who often had been pregnant, though never successfully. At the start of the spring navigational season an English ship brought an experienced midwife to Russia, but the affair received advance publicity and caused Boris problems. He had to resort to stratagem to prevent the boyar council from discussing the sensitive matter. In a letter Queen Elizabeth informed Fedor she was sending an able, seasoned midwife and a doctor to supervise her work to the Russian court in the interests of Irina's health, but only the doctor was allowed to reach Moscow. The midwife was detained in Vologda, and all reference to her was expunged carefully from the queen's letter when it was rendered into Russian. The translation shown the members of the boyar council simply declared that a doctor had come from London whose medical skills were superior to any midwife's.

The Godunov family hoped the birth of an heir would immediately secure the dynasty and its own position at court, but Boris' appeal to people considered heretics of a different faith aroused his enemies, who manifested great concern for piety by refusing to entertain the notion that a female doctor-heretic, as they termed the midwife, might facilitate the birth of an Orthodox heir to the throne. Events in Moscow assumed menacing proportions and Boris was forced to yield. After a whole year in Vologda with no call for her services, the midwife went home. The birth of an heir ran counter to the opposition's calculations, for the royal family had become a pawn in the hands of the mighty boyars and clergy united in their efforts to bring Godunov down.

Boris had both strengths and weaknesses. He had failed to conceal his demarches at the courts of Vienna and London, and by the spring of 1586 it was rumored spitefully in Moscow that the Godunov family was trying to set an Austrian Catholic on the throne and affiance Queen Irina to him while her husband was still alive, or if this ploy failed was set to flee to the Protestants in England. All this provided fresh fuel for the boyars to use in their campaign against Boris, and the situation in the capital became more difficult when Nikita Romanov-Yurev died late in April. A popular rising that ensued almost ruined the Godunov family. Contemporaries who survived the Time of Troubles were fond of recalling how calm and untroubled

Fedor's reign was, but they had chosen to forget a good deal. The epoch of Tsar Alexis Mikhailovich has traditionally been called an age of disturbances, but in fact unrest began soon after Ivan's death. Under the tranquil Fedor popular risings occurred with remarkable regularity and force.

In 1586 the tsar's diplomats abroad categorically denied rumors that the authorities in Moscow ". . . sit in the Kremlin in a state of siege. Such has never been the case and only an idle chatterer would say so. From whom are they hiding? From peasants? The fortress has guards at the gate, but that is nothing new. It is a longstanding practice to ensure the common safety."[17] They were not telling the truth; chronicles and monastery records leave no doubts on that score. The disbursement registers of the Miracles (Chudov) monastery furnish clear, indisputable proof that the Kremlin was besieged: in May, 1586 the monastery purchased military supplies "because it is a time of siege." The monastery servitors obviously were helping fusiliers guard the Kremlin walls while the siege lasted.

The chronicles indicate the rising, which burst out suddenly, caught the leaders unawares. A host of people charged into the Kremlin and packed the square in front of the Palace of Facets. The mob demanded Boris be surrendered to them, for they considered him an incarnation of injustice and oppression. A chronicler reported the people of Moscow wanted to stone the whole Godunov family to death on the spot without mercy. Boris was powerless to protect himself and those close to him. The explosion of elemental popular rage stunned those in power. The boyars did everything they could in order to calm the commons and get them out of the Kremlin, and to do so they had to compose their differences. Metropolitan Dionisii assumed the task of peacemaker and the Shuiskii faction was unable to take advantage of a splendid chance to settle accounts with its enemies. Regent Ivan Shuiskii, speaking for all the boyars, assured the mob they were not angry with Boris, had settled their disagreements, and had no wish to indulge in mutual recriminations in future. A few petty traders tried to contradict him, but the opportunity slipped by and the crowd's attitude altered. As soon as the mob left the Kremlin the boyars locked the gates, stationed fusiliers along the walls, and placed a heavy guard around the royal palace. This began what the diplomatic documents termed the Kremlin siege.

The fate of the Godunov family appeared to hang by a thread and Boris became even more determined to seek safety abroad while his supporters fell away before his eyes. The reason for his failure is clear.

The zemshchina had made him disperse the old court guard and thus deprived him of an effective device to maintain order. He could not control the situation.

The Moscow disturbances paid the Shuiskii boyars substantial political dividends. Whenever an interregnum occurred members of this family inevitably came to the fore, as they had done when Vasilii III and Ivan IV died and would do again after the deaths of Godunov and the False Dmitrii. The Shuiskii clan epitomized the power of the Russian aristocracy; their connections among the gentry were also a source of strength, and traditionally they had enjoyed support among the Moscow population, especially rich merchants. Their party was led by Ivan Petrovich Shuiskii, who was very popular; his sons, Andrei, Vasilii, and Dmitrii, as well as Boyar Vasilii Fedorovich Skopin-Shuiskii, sat on the council.

The truce between the Shuiskii and Godunov factions proved of short duration, for the nobility was anxious to take advantage of Boris' misfortunes, of which everyone knew, in order finally to be rid of him. The Shuiskii forces were behind a new move the zemshchina made against the Godunov family. Russian and foreign sources of quite different origins unanimously affirm that the opposition tried to make Tsar Fedor obtain a divorce, which would shatter Boris' influence. Appearing at court its representatives begged Fedor to send Irina to a nunnery and marry again in order to acquire offspring.[18] Their request was tantamount to an assembly resolution; it was signed by the regent, Prince Ivan Shuiskii, other members of the boyar council, Metropolitan Dionisii, bishops, and leading merchants and traders among the townspeople. They were calling for the tonsure of Irina Godunova, and, consequently, Boris' removal, and the zemshchina interpellation carried weight. However, although in youth Fedor had been terrified of the beatings his father administered, even that arbitrary despot had not been able to compel his weak-willed son to obtain a divorce, and so the boyars and the metropolitan interfering in his private life had even less chance of success. On October 13, 1586 Metropolitan Dionisii was deprived of office, tonsured, and banished to the Khutynskii monastery in Novgorod, and the archbishop of Krutitsa, Varlaam Pushkin, who had connived with him, was confined to the Antoniev monastery in the same city. The disgraced churchmen were able to continue their conversations in quiet solitude.

Fedor's family life was not the sole bone of contention between Godunov's partisans and the boyar faction. Foreign affairs provided a constant source of friction. The nobles favored closer ties with the Rzeczpospolita. Sapieha, chancellor of Lithuania, wrote from Moscow that they supported King Batory, and in 1585 Zaborovskii, the interpreter in the ambassadorial chancellery retailed the same information, supplementing it with significant details. He secretly told Batory that the pro-Polish party was headed by the Shuiskii faction, whose members were devoted to the king and entertained strong hopes because "like elders around an eagle" their estates adjoined the king's realm.[19] There is no question that an official of the Muscovite diplomatic corps possessed good sources of information. The reasons why the Shuiskii faction sympathized with Poland are comprehensible. The Muscovite nobility was impressed with the political system in the Rzeczpospolita, where royal power was limited in the interest of the magnates. The boyars favored the development of a comparable order in Russia, thereby restricting the tsar's autocratic power.

King Stefan Batory was aware of the quarrels among the leading boyars and of the popular disturbances in Moscow. His correspondence with the Jesuit Possevino shows that he was convinced the boyars and the bulk of the people, unwilling to endure Godunov's despotism, merely were waiting for Polish support. Muscovite emigre nobles told the king to lose no time. One of them, Mikhail Golovin, said to Batory: "Wherever you go everyone will support you; no one . . . will raise a hand against you" because of the marked factionalism among the boyars: "When such great dissension and disorder exists no one will serve or fight."[20] The Polish diet met late in 1586, charged with discussing and drawing up plans for an invasion of Russia.

Faced by imminent war with the Rzeczpospolita, Boris openly charged that the leaders of the boyar opposition had made treasonable contact with the enemy. It was known in Lithuania how in the middle of autumn, 1586 Godunov had stated in council that Andrei Shuiskii had gone to the frontier, ostensibly to hunt, but there had met some Lithuanian magnates. Shuiskii reportedly managed to clear himself, but the council meeting purportedly ended with Godunov and Shuiskii fighting and wounding each other. Informed contemporaries declared that disaffected individuals were organizing a conspiracy against Boris. Warkoch, the Austrian ambassador, heard about it from Boris himself. Reporting the conversation, he wrote: "The executors (of Tsar Ivan–R.S.), having acquired many covert supporters, particularly among townspeople and merchants, planned a sudden attack on Boris and all those thwarting them, so as to eliminate

them and henceforth rule as they pleased."[21] During the course of
many years the Godunov family had become expert in political sur-
veillance. It had eyes and ears everywhere. Boris learned of the conspirators' plans in good time, but in no position to interfere could do
no more, as Horsey noted, then surround himself with a strong guard.

Late in December, 1586 word reached the Lithuanian border
fortress of Vitebsk that serious disturbances had broken out in Moscow, and the local commander sent his government two letters concerning these developments. In the first he wrote that the disorders
were instigated by Andrei Shuiskii, who had come to an understanding with Shchelkalov. The second made no mention of Shchelkalov
but stated that Shuiskii had attacked Boris' residence; Godunov and
another great boyar had perished and some eight hundred men had
fallen with them.[22]

The Lithuanians, sympathetic to the Shuiskii cause, had waited a
long time to hear that it had prevailed and thus found it easy to believe Godunov had died and Shchelkalov had gone over to the opposition. These rumors appeared dubious, but the reports of Lithuanian
spies were not entirely without foundation. As the letters from
Vitebsk came in, the Lithuanian government also received formal
notification about events in Moscow. Representatives abroad of the
ambassadorial chancellery officially told Lithuania that Boyar Andrei
Shuiskii had been banished and some petty traders executed ". . . for
brigandage and meddling in affairs of no concern to them." A rising
had clearly taken place in Moscow or had at least been attempted
with the support of townspeople. The effort to storm the Godunov
residence met with failure. Boris was ready and deployed a formidable
force to oppose the attack. Recovering from the fright he had experienced, Godunov ordered six merchants beheaded by the Kremlin wall
to terrify the commons, and many townspeople were exiled to Siberia.
In sharp contrast to the punishments meted out to the ringleaders of
the townspeople the sanctions applied against the Shuiskii faction
were surprisingly mild. The official explanation ran that Prince Andrei
had not formally been placed under displeasure, although he was
obliged to quit the capital. Ivan Shuiskii was packed off to the remote town of Kineshmu, where he had an estate.

After the Shuiskii princes left, the authorities proceeded to investigate the cause and circumstances of the conspiracy. The devices
normal for the times were employed during the inquiry. Conspirators
were haled off to torture chambers and harshly interrogated. Some
arrested courtiers, convinced their cause was lost, soon changed their

colors; Fedor Miliukov, who had served the Shuiskii family, divulged information. The investigation, lasting many months, provided the government with valuable evidence, and after it was over a new statement was released abroad about the Shuiskii affair: ". . . Prince Andrei Shuiskii and his brothers tried to betray their sovereign and plotted wrongs and every kind of evil with the traders. Prince Ivan Petrovich aided and abetted them and perpetrated many wrongful acts against his sovereign."[23] Russian diplomats made no effort to explain to the Poles the exact nature of the treasonable deeds performed by the Shuiskii group and its adherents, the traders, but the Moscow authorities did announce the conspirators had favored close ties with Poland. Warkoch reported from Moscow in 1589: "The executors (of Tsar Ivan—R.S.) wanted, as Boris is now claiming, to come to a secret understanding with Poland to make Russia part of it. There is good reason to assume this was no idle matter."[24]

The upheavals in Moscow aroused Boris to proceed resolutely against the boyar opposition. The country was bracing for fresh political turbulence. The whole horizon was menacingly overcast, but the thunderclap came later.

Chapter Three

BOYAR PERSECUTION

Russia's defeat in Livonia long soured its foreign relations. The treaties it had negotiated failed to ensure a lasting, stable peace. When Ivan died Batory refused to ratify the truce of Yam Zapolskii and expansionist circles in Sweden were concerting plans to make new conquests in Russia, but disputes over Livonia prevented Russia's enemies from making common cause.

Russia's weakness encouraged the Crimeans to renew their attacks. Russian commanders defeated them in 1584 and 1585, but these small encounters presaged a major conflict. In 1587 the khan dispatched his sons with forty thousand knights, but the tsar's forces, advancing in good time, made them retire.

Next fierce internecine struggles in Bakhchisarai afforded Russia an opportunity to meddle in Crimean affairs. Murat-Girei, a son of the deposed khan, turned up in Moscow and was enrolled in crown service. The authorities, determined to establish a Muscovite vassal in the Crimea, while preparing to carry out the scheme sent Murat-Girei with a force to Astrakhan, and Godunov himself ordered a stout stone fortress, one of the best in the country, hastily built there. Russian commanders constructed a fort on the Terek river and a fortress on the strip of land between the Don and the Volga. The new town was named Tsaritsyn in Irina's honor.[1] The military activity in the lower Volga area and the north Caucasus showed clearly that Moscow was anxious to confront the Ottoman empire and intended to win the contest.

The conflict between the Crimea and Russia encouraged the latter's aggressive western neighbors. Batory decided to undertake a new eastern campaign, but late in 1586 he died at the height of the military preparations he had initiated. During the interregnum Russian diplomats proposed electing Tsar Fedor to the throne of the Rzeczpos-polita and turning the two countries' resources against the Turks and Tatars, but a Swedish and an Austrian candidate simultaneously prevailed. After a struggle between them, Sigismund III Vasa, the heir to the Swedish throne, triumphed, and war with Russia constituted one of the main planks in the new Polish king's foreign policy. The personal union of the two countries revived the coalition of Russia's most formidable antagonists, the victors in the Livonian war.

The Muscovite government sought to counter the Polish-Swedish coalition by allying with the Hapsburgs. Godunov sent his emissary, Luca Pauli, to Vienna and the Austrian ambassador, Warkoch, soon arrived in Moscow. Boris invited him to his chambers in a ceremony that bore all the earmarks of a royal audience. A wall of guards stood from one gate to another in the courtyard and courtiers, wearing golden clothing and gold chains, waited in the hall. Warkoch kissed Godunov's hand and gave him a personal communication from the emperor. Boris tried to convince Warkoch it was essential for Russia and Austria to conclude a military alliance and promised to cover part of the empire's expenditures. His style of personal diplomacy displayed characteristic qualities: the subsidies he offered the Viennese court were as large as the tribute Russia had once paid the Crimean khan.

The negotiations with Austria augured a new trend in Russian diplomacy. Western Europe was witnessing the decisive clash between Protestant England and the Catholic Habsburgs. Just before the Spanish attack London sought a rapprochement and sent Giles Fletcher on a mission to Russia. Regarding trade with England as important,[2]

in 1587 Godunov confirmed to the English their right of free trade
in Russia, to the annoyance of the Moscow merchants, but in 1588
he revised his pro-English stance and Fletcher's mission in 1588-1589
met with total failure. The Muscovite government rejected England's
blandishments.

Boris had considerable influence on the country's foreign policy.
Acknowledging this, in 1589 the boyar council passed a decree ap-
proving the personal links Boris had formed with the Austrian and
Spanish Habsburgs, England, and other states in Western Europe.
Boris soon conceived an inflated opinion of his diplomatic prowess:
Moscow learned only later that in March, 1589 Austria had made
peace with the Rzeczpospolita, agreeing not to provide Russia any
assistance. The project to form a Russo-Austrian coalition proved
nugatory and Boris' personal diplomacy had suffered a setback. Russia also had lost a potential ally in England and could not break out
of international isolation.

In summer, 1589 the country was menaced with the danger of invasion. John III, the Swedish king, concentrated virtually all his land
forces, calculated at some ten thousand men, and a fleet of forty
ships at Reval, where he was joined by the Polish king, Sigismund III.
The allies planned a show of force to compel Russia to make terri-
torial concessions. They proposed summoning Fedor to the frontier
for a meeting at which he would be told to hand over the principal
border fortresses of Smolensk, Novgorod and Pskov as well as other
parts of Russia to Sweden and the Rzeczpospolita. John III and his
son intended to dismember the country.

Russia had no resources available to fight this hostile coalition.
The country's finances were in ruins and the number of gentry military units had declined sharply. Early in the Livonian war the high
command had been able to field more than eighteen thousand men,
but no more than ten thousand toward the end of it. Much land belonging to service-tenure holders had been abandoned and forests
covered areas that once had been under cultivation. Five years had
elapsed since the peace, but very little abandoned land was again
being farmed. Peasants and small feudal landholders were feeling the
ruinous consequences of agrarian disaster. The amount of land available for service-tenure holders had contracted. Economic stabiliza-
tion had been arrested by the spontaneous revolts engulfing the
country in 1587-1588. Bad weather destroyed crops and the price of
bread rose steadily in Moscow, Novgorod, Vladimir and Kholmogory.
Peasants were moving to the fertile south. Officials reported that

вичешꙋиско кнsю иваноу тꙋрани
нꙋ. вдомъ прчⷭтые бⷰцы чютворцꙋ
кирилꙋ вкладꙋ. н. рꙋбле денегъ.
дашбразоⷡ иснитъ иплатьꙗ
на. н. же рꙋбле. ивсеⷢтопоне
дано. р. рꙋбле. изатодаꙗние
кнзь иванъ войноцехъ нѣтъ, на
писанъ всенаниⷭ. акормъ по
немъ кормити напреставление
его. ноꙗбрⷶ в. ѕі. доколеимо
кастырь стойтъ.
лѣта зрчи. боꙗрина кнsа ва
силья федоровича скопина кнаги
ни елена петроⷡна. дасынаиⷯ
боꙗрина кнsа михаила василье
вича кнатини алеѯандра василевна
дали покнsе василіи федоровиче
дапокнsе михаиле васильевиче.
вдомъ прчⷭтые бⷰцы. кирилꙋ чюдо
твоⷰцꙋ вклꙋ. р. золотыꙗ запꙗ

Manuscript Excerpt Concerning the Death of Ivan Petrovich Shuiskii

many members of the gentry had become paupers, and ruined serving-
men with their families left their fallow land, indentured themselves
to boyars, rarely occupied peasant plots, and increasingly subsisted
on charity. The discontent of the lesser gentry portended political
crisis.

A famine in 1588 rendered the situation in Moscow more difficult.
Gangs of beggars and tramps roamed the streets. The people held
Boris Godunov, formerly considered primarily a usurper of power,
responsible for their misery and chided him overtly and covertly. In
1588-1589 Fletcher saw a Moscow mob eagerly listening to a holy
fool impugning Boris: "At present a man walks naked about the
streets of Moscow stirring up everyone against the government, especially the Godunov family, which he considers is oppressing the whole
country."[3] By 1589 the famine had abated but the situation in Moscow remained disturbing. Early in spring the government, fearing
street incidents, ordered strong military units assigned all over the
city.[4]

In 1588-1589 Moscow was full of rumors extremely unpleasant
for Boris Godunov that were picked up and circulated abroad. Late
in 1588 the Vatican representative in Cracow transmitted two sensational communications to Rome. The first stated that the ruler of
Muscovy had ordered his brother-in-law beaten with staves, but Boris,
grasping a knife, twice wounded the tsar and the latter fell seriously
ill. The second reported a highly untrustworthy rumor that Fedor
had been murdered by his own courtiers, a possible allusion to Godunov and his supporters.

The news from Moscow was reflected in an official exchange involving Chancellor Sapieha of Lithuania. The source of his information was a member of the Polish gentry stationed on the border, who
engaged in a conversation with Russian guards. Their Lithuanian acquaintance reported: "The Muscovite princess had a daughter. The
Godunov family was displeased and secretly substituted the newborn
son of a fusilier's wife for the queen's daughter. One Godunov partisan, who knew of this, informed on them to young Prince Dmitrii,
the brother of the present Muscovite sovereign, and other boyars,
who then told the sovereign himself. The sovereign ordered his wife
tonsured for her transgressions. Fearing the same would happen to
them, members of the Godunov family in all probability actually
killed the sovereign, as the Russian guards reported."[5]

Two months later Barakovskii, the vice-chancellor of Lithuania,
sent a letter to the Polish legate in Rome with further spicy details

about the Moscow scandals. Here is a summary of them: when Tsar
Fedor left Moscow on a pilgrimage to a monastery somebody made
the queen pregnant, and Fedor wanted her tonsured. Boris Godunov,
the queen's brother, quarreled with Fedor over his sister. During the
altercation the tsar struck his brother-in-law with his staff and the
latter stabbed Fedor several times with a knife. The tsar's condition
is poor. Some claim the grand princess tried to poison her husband
for fear he might tonsure her.[6] The malicious gossip abundant in
Moscow most likely formed the basis of the chancellor's statements.
After their petition to Fedor failed to dislodge Queen Irina the boyars
tried to circulate spiteful rumors charging the pious queen with being
unfaithful, substituting another child for the royal one, and intend-
ing to poison her husband. These insinuations damaged the Godunov family's prestige. Previously unpopular, Boris now became a
target for every conceivable attack, and even those wishing him well
harbored no illusions concerning his future. Warkoch wrote in 1589:
"If anything happens to the grand prince, Boris' enemies would move
against him again . . . and if he tried to make himself ruler he would
be unlikely to succeed."

Godunov's ambition estranged his closest allies. His unceremonious
intrusion into the affairs of the diplomatic corps offended the head
secretary of the ambassadorial chancellery, Andrei Shchelkalov. In
1587 Queen Elizabeth carelessly addressed a letter to Godunov and
Shchelkalov as joint rulers. Boris at once expressed irritation and
told London it was improper to confuse him with a crown secretary;
to do so "is highly detrimental to my princely rank and dignity."[7]
Shchelkalov, who enjoyed genuine popularity in the zemshchina, refused to acknowledge that Boris stood higher. He observed in a discussion with Fletcher in 1588 that Boris "had to perform all duties
pertinent to the country's interest . . . under a mandate from the
tsar." He was in effect saying Boris was merely another chancery
figure like himself. Their rivalry broke out in the open in 1588 and
led to a brief period of disgrace for Shchelkalov. A year later Warkoch,
during his sojourn in Moscow, noted: "Andrei Shchelkalov no longer
occupies a place of honor and Boris Fedorovich is by no means
favorably disposed towards him. The secretary is under investigation
and not much trusted."[8]

During these domestic and foreign crises the boyars rose in opposition. In a confidential chat with Horsey, Boris complained that the
Nagoi family and the Shuiskii faction had made common cause and
were conspiring against him.[9] The members of the Nagoi family, who

previously had served in the oprichnina, and the noble Shuiskii princes were politically poles apart, but both groups brimmed with hostility for Godunov. His prospective isolation stimulated Boris to use force to put down his enemies. The repressions revealed the government's weakness. In Kliuchevskii's apposite phrase, the Muscovite chronicles fully understood how difficult Boris' position was under Tsar Fedor: he had to hit so as not to be hit. Regent Ivan Petrovich Shuiskii was the first victim. Prince Ivan Turenin, a courtier devoted to Boris, apprehended Shuiskii on his estate and took him under heavy guard to Beloozero, where he was forcibly tonsured in the Kirillo-Belozersk monastery, now the place where two of Ivan's executors were confined. Shuiskii, now Elder Iov, did not long survive in this remote northern retreat. The whole country heard he had died by late 1588: Fletcher, Horsey, and the Moscow and Pskov chronicles declared the mighty boyar had been murdered on Boris' orders. Who knows whether they were reporting credible information or merely retailing malicious gossip? Trustworthy documents I discovered in the Kirillo-Belozersk monastery archives help dissipate the confusion.

The monastery's revenue records show that the adjutant, Prince Turenin, arrived on November 12, 1588 and made a substantial contribution to remember Prince Ivan Shuiskii's soul on November 28. The elders noted: "Prince Shuiskii needed no further sustenance after November 16."[10] Turenin obviously could not have committed money to commemorate a disgraced person unless the tsar had specifically approved, but he needed at least a month to hear from Moscow. This means he could not have obtained a decision before mid-December. How then could Turenin offer alms for Shuiskii's soul in November, less than two weeks after he died? The inescapable conclusion is that Boris ordered Turenin to convey Shuiskii to Beloozero and there suffocate him with smoke, or, to put it otherwise, poison him with coal gas. The mode of execution shows that Boris hoped to eliminate his rival without fuss or publicity. This is also the reason why he went through the facade of tonsure. Shuiskii's execution might genuinely be termed a pious one. Muscovite sovereigns always had desired to don a monk's habit before they died, although not all were successful; Ivan was not tonsured until after his death. People of that period believed resemblance to an angel would facilitate their entrance into the other world. Although the situation was critical, it was fear, not sober political calculation, that occasioned Shuiskii's murder. His tonsure ended his secular career, for he could never return to the world as a defrocked monk. Horsey claimed everyone lamented the eminent commander's demise. Godunov's reputation was destroyed, for rumor now immediately would attribute any death or disaster to his evil designs. Junior members of the Shuiskii family dispersed among their villages were harassed, arrested and imprisoned. Andrei was confined in Buigorod, Vasilii in Galich, and two brothers were left in Shuia-selo. Court records of late 1588 refer to the dispatch of Escorts Zamytskii, Okinfov, and Vyrubov to accompany arrested members of the Shuiskii family. Andrei, the recognized leader of the anti-Godunov conspiracy, caused Boris great apprehension, and this finally decided his fate. The Shuiskii family archives record his murder in prison in June, 1589.

Besides the Shuiskii clan, many other nobles were persecuted. The prominent boyar Fedor Sheremetev, "who together with Prince Ivan Petrovich Shuiskii betrayed the sovereign, Tsar Fedor"[11] (while a Polish prisoner he had taken an oath to Batory), was confined to a monastery. A distinguished commander, Shuiskii's close associate Ivan Kriuk-Kolychev, was immured in a stone prison in Nizhegorod. Members of the gentry suffered also. Tradition holds that the Shuiskii affair caused a lesser boyar from Rostov, Averkii (Avraamii) Palitsyn, who subsequently became a famous writer during the Time of Troubles, to be confined to a monastery. However, harassment of the Shuiskii family and its supporters failed to silence the opposition. Uglich, the home of Tsar Ivan's youngest son, remained a center of agitation against Godunov and relations between the courts in Moscow and Uglich daily grew worse. One consequence of this was a small but significant episode involving Ivan's will.

Still-unpublished documents in the Vienna archives reveal a few facts concerning this incident. The first is a report sent from Moscow by Luca Pauli. Boris had sent this Austrian, long a resident of Moscow, to Vienna, where he fascinated imperial officials with tales about the portion of the tsar's will pertaining to Austria. The Habsburgs sent their envoy, Warkoch, to Russia with instructions to do whatever was necessary to learn the contents of the will. After herculean efforts Warkoch managed to obtain the required information. He wrote that Boris Godunov had detected and suppressed a boyar conspiracy against him, severely punished Ivan's executors who were guilty of sedition and, it was said, had destroyed the tsar's will. Pauli augmented the envoy's account with dramatic details. He said that Savva Frolov, the secretary who had transcribed Ivan's will, had died suddenly and it was suspected he had been poisoned to prevent the contents of the will from becoming known.[12] It is hard to evaluate this information, although superficial factual correspondences exist. Horsey, who was present when Ivan died, asserts the tsar dictated his will to Savva Frolov, a confidential secretary. Pauli heard that the will was still extant in April, 1588, but by November of the following year, precisely the time when the career of Secretary Frolov was cut short and his name disappeared from all documents, the Austrians learned that it had been destroyed. In those days the destruction of a tsar's will was unprecedented. What impelled Boris to take such an action? Perhaps it was because in the will Ivan ordained that the regents were to enjoy plenipotentiary powers and specified the rights Dmitrii, Fedor's younger brother, was to possess.

If the childless Fedor died Dmitrii would become the sole surviving member of the royal house. The Nagoi family realized he might accede to the throne at any time and in preparation deliberately encouraged the lad's hostility to Tsar Fedor's councillors. Dmitrii, an epileptic, early displayed traces of his father's cruel temper. In winter he would make snowmen to which he gave the names of leading boyars, and as soon as he finished them he would savagely cut off their heads, intoning: "This is Mstislavskii; this is Godunov!" The boy's antics caused annoyance and aroused fear in Moscow, and the suspicions the two camps harbored of each other assumed extreme forms. The court at Uglich sowed rumors (which Fletcher reflected in 1588-1589) everywhere that the tsar's relatives, calculating they could win the throne if Fedor died without issue, were trying to poison Dmitrii. These rumors were so persistent that they found their way into chronicles of the seventeenth century.

The Muscovite court took countermeasures. No later than 1588 the authorities sent a circular to all churches forbidding priests to mention Dmitrii during service because, as a product of the tsar's sixth marriage, he was illegitimate. The English envoy asserted that Boris Godunov had insisted the tsar personally issue such an order to the clergy. Canon law sternly prohibited Orthodox from marrying more than three times. As long as Ivan was alive no one dared express doubts concerning the validity of his final union, but things were different after he died. Dmitrii's relatives could only hope that in his will the father had blessed his son, which would suffice to confirm him as the lawful successor, but the destruction of the will robbed the prince of Uglich of legal grounds to press a claim to the throne. It is not clear whether, as Boris claimed, the Nagoi family had concerted with the Shuiskii faction, but in any event both were persecuted at approximately the same time. No later than 1588 the authorities arrested Petr Nagoi, son of Ivan's favorite Afanasii Nagoi, and shut him up in a monastery. Although it was believed Afanasii had been murdered as soon as Ivan died, Tsar Fedor's court register discloses that he was confined in Yaroslavl under the supervision of an escort, the courtier Zherebtsov, whom Boris trusted.

Godunov's policies were not generally well received, and they met with stubborn opposition from the appanage and boyar nobility; thus, it is not surprising that he strove to weaken the aristocracy's political power. In the late 1580s the treasury confiscated the estates belonging to Mariia Staritskaia, the queen of Livonia,[13] a cousin of Mariia Nagaia, who was tonsured forcibly and immured with her young daughter in a nunnery. Mariia Nagaia's rights also were infringed; the principality of Uglich, which she controlled, was placed under the Moscow chancery administration, which sent a crown secretary, Mikhail Bitiagovskii, to oversee it. Tsar Simeon Bekbulatovich was deprived of his title of grand prince of Tver and lost his estate. The Vorotynskii princes were allowed to keep their holdings but were forbidden to reside in Moscow. Besides the appanage nobility, the Golitsyn and Kurakin princes and the old non-titled Moscow families of Sheremetev and Buturlin also were harassed. For years Godunov would not suffer members of the distinguished Morozov, Yakovlev and Kolychev families to enter the boyar council. The cleavage between Boris and the boyars, the discontent of the impoverished gentry, and urban disturbance created a situation in some ways reminiscent of the oprichnina years. Contemporaries were alive to the danger. One of them, after carefully describing the methods Ivan had used during that time, observed that the Godunov interests were employing comparable techniques to humble and extirpate great nobles. Boris' activities did indeed assume a distinctive anti-boyar animus, but his clash with the nobility never led to a replay of the oprichnina. Ivan's protégé prevailed over the boyars without resorting to the methods of the oprichnina because he could profit from its results; his triumph was due to the political centralization successfully achieved by the end of the sixteenth century. Without support from the strong chancery apparatus Godunov would probably not have been able to cope with the outburst of aristocratic reaction. One should take contemporary remarks about a new oprichnina under Boris with a grain of salt. Godunov's policy was different; refusing to call out the praetorians, the privileged guard corps from whose ranks he had himself emerged, he relied on the mass of the gentry.

Fletcher, author of a comprehensive work about Russia, wrote that the Russian government taxed all levels of society unmercifully, but the gentry and clergy solved the problem by transferring the burden to the commons. The English jurist appears to have grasped one of the secrets of the Muscovite taxation system; he concluded: "Traders and peasants [this is how he characterized the commons] have recently been weighed down by heavy, intolerable taxation," and that Moscow regarded the Godunov faction as an oppressor of the entire country.[14] His observations sharply contradict the explanations of Boris' taxation policies offered by the ambassadorial chancellery. When Fletcher's report was published in London, Russian diplomats in Poland were saying that Boris had brought justice to the people and freed them from ruinous imposts and obligations. The envoys declared that all over the country "Boris has reduced land taxes, lowered immunities, exacted no tribute, and abolished corvée."[15] From 1583 to 1588 taxes formally increased one and a half times and the lower ranks obtained no particular reductions. The heads of the ambassadorial chancellery obviously were referring to measures Godunov had initiated exclusively to benefit the upper classes.

Unlike great privileged landowners, petty service-tenure landholders enjoyed no financial advantages and had to pay taxes to the treasury on all lands they held on service-tenure. This system did not prove deleterious to the gentry until the period when numerous disasters depopulated the countryside and disturbed the yield ratio between general tillage and private plots on service-tenure estates occupied by ordinary serving-men; their private plots now no longer were able to furnish adequate sustenance while taxed as heavily as peasant holdings. Taxation of personal plots was ruining the petty service gentry, and its members grumbled. The government realized that it could never achieve real stability without significant concessions to the lesser gentry. The statements issuing from the ambassadorial chancellery were based on fact; Godunov did offer serving-men financial concessions. The treasury began to exempt private plots of landholders rendering military service from taxation. It is uncertain when this policy came into general use, but it was widespread by the early 1590s, as revenue records from the Bezhetskii region southeast of Novgorod amply demonstrate.

Godunov's tax program was clearly aimed at the mass of the gentry, and petty service-tenure landholders considered the privileges they had obtained substantial. Freeing general tillage from taxation meant they could survive and be saved from penury when times were hard, but one should not think the new policy benefited the lesser gentry exclusively. The general tillage units exempted by the treasury increased in proportion to the size of service-tenure estates members of the gentry controlled, and so the tax reform brought greater profit to the middle rather than to the lesser gentry.

Peresvetov had once told Ivan to treat his soldiers as a father treats his children: "Generosity to his soldiers is a sign of a tsar's wisdom," and in Fedor's day the service ranks continued to believe this as strongly as they had during Ivan's reign. They advanced their needs with increasing insistence, but for the nonce the ruling group failed to respond to their demands.

The boyar regime began by abolishing the immunities great landowners enjoyed, a move ostensibly dictated by concern for the impoverished gentry but in point of fact designed mainly to enrich the treasury. Having reached the summit of power, Boris wanted to forget his humble origins and at first did not favor the gentry, but his domestic policy soon shifted after he quarreled with the boyar aristocracy and the strength of the guards corps associated with the court declined. Tax exemption for gentry lands and preliminary moves to enserf the peasantry showed that the basic contours of his new course had already been outlined. The tax reform had significant social consequences: for the first time a clear line was drawn between upper, privileged feudal landowners and the lower, tax-paying dependent peasantry.

Chapter Four

ESTABLISHMENT OF THE PATRIARCHATE

The antifeudal revolts, boyar dissension, and Tsar Fedor's incapacity weakened the autocratic administration, and division between secular and ecclesiastical authority, exemplified in the removal of Metropolitan Dionisii, deepened the crisis. Monasteries resisted attacks on their privileges and immunities. In a difficult position, the government tried to gloss over contradictions and avoid further confrontation with church leaders. Boris Godunov managed to install his protégé, Iov, as metropolitan, but the new prelate lacked influence and enjoyed little popularity. Boyars and clergy never forgave him his past involvement in the oprichnina.

The *History of the Most Holy Patriarch* relates how wise, pious Tsar Ivan conferred upon Iov his first ecclesiastical office in Staritsa.

It can be determined that this occurred at the height of the period of executions, when Ivan made Staritsa his temporary residence and examined the local population. The post of abbot of the Dormition monastery in Staritsa chancing to fall vacant, Iov was appointed to it. A man of mediocre ability, he failed to advance rapidly although Ivan was able to observe him constantly. In 1581 he became bishop of Kolomna and apparently had gone as far as he could until everything changed when Godunov came to power; Iov became an archbishop and, a few months later, metropolitan. Unlike the skilled scholar Dionisii, the new head of the church was not remarkable either for education or intelligence, but his devotion to Boris was a good substitute for talent. In addition, Iov could read the longest prayers aloud impressively and without faltering, "like a wondrous clarion, to the delight and pleasure of all."[1] Boris was prepared to do anything necessary in order to exalt Iov. Without strong leadership the church could not reacquire the influence it had earlier possessed, but the severe social crisis demanded recrudescence of a vigorous church organization, and so the secular authorities seized the initiative and established a patriarchate in Russia.

The time had long passed since the ecumenical Orthodox church headed by the patriarch of Constantinople could consider the Russian metropolitan see a second-class, peripheral eparchy. The collapse of the Byzantine empire had reversed their respective roles: the once-mighty Byzantine church had declined and fallen under the control of the victorious Turks, and the Russian church came to the fore. Muscovite metropolitans enjoyed incomparably greater scope and resources than the patriarch of Constantinople, which now was ruled by heretics, and the junior patriarchs in Alexandria and Antioch were in a parlous position. During the sixteenth century the eastern patriarchs asked Moscow for more and more assistance and the number of suppliants annually increased.

Such new realities found expression in the works of those Russian writers who devised the doctrine of Moscow—The Third Rome. The collapse of the second Rome (Byzantium) made Muscovy (the Third Rome) the principal bastion of Orthodoxy. In time apologists of church power added a new formulation to this concept: since Russia was now the center of ecumenical Orthodoxy, its church must be headed by a personage of high ecclesiastical rank; the Orthodox autocrat needed a patriarch, as had the emperor in Constantinople. Leaders of the eastern Orthodox church had no sympathy with this but hesitated openly to reject it because haggling over a patriarchate might provide them with substantial benefits. After Fedor ascended the throne, Joachim, patriarch of Antioch, came to Moscow with the usual requests for subvention and was received with great honor, but before turning to money matters his hosts proposed establishing a patriarchate in Russia. Joachim most reluctantly promised to communicate their desire to a general council. After he left an emissary from Theoleptos, patriarch of Constantinople, arrived. The Greeks clearly had no wish to put anything in writing concerning a Muscovite patriarchy. Theoleptos' letter touched mainly on financial problems, but the emissary stated verbally that the ecumenical patriarchs would decide the issue involving Moscow very soon.

Relations with Constantinople took a new turn after the Turks deposed Theoleptos, who was succeeded by Jeremiah. The new head of the universal church set out for Moscow in person. Moscow had not been informed of the change in church leaders and first suspected Jeremiah was an impostor, but the Greeks soon disposed of these suspicions and were received in the Kremlin on July 21, 1588. Jeremiah was presented to the tsar and then escorted to a special chamber for an intimate chat with Boris Godunov and Andrei Shchelkalov. The discussion disclosed some highly unpalatable facts. The Russians assumed the patriarch had brought a general council decision with him, but circumstances turned out to be much more complex.

The Moscow negotiations dragged on for more than six months, and sources have evaluated them differently. Muscovite ecclesiastical writers distorted the truth by claiming the patriarch had brought a positive decision by the general council,[2] and the official record of the ambassadorial chancellery contains major omissions. Byzantine participants assisting the patriarch, Metropolitan Dorotheos and Archbishop Arsenios, have left two mutually exclusive versions of the discussions conducted in Moscow.

Arsenios, archbishop of Elassoniki, was determined to glorify Patriarch Jeremiah and sing praises of the tsar's magnanimity. He composed his impressions of Moscow in verse because, as he expressed it, what he saw was not susceptible of description in prose.[3] What inspired him? It is not hard to guess. At Patriarch Jeremiah's audience in the Kremlin the tsar bestowed lavish gifts on all the former's followers except Arsenios. This omission is explained by the fact that the archbishop already had visited Moscow and been given a large sum of money to pray for Tsar Ivan's soul, but had disposed of it improperly. Such gifts were to be used solely in one's own diocese, but after Arsenios left Russia he spent time in hostile Lithuania.[4] It was thus understandable that when he came to Moscow again he was received in a cold and unfriendly manner, but during the course of the protracted negotiations in the capital Arsenios managed to win back the Muscovites' favor. At a final audience the tsar said to him: "Rest assured I shall never forsake you. I shall entrust you with many towns and districts, where you will serve as bishop."[5] The tsar's unexpected generosity stems from the fact that Arsenios seems to have rendered him substantial services in bringing the negotiations concerning a Russian patriarchate to a satisfactory conclusion before he departed for Constantinople, where Jeremiah was faced with the disagreeable task of explaining his actions to a general council. Arsenios' account, in which he emerged as Jeremiah's apologist, assisted the patriarch in extricating himself from a difficult position, while Metropolitan Dorotheos remained critical of him. Dorotheos compiled a chronicle which contained a report on the Moscow parleys and his brief entry, which is devoid of literary merit, deserves greater credence than Arsenios' poetic effusion.[6] He contended that the debts incurred by the Constantinople patriarchate constituted the real reason why Jeremiah went to Moscow, but the question of subsidies was shunted aside immediately because the Russian government insisted the issue of a native patriarchy must be resolved first.

Jeremiah's arrival forced Moscow to make a choice. The alternatives were to dismiss the patriarch without a subvention and lose any advantage that might accrue from the first visit to Russia of the head of the Orthodox church, grant the patriarch generous alms (although the experience with Joachim had shown it was risky to rely on the Byzantines' verbal assurances), or retain Jeremiah and compel him to make concessions. Moscow had good reasons for choosing the third course.

On their way to Moscow, Jeremiah, Dorotheos and Arsenios passed through Poland and Chancellor Jan Zamojski invited them to Zamoste, where he sounded them out about moving the patriarchal see from Constantinople to Kiev, then part of the Rzeczpospolita. After his talk with Jeremiah, the chancellor noted: "It seemed to me he would not be averse to this."[7] Arsenios alerted Moscow to the interview with Zamojski and his news alarmed the Russian authorities and aroused them to vigorous measures. Deciding to hold the Greek party for some length of time, the Muscovite authorities deliberately tried to isolate them. Escorts and guards allowed no one access to Jeremiah, who was literally forbidden to leave his residence, while his servants were accompanied by guards whenever they went out to procure supplies. Although shown every honor and provided with all amenities, the Greeks were prisoners. The patriarch was installed in ample chambers, regally furnished, where divine service might constantly be celebrated, and the palace supplied him with choice food and abundant drink—three flagons of intoxicating hawthorn, cherry and raspberry mead, a barrel of thick mead, and a half-barrel of kvas, but the Kremlin stopped summoning the Greeks and seemed to have forgotten their existence.

Although Jeremiah found Muscovite hospitality galling, he nevertheless valued it. The aged patriarch, who had experienced the vicissitudes of fate, been betrayed by his bishops, endured the haughtiness of conquerors of a different faith, and been robbed and expelled from his residence, was not at heart averse to moving to Moscow from Constantinople. In a conversation with his closest counsellors Jeremiah once said he was unwilling to establish a patriarchate in Moscow, "but if I do, I shall remain here as patriarch myself." Noting down his words, Dorotheos observed that the patriarch's entourage included "ill-intentioned dishonorable people, who report everything they hear to the interpreters, who in turn inform the tsar."[8] In alluding to dishonorable counsellors Dorotheos was thinking of Arsenios, now a fervent partisan of the Moscow project.

Once the authorities learned of the patriarch's desire they hit upon an ingenious stratagem, suggesting to Jeremiah that a brilliant future awaited him in Moscow: "Master, if you are minded to stay here, you will be our patriarch." However, such statements emanated only from the escorts attending him, not from the tsar or his boyars. Falling into the trap set for him, without waiting for an official invitation Jeremiah said to them: "I shall remain!"

Godunov's secret diplomacy apparently had produced good results and the question was referred immediately to the boyar council. Informing it of Jeremiah's acquiescence, Tsar Fedor attached various conditions. A secretary read his speech: "Jeremiah, patriarch of Constantinople, has signified he wishes to stay in our land; he will be patriarch in the primary see of Vladimir, while the metropolitan will be in Moscow as before. If Jeremiah does not care . . . to live in Vladimir, only a Moscow council can create a patriarch in Moscow."[9] It was Godunov, of course, not the simple-minded Fedor, who was the author of these conditions. His scheme meant that Jeremiah might establish a residence in remote Vladimir while Metropolitan Iov remained the real head of the church. Boris had obviously no intention of sacrificing his friend, and personally communicated the council decision to Jeremiah. Arsenios was present at the interview.

He observed that Boris affected a downcast mien as he "with fear, but honorably and properly" described the situation. Boris conducted the conversation so artfully that the patriarch, strongly moved by his friendly words, virtually agreed to all the proposals until members of his retinue pointed out that he would have to reside in Vladimir, not in Moscow: "Vladimir is worse than Kukuz"[10] (the Armenian fortress thought to be the place where St. John Chrysostom was confined). The patriarch's final word was that he would establish his residence only in Moscow, "for patriarchs are always with the sovereign; it is totally impossible for a patriarch to live apart from his sovereign."[11] After hearing Jeremiah's ultimate position Boris replied that the patriarch of Moscow must be a Russian, but the former, relying on the fact that he alone could dispose of his seat, rejected this notion as well: "It will be unlawful to consecrate another if I myself cannot occupy both sees." Witnesses believed Boris was disappointed when he quitted the patriarch's abode.

Since diplomacy had failed the Muscovites adopted other tactics. Godunov absented himself temporarily and the brothers Andrei and Vasilii Shchelkalov took over the thankless task, attempting to buy the patriarch's assent with lavish promises of costly gifts, rich maintenance, and towns and districts to rule, but also by giving Jeremiah to understand he would not be allowed to leave Moscow until he made concessions. At last they took a hard line with the Greeks; when Dorotheos refused to sign the charter consecrating Iov, Andrei Shchelkalov threatened to drown him. The negotiations had received wide publicity. Boris could not afford to break them off and tried to conclude them as quickly as possible. The boyar council, again assembling in the palace, formally rejected Jeremiah's request to become patriarch in Moscow and resolved to deprive him of the right to designate patriarchs and create new metropolitanates, archbishoprics, and bishoprics even before it received the patriarch's formal agreement. On January 13, 1589 Godunov and Shchelkalov told Jeremiah what they had done. The discussion lasted a long time. The official account states: "Patriarch Jeremiah spoke about this and took great counsel with Boyar Boris Fedorovich." He gave way on all counts, asking only that "the sovereign pious tsar might graciously suffer him to depart." The Greeks capitulated in order to deliver themselves from captivity in Moscow. Dorotheos observed: "Without enthusiasm Jeremiah at last laid his hands upon the patriarch of Russia." Archbishop Arsenios declares that from the first the Muscovite clergy had participated in the negotiations with Jeremiah, but the sources contradict this pious legend. The authorities did not convoke an assembly of clergy until the difficult negotiations had been crowned with success. Boris Godunov saw no need to consult with "the sovereign's pilgrims" over electing a candidate to the patriarchal throne.

Jeremiah furnished the government with a minute description of the ceremony for consecrating a patriarch. Custom dictated that the tsar and the spiritual assembly secretly should choose three candidates, one of whom the tsar subsequently would confirm. This method of selecting the head of the church seemed clumsy to the Muscovites, but at Jeremiah's insistence they agreed to hold a secret election. The whole procedure was a mere formality. The authorities defined the duties of the electoral council down to the last detail, including the secret election: Jeremiah was to meet apart with the Muscovite bishops and "choose three . . . Metropolitan Iov of all Russia, Archbishop Aleksandr of Novgorod, and Archbishop Varlaam of Rostov." The decree went on to state: "Next from these three pious Tsar Fedor will choose only Metropolitan Iov to be patriarch."[12] Jeremiah unswervingly fulfilled Godunov's prescriptions pertaining to the secret election and on January 26, 1589 elevated Iov to the patriarchal chair of Muscovy.

The Greeks hoped they could now at last return home but instead were told to make a pilgrimage to the Trinity-St. Sergius monastery. When they came back they begged to be sent to Constantinople, but Godunov declined on the pretext it was disagreeable to travel in spring, when roads were bad. The Greeks continued to be held because Moscow was occupied with carrying out the assembly decree to establish the patriarchy. The council that ostensibly had drawn up the document scarcely ever sat with a full complement. Its enactment listed Jeremiah and Dorotheos as members, but Dorotheos reported that when the final decree was brought to the Greeks' residence they could not understand it, because no translation had been provided. He was forced by threats to sign but at once advised the patriarch secretly to lay a curse on the decree.

After spending almost a year in Moscow, on May 19 the patriarch finally was granted permission to return home. Boris rewarded his former captives generously. In obvious admiration Arsenios wrote that the puissant tsar and his queen had made them all rich, but a subsidy to build a new patriarchal palace in Constantinople, the original reason why Jeremiah had come to Russia, was not forthcoming until the last moment. Godunov did not remind the tsar of it until after the patriarch had departed, and then one thousand rubles were hastily sent to the Greeks for a new patriarchal church. To celebrate the establishment of the Muscovite patriarchate a great holiday was declared. During the procession the newly-consecrated patriarch rode on a donkey from the Frolov gate and toured the Kremlin. Boris led a donkey, and a throng accompanied them.

After Iov's accession the authorities composed a charter, ostensibly confirming his election, that alluded to the historic role Russia had played as a bulwark of the ecumenical Orthodox church: "Ancient Rome fell due to the Apollinarian heresy[13] . . . the second Rome, which is Constantinople . . . was overwhelmed by the godless Turks, but, O pious tsar, your mighty Russian kingdom, the Third Rome, surpasses all others in piety. Our whole pious kingdom is concentrated in you alone. You alone beneath heaven, O Christian tsar, are glorious throughout the ages and among all Christians."[14] For many years Muscovite writers had been propounding the theory of Moscow the Third Rome in unofficial works. Although he claimed unlimited power Ivan IV had not adopted the concept because it was designed to enhance the church's authority. After his death the successful policy of centralization subordinated the church in Russia once and for all. The alliance between Metropolitan Dionisii and the boyar opposition was but a brief episode, which culminated in the spiritual leader's deposition, and Iov completed the final subjugation of the church to the secular arm. During his administration the theory of Moscow the Third Rome first found reflection in crown documents and became official doctrine. Boris' closest associates were involved in the metamorphosis. Church books his uncle, Dmitrii Godunov, distributed to monasteries bore the notation that they had been copied "in the God-preserved, preeminent and regal city of Moscow, the Third Rome, magnificent in its piety."

What did Moscow the Third Rome mean when it became official doctrine? It is possible to think that in Godunov's time Moscow was planning to become the center of a new world empire succeeding ancient Rome and Byzantium, but such an interpretation is utterly fallacious. Russia had experienced disastrous defeat in the Livonian war, and afterwards the government's primary concern was to protect the frontiers and recover lost territory. It is also possible to assume that the doctrine of Moscow the Third Rome mirrored the aspirations of the Russian church to lead the ecumenical Orthodox movement, but this assumption is likewise untenable. In spite of its bombast the theory of Moscow the Third Rome was designed simply

to overcome Moscow's inferior position among the centers of Orthodoxy. The establishment of the patriarchate heightened the Russian
church's prestige and testified to the new alignment of forces within
the Orthodox hierarchy.

Contemporaries regarded Godunov's church reform as his first
major success. Secretary Timofeev wrote: "Its accomplishment was
the beginning of his exultation." Establishing the patriarchate was
unquestionably a landmark in Boris' career. His policy of creating a
national church pandered to his subjects' vanity, acquired him a
measure of popularity, and disposed the princes of the church in his
favor. Godunov prized this initial victory highly. Numbing anxiety,
humiliating weakness, and crushing failure now seemed things of the
past.

Chapter Five

FOREIGN POLICY

In the Baltic area Godunov's government continued Ivan's foreign
policy but refrained from active moves as long as there was danger of
an alliance between Poland and Sweden. When that peril became less
immediate after the Rzeczpospolita refused to join an anti-Turkish
coalition because of wars with the Tatars and Turkey, Russia lost no
time in striking at Sweden. Moscow was determined to recover the
territory the Swedes had seized, above all the port of Narva. The Russian command employed all the forces at its disposal to mount the
attack. Meek Tsar Fedor personally assumed command and Queen
Irina, who dominated her husband, accompanied him from Moscow
to Novgorod.

In January, 1590 Russian units occupied Yam, blockaded Kopore,
and moved on Narva, near which the commander, Prince Dmitrii
Khvorostinin, defeated the Swedish battalions that had advanced to
engage him. Boris Godunov took personal charge of the siege of the
enemy fortress. His opponents immediately suspected him of treason,
alleging that Fedor had failed to recapture Narva from the Swedes
solely because Boris was in collusion with them. In fact, Boris' dis-
positions at Narva are explainable by his lack of military experience,
not his concerting with the enemy. Witnesses saw how he ordered

cannon to concentrate fire to breach the walls "but did not order towers and conduits shelled."[1] The artillery the enemy had positioned in the towers was not put out of action soon enough and caused enormous losses among the soldiers trying to storm the town. The besiegers of Narva paid a heavy price for Boris' ineffective leadership.

On February 19 the Russians mounted a general attack. Possessing overwhelming superiority in numbers they stormed the fortress at seven places simultaneously, and the force charging the main breach was reckoned at five thousand men, including one thousand cossacks and almost two thousand fusiliers. Although the Swedes managed to repulse their onset and both sides suffered severely, when the Russian command readied fresh troops the Swedes could no longer compensate their losses. The garrison had been so weakened that the Narva command, despairing of success, sued for peace without waiting for another attack.

The condition of the Swedes was such that a determined assault would have decided their fate in a matter of hours but Boris, in full charge of operations, felt the risk was too great and hesitated, preferring to negotiate in hope of persuading the Swedes to capitulate. The Swedish command tried to protract the talks and the tactic succeeded, placing the Russians in a difficult position. Winter was coming to an end; the ice on the Narova was melting, and water forming on its surface might divide the army, which was strung out along both banks of the river. Boris soon grew convinced words alone could not induce the Swedes to surrender the fortress and instructed his representatives to go back, win over the Swedes on the question of Rugodiv,[2] and then make a truce on the enemy's terms.[3] Godunov's caution, which had rendered him invulnerable in the arena of political intrigue, proved abortive in war; victory had escaped from his clumsy hands. The truce concluded at Narva provided the Swedes should evacuate the Russian fortresses of Ivangorod and Kopore they had seized earlier. Russia got back the coastline between the Narova and Neva rivers but failed to acquire Narva and rebuild the port. The campaign's basic objective was not achieved.

John III, the Swedish king, refusing to accept the fact that Russia had defeated him, prepared for revenge. Unable to obtain support from the Rzeczpospolita, he formed an alliance with the Crimea and carried out the largest muster that had taken place since the Livonian war; by 1591 Sweden had massed some eighteen thousand soldiers on the Russian frontier. The Crimean khan, Kaza-Girei, backed by the Ottoman empire, dispatched even stronger forces—as many as one hundred thousand knights—including Crimeans, the Little Nogai horde, detachments drawn from the Turkish fortresses of Ochakov and Belgorod, Janissaries, and Turkish artillery—to attack Moscow. Should these forces prevail, the Crimea and Turkey would be able substantially to expand their sphere of influence in Eastern Europe.

When the Russian command learned the size of the enemy's forces it decided not to await them on the Oka and withdrew units from border strong points towards Moscow. Early in the morning of July 4, 1591 the Tatars, advancing along the Serpukhov road, took Kotly. Russian troops stationed in a movable fortress south of the Danilov monastery gave battle all day and at night the Tatars retired. Sources have interpreted the defeat of the Tatars in different ways. The Military Register for 1598 provides the official version: the Russian commanders attacked the khan and the horde as they were approaching the movable fortress, "fought all day from morning to night,"[4] and when it grew dark Boris Godunov withdrew troops from the movable fortress and artillery, marched on Kaza-Girei's camp and suddenly opened fire, forcing the Tatars to flee. Eyewitnesses dispute this version. Ivan Timofeev, serving in the artillery chancellery, who probably participated in the enemy's defeat, declares that although the Tatars were frightened by a heavy night artillery barrage, Godunov never ordered a nocturnal attack. The Moscow chronicles agree with him.

Another source, the contemporary lists of the Military Records Office, provides a full, credible narrative of the action. Unedited in the royal chancellery, they show the fighting during the day bore no resemblance to a general conflict. In no hurry to commit his main force the khan sent his sons to harry Russian troop movements and "took no direct action nor moved his regiments."[5] The commanders ordered cavalry from the movable fortress to attack the Tatars and the day passed in fierce clashes. In the evening the Crimeans withdrew towards Kolomenskoe and struck the camp they had built there on both sides of the river Moscow. Though ready to move, the tsar's commanders remained stationary for the time being as there was no reason to leave their fortified posts at night; it was difficult, if not impossible, to direct troops and transport artillery in darkness.

Long after midnight a great disturbance suddenly broke out in the movable fortress; the men sleeping by their weapons jumped to their places and opened fire, and next heavy artillery on the walls of Moscow began to fire after the small arms.[6] Puffs of smoke enveloped the city; the noise was deafening and the salvos lighted up the entire region. To find out what was happening the commanders dispatched gentry units towards Kolomenskoe. The murderous fusillade and the appearance of the Russians near their camp terrified the Tatars, for no one knew the approaching enemy's numbers and they had not forgotten the terrible losses they had sustained at Moscow in 1572.[7] Fear of a night attack caused the Tatars to panic; the khan could not restrain them and they fled in disarray from Kolomenskoe to the Oka. Had the commanders taken advantage of the delay the Tatars must suffer in fording the Oka they might have organized a real chase, but they confined themselves to sending a few gentry units in hot pursuit. These overwhelmed the Tatar rearguard and, according to one source, took four hundred or, according to the official one, one thousand prisoners. Many Crimeans drowned crossing the Oka, and the light wagon carrying the khan away from his camp sank. The roads the Tatars followed as they fled were littered with abandoned equipment. The khan returned to Bakhchisarai at night with a bandaged hand. Since he had not participated in the battles with the Russians he must have been wounded during the nocturnal turmoil or the swift flight.

As in the case of the siege of Narva, Boris Godunov had not acted decisively and vigorously in the struggle with the Tatars but he reaped the glory after the victory. Moscow and the court hailed him as a hero. At a celebration in the Kremlin Tsar Fedor removed a golden chain and fastened it around his brother-in-law's neck. Godunov's other awards included a gold vessel found in Mamai's camp after the battle of Kulikovo Field,[8] one of the tsar's own fur coats, and landed estates. Boris longed to be regarded as a great and glorious military leader but the loud praise and rewards he received deceived no one. In the flowery language of the times contemporaries wrote that Godunov "is clumsy in battle" and "unskilfull in bearing arms."[9]

The Tatar defeat at Moscow doomed the Swedish attack on Novgorod and Pskov. Field Marshal Fleming's large army approached Gdov, not far from Pskov, but could not take even this small fortress. Other Swedish units marched on Novgorod, but the Russians laid waste the frontier region, thus further contributing to the failure of the king's forces. The clashes on the Russo-Swedish border lasted another year, when military action gave way to peace negotiations. In May, 1595, in Tiavzin, Russian envoys signed what was termed a perpetual peace with Sweden. The latter country agreed to return the fortress of Korela, a valuable defense outpost and the sole piece of territory Russia had retained after the Livonian war west of the Neva. Control of the mouths of the Neva and Narova rivers meant that Russia had outlets to the sea, but could not build ports because the Swedish fleet continued to dominate the Baltic. Swedish representatives sought to make the peace treaty embody the principle of naval blockade applicable to the Russian littoral around Ivangorod; thus, the plan to make the town Russia's maritime gateway met with no success.

The peace of Tiavzin was harmful to Russia's economic interests for the country needed to expand trade with Western Europe. Muscovite diplomacy had appraised incorrectly the situation in the eastern Baltic region and made concessions to Sweden although the union between Sweden and the Rzeczpospolita was less stable than Moscow had assumed.[10] When Boris finally realized this he refused to ratify the treaty, but his action did not change anything and the Baltic question remained unresolved. Platonov has exaggerated Godunov's achievements in foreign policy: "As the formulator of Moscow's policies Boris could take pride in the fact that he had forced his neighbors to recognize the revival of Moscow's political strength after the defeats it had endured."[11] In reality, in Godunov's time Russia was striving to achieve partial readjustment of the consequences of the disastrous Livonian war. From time immemorial Russia had recovered lands it had lost, but this time it failed to acquire an outlet on the Baltic sea, so vital to its economic development. Boris' eastern policy met with greater success. Russia repulsed the Tatar invasion and made the southern borders safer by advancing defense lines into the Wild Field,[12] where the new frontier fortresses of Voronezh (1585), Livny (1586), Elets (1592), and Belgorod, Oskol and Kursk (1596) quickly were constructed.

Boris Godunov was at last able to assign larger forces to the systematic subjection of Siberia, for Ermak's famous expedition had been merely the beginning of the great Siberian epic.[13] Fusilier squadrons dispatched across the Urals in 1584-1585 could not consolidate a position, but the Siberian khan, Kuchum, was defeated by Seid-khan, one of his rivals, and forced to give up Kashlyk, or Isker, the capital of the khanate. In 1587 the Russians built the town of Tobolsk near Kashlyk; Seid-khan was captured, and the ancient Tatar capital abandoned. In order to establish a decisive presence beyond the Urals the tsar's commanders built a host of small forts along the Ob river; fortified towns such as Berezov, Obdorsk, Surgut, Narym, and Tara rose at places deep in the taiga and the way lay open for the Russians to penetrate the depths of the unknown continent. The acquisition of Siberia was fraught with significance for the fate of Russia.

Chapter Six

DRAMA IN UGLICH

Since the days of Karamzin it has been a matter of course to charge Godunov with complicity in the murder of Dmitrii. What Pushkin termed the "cruel murder" is an invisible presence in the main scenes of his tragedy, *Boris Godunov*. Karamzin suggested to Pushkin that he should portray Tsar Boris as a "savage blend of piety and criminal passions," and influenced by this concept Pushkin, as he himself noted, detected a poetic side to Boris. Silly, spiteful gossip could not frighten the intelligent and firm regent, but he was tortured by remorse. For thirteen years he dreamed of the dead child, and the torments of conscience were unbearable:

> The reproach pounds like a hammer in his ears
> And everything disgusts; his head spins,
> The blood of children in his eyes . . .[1]

Did the death of Dmitrii really play the role in Boris' life that has been attributed to it? The facts must be examined in order to answer the question.

Ivan the Terrible's youngest son Dmitrii died in Uglich on Monday, May 15, 1591. Tales and stories from the Time of Troubles are filled with vivid details of his murder, but none of their authors was an eyewitness to what actually had happened. The most they had seen were Dmitrii's relics which were exhibited in Moscow fifteen years after his death when the church proclaimed him a saint. The new tsar, Vasilii Shuiskii, who had led a conspiracy against the False Dmitrii, was obliged to do everything in his power to prove the latter was an impostor and the real Dmitrii had died in Uglich long ago. Directly after False Dmitrii's death the boyars announced to the people: "Dmitrii did indeed die and was buried in Uglich." Their rescript was composed with Shuiskii's approval and at his behest, since he no longer needed to revise the version of Dmitrii's death a commission once chaired by him had prepared. Some two weeks later, however, the authorities began to assert that Godunov had murdered Dmitrii;[2] the clergy expended great energy to show that Dmitrii had been an innocent martyr, and official propaganda started classifying rumors he had committed suicide as heresy.

Since an involuntary suicide could not be a saint, the fabricators
of the myth claimed Dmitrii had not been playing with a knife when
he died but with a handful of nuts. Shuiskii's commission had not
said a word about nuts but this did not stop Shuiskii, once he became
tsar, from telling the people: "They say that while he [Dmitrii—R.S.]
was playing he was enjoying eating some nuts and when he was killed
his blood stained the nuts. This is why these nuts were placed in his
hand and they are uncorrupted."[3] When Dmitrii's relics were brought
to Moscow and placed on view in a church everyone could see nuts
in the grave and witnesses were found to claim having discerned
blood on them.

Is such testimony credible? How can it be proved that nuts lying
underground with a decomposed corpse for fifteen years would remain in a state of preservation, or that a witness, elbowing his way
forward to the grave for an instant, could catch sight of blood on
withered nuts which according to the laws of nature should long
before have become dust? There are two solutions: either the witnesses viewing the relics fifteen years later were mistaken, or the
grave actually contained nuts that had obviously been tampered with.
This evidence, clumsily fabricated by those who opened the grave,
misled them.

The earliest lives of the new saint declared Dmitrii was attacked
by wicked youths, one of whom snatched away his knife and cut his
throat, but feeling this brief version unsatisfactory church propa-
gandists composed an emotional narrative abounding in dramatic but
entirely fictitious details: one of the wicked boys, seeing Dmitrii
wearing a necklace, asked the latter to display it. When Dmitrii trust-
ingly thrust out his neck he struck with the knife but missed the
throat. The two other miscreants then slaughtered Dmitrii like a
lamb. Those who contrived such a legend, disappointed in the prosaic
details of the incident, tried to embellish it, moving the action from
an unexciting location—the rear courtyard—to the Red Porch and
ultimately to the main palace staircase, where a pathetic scene was
supposed to have occurred: like an evil viper Secretary Mishka Bitiagovskii jumped onto the staircase and grasped Dmitrii by the legs
while Mishka's son seized his noble head and Kachalov cut his throat.[4]

It is idle to seek trustworthy facts in the lives; the investigative
report compiled at the scene a few days after Dmitrii died is far more
credible, but suspicion long has existed that the original document
was tampered with, for even brief scrutiny reveals traces of hasty revision. Someone cut out pages and glued them back elsewhere, thereby placing them out of sequence, and the preamble has vanished.

V.K. Klein, the editor of this source document, undertook to reconstruct it. He noted the presence of rust marks on its pages which, though of differing sizes, showed similar configurations. Klein suggested the work had been exposed to moisture while kept in the archives rolled up like a scroll. The outside pages were damaged most; the size of the marks diminished closer to the middle and disappeared completely inside because water did not penetrate so far. Using the size of the marks as a guide Klein put the pages in their proper order and thus managed to reproduce a full, coherent text with only the first pages missing. It is logical to assume that these pages had served as the scroll's cover, had grown damp, and fallen away of themselves. When old manuscripts were rolled up their final pages formed the outside cover to which new pages were subsequently fastened, but in the Uglich scroll it was the beginning, not the end of the manuscript that was soaked. What is the reason? After another section was added the scroll was again rolled up. People then read, as they do today, from left to right and the archives maintained documents ready for perusal. This also explains why it was the first, not the last pages of the Uglich scroll that grew damp. In Peter the Great's time archives adopted a new system of keeping documents. His archivists combined large awkward scrolls into bundles and had to cut the Uglich scroll into separate sheets, which later got mixed up. This is how the record of the Uglich affair acquired its present form.

There is a school of thought holding that the extant Uglich materials are a copy composed in Godunov's Moscow chancellery and the original draft of the interrogation has not survived. Paleographical analysis of the manuscript contradicts this view. The Uglich inquiry displays the handwriting of some six scribes and the signatures of at least twenty witnesses, inhabitants of Uglich, are affixed to the document. The signatures are strongly individualized, reflecting the signatories' degree of literacy. Witnesses who never left Uglich could not have signed a copy compiled in Moscow.

Some believe Godunov sent trusted lieutenants to Uglich to quell rumors to the effect that Dmitrii had met with a violent end, not to discover the truth. Such a view omits a number of important considerations. Prince Shuiskii presided over the investigation, and he was perhaps the ablest and most resourceful of Boris' opponents. One of his brothers, it may be recalled, had been slain on Boris' orders and the other had died in a monastery. Vasilii Shuiskii himself had spent years in exile and had returned but a short time before the Uglich affair. The boyar council took the initiative in appointing Shuiskii, who confused investigators by changing his testimony several

Excerpt from the Report of the Uglich Commission of Inquiry

times. He originally swore Dmitrii's death was an accident but later started talking about murder. The shifts in Shuiskii's testimony might merit attention if he had witnessed the crime, but he was only an investigator and, furthermore, not working alone. The church leaders had sent Metropolitan Gelvasii to supervise his activity, and his commission included Associate Boyar Kleshnin and Conciliar Secretary Vyluzgin. Kleshnin was a friend of Godunov but also the father-in-law of Mikhail Nagoi, who had figured prominently in the Uglich affair. Vyluzgin, a leading official, was in charge of the land-tenure chancellery and had numerous assistant secretaries at his call, who were responsible for conducting the practical work of investigation. The commission members held various political views; each closely watched his associates' activities, ready to take advantage of any sign of inadvertance.

The investigative report proves Boris had nothing to do with Dmitrii's death, and this is precisely why historians will not believe it to be true. Dmitrii's death was fraught with major political consequences and, above all, the question of *cui bono,* a splendid test of political expediency, is involved. The unshakeable conviction that the disappearance of the sole surviving heir of the original Muscovite dynasty could benefit only Godunov has detracted greatly from the importance that should be assigned to the Uglich investigative report; strong grounds exist for believing it has fallen victim to the retrospective view of history.

Until Dmitrii died the possibility always remained that Fedor might produce a lawful heir and no one could predict to whom the throne might pass. Among the tsar's close relatives it was the Romanov family, not Godunov, upon which fortune was most likely to smile. The government was confronted with a critical situation at the time of the Uglich affair. Directly threatened by Swedish and Tatar forces, the authorities were preparing to fight both foreign and domestic foes. A week or two prior to Dmitrii's death augmented military units had been assigned to patrol the streets of Moscow, and other police measures were taken in case popular uprisings should occur. The least rumor would cause the people to revolt, and this meant disaster for Godunov. Under the circumstances Dmitrii's death proved disadvantageous, indeed extremely dangerous, for Boris. The facts controvert the traditional view that Boris' political position required the elimination of Ivan's youngest son and also negate previously held opinions concerning the nature and effectiveness of the Uglich investigation.

The investigative material contains at least two versions of Dmitrii's death. One comes from the deceased's kin, the Nagoi family. During the entire inquiry Mikhail Nagoi stubbornly maintained that Secretary Bitiagovskii's son, his nephew Nikita Kachalov, and his niece's husband, Osip Volokhov, had killed Dmitrii. Mikhail's brothers gave more cautious testimony. Grigorii Nagoi said that a large crowd had collected around Dmitrii's body and unknown members of it began saying he had been murdered. Although Mikhail and Grigorii arrived at the scene much later, they claimed Dmitrii was still alive and expired in their presence. They were obviously confused. Andrei Nagoi, who was dining with the queen in the palace, heard shouts outside the window that her son was dead. Running out into the yard, he was certain Dmitrii was dead in the arms of his nurse and heard people crying he had been killed, but "he did not see who killed him." Mikhail's and Grigorii's error is quite understandable: a few who saw them close up independently testified that when Mikhail ran or galloped on his horse into the yard he was dead drunk. Grigorii had been carousing with his brother.[5] The form the interrogation took reveals that the Nagoi family wanted to establish that Dmitrii was murdered, for they hoped to use their version to settle accounts with Crown Secretary Bitiagovskii.

On Monday, May 15, when Queen Mariia went to dine she sent her son out to play with four other children. They were playing in the corner of a small back yard between the palace and the fortress wall, supervised by Vasilisa Volokhova and two other nurses. Dinner had just begun when suddenly loud shouts were heard from the yard. Running down, the queen saw with horror that her only son was dead and, beside herself with grief, began to pummel Vasilisa. Believing the nurse had failed to protect her son, Mariia thirsted to punish her as savagely as possible, and as she beat the nurse about the head with a stick she screamed that Vasilisa's son Osip had murdered Dmitrii.[6] These words were the equivalent of a death sentence.

Mariia ordered the bells rung to summon the people. The incessant peal of the tocsin aroused the whole town and the square before the palace filled with an excited throng. Bitiagovskii, the chief secretary in Uglich, hearing the noise, galloped to the Kremlin, rushed upstairs when he learned Dmitrii had been conveyed there, and hastened past the body to the belltower in the shrine. Bursting in, he ordered the ringers to stop tolling the bells, but the sacristan, as he later reported, locked the belfry door and refused to let him in.

The secretary's opportune arrival saved Volokhova and her son. Servants in the secretariat told how Nikita Kachalov intervened on behalf of Osip Volokhov, saying, "You must not kill my brother-in-law."[7] Young Kachalov's daring cost him his life, but his action was entirely understandable. Relying as he usually did on his powerful uncle, he interceded for his brother-in-law while Bitiagovskii was still running through the square to find out what was happening. Osip Volokhov took advantage of the moment to hide in the Bitiagovskii residence, the only place he could be safe from the queen's rage.

Relations between Bitiagovskii and the Nagoi family had become strained almost as soon as he arrived in Uglich. The family had been deprived of control over the revenues produced by their estates and was supported by monies received from the treasury. The queen considered the government's subsidy inadequate and dependence on a secretary degrading. Her lady-in-waiting and others told the commission that Mikhail Nagoi was "constantly asking the treasury for more money than the crown had allotted," and Bitiagovskii kept refusing him, so that quarrels and arguments ensued.[8] The most recent clash had occurred the morning of May 15.

In the courtyard the secretary first tried to address the crowd but then turned and urged Mikhail Nagoi "to stop the unseemly racket of which he was not the cause." With Kachalov's aid Bitiagovskii and his men prevented Volokhova and her son from being lynched; this drove the queen and her brothers into a frenzy and they incited the mob against Bitiagovskii and his supporters. Vasilisa Volokhova, severely beaten and thrown into the square, saw the queen egging the crowd on against Bitiagovskii and his men and murmured, "So be it; they murdered Dmitrii."[9] Tipsy Mikhail Nagoi was getting ready to lead a posse to lynch the secretary when relatives and slaves came to the aid of Bitiagovskii and his men. Later Mikhail boasted to his cronies that he had commanded the secretary and his son be put to death, and "I ordered Kachalov, Daniil Tretiakov, and their men slain because they had spirited Mikhail Bitiagovskii and his son away from me."[10]

After escaping Nagoi, Bitiagovskii and his followers locked themselves inside the secretariat, but their pusillanimity destroyed them. The mob smashed down doors, sacked the building, and slew those it found there. A courtier in the queen's service was forced to admit to the commission that the rabble had killed the chancery people "at the behest of Mikhail Nagoi."

The crowd ran from the square to the Bitiagovskii residence, ransacked it, and "after drinking the liquor stored in the cellar smashed the barrels." They "beat the secretary's wife and dragged her naked and bareheaded" with her children to the palace, where they also had conveyed Osip Volokhov, who had been found in Bitiagovskii's house.

At the height of the commotion two high churchmen, Archimandrite Feodorit and Abbot Savvatii, arrived at the Kremlin. That day they had both been celebrating mass in a monastery but, hearing the tocsin, sent servants who returned and told them: "We heard both in town and in the countryside that Dmitrii has been murdered, but nobody knows who killed him." The servants were soon followed to the monastery by a deacon, who told the elders in the queen's name to come to the palace. The abbot testified he found the queen beside the body of her son in the church of the Salvation: "Dmitrii lay dead in Salvation church, and the queen said: 'Mikita Kachalov, Danilo Mikhailovich Bitiagovskii, and Osip Volokhov murdered him.'"[11]

The monks' arrival temporarily checked the excesses. The mob tried to attack Bitiagovskii's widow, but the elders, as they put it, "seized her and her daughters, removed them, and would not allow them to be slain." They saw Osip Volokhov in the shrine, standing behind a pillar, seriously wounded, near Dmitrii's corpse while his mother was making a desperate effort to save him. She begged the queen: "Grant me a fair hearing," but Mariia was inexorable. As soon as the elders quitted the shrine she consigned Osip to the mercies of the mob with the words: "Here is Dmitrii's murderer."

The story that Dmitrii was brutally murdered got about at a time when mob rule prevailed, and the Nagoi family espoused it as a pretext to eliminate Bitiagovskii and his men. The allegations against the crown secretary cannot stand critical scrutiny. The Bitiagovskii family could not have been involved in the crime. At a hearing the secretary's widow related how the members of her family were dining at home with a guest, the priest Bogdan, when the bells began ringing. Since he was Grigorii Nagoi's confessor Bogdan did all he could to exculpate the queen and her brothers, but he unabashedly affirmed to Shuiskii's commission that he was seated at the same table with Bitiagovskii and his son when the tocsin sounded, thereby providing the family with a watertight alibi.

Fifteen men died during the day's riot and their bodies were thrown into a ditch by the fortress wall. Two days later government troops entered Uglich in the evening and the Nagoi family now realized its members would be held responsible for the murder of the chief official representing the crown in Uglich. Late during the last night before Shuiskii's commission arrived Mikhail Nagoi, summoning trusted retainers, told them to procure knives. Rakov, the town clerk, went to market and got two knives from townsmen; Grigorii Nagoi brought a Tatar dirk, and the Bitiagovskii residence yielded an iron cudgel. After these weapons were assembled Nagoi's men killed a chicken in a storeroom, smeared its blood on the knives and cudgel, and took them to the ditch in which the disfigured corpses lay. Rakov, who was directly in charge of the operation, told the commission: "Mikhail Nagoi had me place the knives by Mikhail Bitiagovskii, his son, and Mikita Kachalov, and the cudgel by Osip Volokhov."[12]

The false evidence manufactured by the Nagoi brothers misled witnesses but failed to fool the commission. Admitting his guilt, Rakov described the nocturnal foray to Shuiskii; Mikhail tried to deny it but was soon exposed for, when confronted by Rakov, the servant who had killed the chicken in the storeroom confirmed the former's testimony. Unlike his brother, Grigorii Nagoi did not attempt to lie and admitted he had brought the Tatar dirk from his home, where it was kept under lock and key, and had helped fabricate other evidence. The examination of the principal witnesses decisively refuted the contention that the murder of Dmitrii had been planned in advance.

Dmitrii died at noon on a clear day in the presence of numerous spectators. The commission had no difficulty finding eyewitnesses. Shuiskii examined Nurse Volokhova, Wetnurse Arina Tuchkova, Lady-in-Waiting Mariia Kolobova, and the four lads who had been playing knife-toss with Dmitrii. Attaching great importance to the boys' testimony, investigators put the same question to them twice in order to obtain a clear, accurate answer. The first question was: "Who were then standing behind Dmitrii?" The boys replied: "Behind Dmitrii then stood only we four, the wetnurse, and the lady-in-waiting." On hearing their answer the commission inquired openly: "Were Osip Volokhov and Daniil Bitiagovskii standing behind Dmitrii at the time?" The children replied that they were not and went on briefly, vividly and accurately to recount what they had seen: "Dmitrii was using a penknife to play toss with us in the back yard when an illness came upon him [an epileptic fit] and he fell on his knife."[13]

Could the boys have lied to despite Mariia or contrived a tale of illness to please Shuiskii since they had nothing to fear from the angry queen? The testimony of the adults furnishes no support for either assumption. Underchamberlains Larionov, Ivanov and Gnidin of the queen's court deposed as follows: "When the queen sat down to dinner we were stationed in the upper chamber behind the chairs

when the minor junior courtier Petrushka Kolobov ran up and exclaimed: 'Dmitrii was playing knife-toss with us in the yard when
he had a fit . . . and then, while it was upon him he fell on his knife
and this caused his death.'"[14] Petrushka Kolobov, the oldest of the
boys playing with Dmitrii, speaking for all of them, repeated to the
commission what he had told the underchamberlains just after Dmitrii died. Mariia Kolobova, Nurse Volokhova and Wetnurse Tuchkova
also supported the testimony of Petrushka and his comrades, and the
latter displayed surprising candor. To Shuiskii and the queen she declared she was responsible for the misfortune: "I was not on guard
when the dark illness fell on Dmitrii . . . and he fell on his knife."[15]
Tuchkova enjoyed the queen's confidence; it was not she but Volokhova whom Mariia tried to kill when her son died, although both
women were equally responsible for not having kept a close eye on
him.

Seven persons standing in the yard near Dmitrii also witnessed his
death and an eighth appeared later before the commission, although
he did not come forward at once. On questioning Protopopov, a
clerk, the commission discovered that he had first learned details of
Dmitrii's death from Tulubeev, a chamberlain. Summoned to testify,
Tulubeev cited Yudin, a gentleman-in-waiting, and when the two
men confronted each other the affair was finally unravelled. On
Monday, May 15, Yudin, at his post in an upper chamber, was look-
ing out of the window at the inner yard. The tragedy unfolded before
his eyes. He stated that Dmitrii was playing knife-toss in the yard
when he fell on his knife, "and he (Yudin—R.S.) . . . saw it happen."[16]
He mentioned what he had seen to friends but, aware that the queen
was alleging murder, deemed it wise to avoid testifying until chance
revealed him to the investigating commission.

The testimony given by the principal witnesses in Uglich agreed in
essentials but was expressed with sufficient individuality to create a
presumption of veracity. The testimony of the minor witnesses, more
than one hundred in number, produces a different impression by re-
vealing a disturbing pattern of similarity that has long bothered
scholars. When several people employ the same expressions they may
be suspected of bearing false witness, but the stock phrases appearing
in the investigative report can be explained. The questions put to the
primary witnesses elicited a full picture of what had occurred, and
the testimony of those who knew of Dmitrii's death only at second
hand added nothing new. The commission mainly examined court servants, who were largely uneducated and spoke poorly, like Chekhov's

malefactor,[17] and a great deal of time would have been needed in order to extract intelligible answers from them; but time was just what the investigators lacked, so they employed stereotypes in their questions to prompt these secondary witnesses to answer. The chanceries at that time often used such a technique.

The version of Dmitrii's unexpected death reconstructed from the testimony of the principal witnesses contains two points susceptible of incontrovertible proof. The first is Dmitrii's illness, which witnesses termed "black ailment," "falling sickness," or "falling weakness." To judge from their descriptions of the sequence of his seizures, Dmitrii was an epileptic. Carriers declared: "Before this . . . he would have that sickness for months on end." Dmitrii had experienced a violent attack about a month before he died. Nurse Volokhova testified that before Easter Dmitrii, while ill, "bit the hand of Andrei Nagoi's daughter, until they removed her . . . from him." Andrei Nagoi confirmed this, saying that Dmitrii "during the great fast chewed my daughter's hand," and had previously bitten his own hands, as well as those of his companions and attendants: "Whenever they try to restrain Dmitrii, he eats like a glutton; this is why he falls ill." Bitiagovskii's widow told the same story: "Many times it happened that when this illness afflicted Dmitrii, Andrei Nagoi, his wet-nurse, and boyar ladies would try to restrain him, and he . . . would bite their hands or devour anything his teeth fastened upon."[18]

She further testified that Dmitrii's last epileptic attack endured for several days. It began on a Tuesday; when three days later he was somewhat recovered his mother took him to church and then let him walk in the yard. On Saturday Dmitrii again went for a walk when he suddenly experienced another seizure. His uncontrolled actions so frightened his nurses that they were slow to grasp his hands after the attack occurred when the queen was absent in the palace. This explains why the child fell to the ground and beat it for a long time, as those who saw him reported. He was writhing on the ground and the nurses clustered around him. When his wetnurse lifted him up it was too late.

The second point is that Dmitrii was playing with a knife. Witnesses described his game in great detail: he was "throwing a knife across a line," he was "jabbing with a knife," and he was "walking about the yard and throwing a sharp-pointed knife into a circle." Knife-toss was played like this: players took turns throwing a knife into a circle drawn on the ground; the knife was usually held by its sharp edge and had to be flung so skilfully that it would describe an

arc in the air before sticking in the earth. His comrades standing near-
by said the child fell on the knife. Vasilisa Volokhova described the
incident more closely: "Dmitrii fell on the ground and there he himself cut his throat with the knife." Other witnesses agreed that Dmitrii
cut himself when he stumbled or fell to the ground, but no one knew
exactly when he wounded himself, whether while falling or when
thrashing in convulsions on the ground. They were certain of only
one thing: he had himself inflicted the wound in his throat. Medicine
gives an unequivocal answer to the question of whether a small wound
in the throat can cause death. The carotid artery and the jugular vein
lie just below the skin in the neck. If a child strikes one of these ves-
sels it is not only likely but certain he will die. The adults should have
run to Dmitrii and staunched the flow of blood but no one in the
sixteenth century would ever have thought of doing so. Even the
finest doctor in Europe, had he chanced to be in the yard, could not
have saved the boy.

It is sometimes alleged that the knife was placed in Dmitrii's hand
at the right moment and his death was not an accident. This theory
is groundless because it fails to take the customs and temperament
of the swashbuckling feudal nobility into consideration. Its members
were never parted from their weapons. The accoutrements of knife
and sword were a sign of noble birth. Sons of noble families grew
accustomed to carrying weapons in early childhood. Young Dmitrii
was smartly fitted out with a small sword and used a little iron cudgel
to kill hens and geese. A small knife was often found in his hand
when he experienced epileptic seizures. Bitiagovskii's widow testified
that once, in March, "Dmitrii was overcome in his room with his sickness and . . . stabbed his mother, the queen, on that occasion." Nurse
Volokhova also recalled the fit during which "Dmitrii stabbed his
mother, Queen Mariia, with his dagger."

Should the commission be faulted for failing to find the ill-fated
dagger that wounded Dmitrii? It should not, for it is difficult to believe that the Nagoi family, which stooped to faking clues, made no
effort to conceal genuine evidence. Dmitrii's toy dagger bore little
resemblance to a murder weapon; Nagoi partisans substituted a real
one, the Tatar dirk, and the long bloodstained knives they threw into
the ditch were intended to convince the investigators that an in-
veterate gang of assassins had been at work outside the palace win-
dows.

The investigators interrogated the principal witnesses in the presence of the queen. She had the right to object to false or misleading

testimony but instead made a humble appeal to Shuiskii's associate, Metropolitan Gelvasii, to intercede with the tsar on behalf of the humble retainers Mikhail and his brother had suborned: "Forgive them for slaying Mikhail Bitiagovskii and his son. In truth they are guilty of a sinful act."[19] Mariia was no longer insisting the secretary and junior court officials had murdered her son.

In addition to the inquiry Shuiskii conducted on the spot, foreigners also reported Dmitrii's death. The majority was content merely to retail subsequent rumors, but two were in Russia at the time of the Uglich tragedy. The Vienna archives have preserved a dispatch Luca Pauli (to whom reference has already been made) sent to the Viennese court: "Incidentally, it has come about that Prince Dmitrii, the grand prince's brother . . . who resided in Uglich, died or committed suicide."[20] Pauli's cautious observation may be interpreted in two ways, but he refrained from stating openly that Dmitrii had been murdered. Sir Jerome Horsey was better informed about Dmitrii's death than Pauli or other foreigners, for he was in Yaroslavl, near Uglich, in May, 1591, where he learned what had happened sooner than Moscow did. Horsey related what he had heard in a letter of June 10, 1591, to Lord Burleigh, in which he informed London confidentially that Dmitrii had been brutally and treacherously murdered on May 19 [sic—R.S.] when his throat was cut in the presence of his mother.

In order to assess the validity of Horsey's statement its source must be identified. Horsey's later writings, in which he carefully formulated the impressions he gathered in Yaroslavl, facilitate this task. All his life Horsey remembered an incident that occurred to him there in May, 1591. In the middle of the night there came a loud knocking on his door. Seizing his pistols he looked into the street and the light of the moon helped him to recognize Afanasii Nagoi, an old acquaintance, who told him: "Dmitrii is dead; the secretaries cut his throat at six o'clock, and one of their servants has confessed under torture that Boris sent them. The queen has been poisoned and is near death . . . ." Horsey's June 10 letter obviously reflects no more than the Nagoi family's version of Dmitrii's murder.

It has been claimed that threats and violence were used to extract testimony from inhabitants of Uglich concerning the sudden death of Ivan's youngest son. Many sources allege that residents of Uglich endured cruel persecutions, but it can be successfully established this took place several months after Shuiskii finished his work. His commission did not harass witnesses with one exception, duly entered in

the record. During an interrogation held in the palace one of Bitiagovskii's servants apprehended the queen's groom and charged him with
stealing the secretary's goods. The charges were substantiated and
the groom and his son were arrested. This was the sole example of
repression experienced by the inhabitants of Uglich during the investigation. The remarkably complete and credible investigation of
the circumstances surrounding Dmitrii's death leaves no room for
doubt, but during the Time of Troubles Dmitrii's name was assumed
by a bold adventurer who acquired the Muscovite throne and made
Dmitrii's death an enigma.

The Nagoi family sought to take advantage of Dmitrii's death to
mount an intrigue and strike at Godunov. Afanasii Nagoi took the
initiative. Emissaries from the queen reached him in Yaroslavl the
night of May 16 and Horsey saw what followed. He relates that in
the middle of the night a tocsin aroused the people of Yaroslavl and
Nagoi supporters told them Ivan's youngest son had treacherously
been slain by assassins sent from elsewhere. They calculated this
would incite an uprising, but it failed to materialize.

Defeated in Yaroslavl, Nagoi partisans made a desperate attempt
to arouse Moscow against Boris. Late in May major fires broke out
there and thousands of people lost their homes. The disaster threatened to provoke an uprising at any moment and the Nagoi family
tried to channel popular discontent against Godunov by circulating
rumors that the Godunov family was responsible both for the murder
of Dmitrii and deliberately setting fire to the capital. The rumors
spread all over Russia and abroad. Diplomats sent to Lithuania officially had to deny statements to the effect that Godunov's men had
set fire to Moscow.

The government made haste to investigate the cause of the fires
and by the end of May charged the Nagoi group with complicity in
them and of fomenting disorder. A boyar court questioned a number
of the arsonists, mainly boyar slaves, and announced that Levka, a
bathhouse attendant, and his confederates were chiefly responsible
for the fires. Under interrogation they testified: "Afanasii Nagoi sent
Ivanko Mikhailov and others to us, told us to buy up incendiary devices and torch many parts of Moscow's business district . . . and
Afanasii Nagoi sent men to many other towns, told them to buy devices and to fire those towns and their business districts."[21]

Godunov and his supporters took advantage of these developments to eliminate the Nagoi family. Secretary Shchelkalov read
church leaders convening in the Kremlin on July 2 the full report of

the Uglich investigation. The church served as a high court in this affair, as it did in all matters pertaining to the royal family, and Patriarch Iov expressed the church's entire agreement with the commission's conclusion that Dmitrii had died an accidental death, noting parenthetically that he had "met death by God's judgment." The patriarch was much more interested in the treasonable activities of the Nagoi faction, whose members had for no reason killed local peasants and employees of crown chanceries, "who uphold the law." The Nagoi family's treason by now transcended the circumstances of Dmitrii's death. Acting on the patriarch's representation, Tsar Fedor had the Nagoi family and inhabitants of Uglich thought to be implicated in the affair arrested and brought to Moscow. Shuiskii's commission reported to council and dissolved. Others unknown investigated the Moscow conflagration and the role played by the Nagoi interests in it. The materials they compiled were not part of the Uglich inquiry and have not survived.

Diplomatic communications from the ambassadorial chancellery establish that the inquiry into the treasonable dealings of the Nagoi faction culminated in July, 1591 and was concluded somewhat later. In July Russian envoys abroad stated: "Peasants, thieves, and Afanasii Nagoi's and his brothers' men were responsible for the Moscow fires; a trial has been held in Moscow, but sentence has not yet been pronounced in this matter." In 1592 the chancellery made it known that the guilty had been punished: "All who behaved like bandits have been executed."[22]

This shows that Dmitrii's relatives were persecuted for many months after he died. Fedor had Dmitrii's mother forcibly tonsured and sent to a remote part of Beloozero. Afanasii Nagoi and his brothers were imprisoned and many of their slaves were executed. Hundreds of the inhabitants of Uglich were exiled to Siberia. Boris was unwilling to forgive Uglich for the terror he felt in May. Perhaps this may explain a symbolic gesture. The great bell of Uglich was punished: part of it was lopped off and in this condition it too was banished to Siberia.

Chapter Seven

CROWN REGENT

With the opposition shattered and the Uglich appanage principality liquidated, the worst of the political crisis appeared to be over. Taking advantage of the situation, the Godunov family made deliberate moves to consolidate its power. Devoted to his numerous clan, Boris filled the boyar council with relatives. Members of his family took over the most important chanceries—the Stable, and the Great Court, which administered the farflung possessions of the royal family.

Boris had established his reputation and improved his own circumstances. The treasury had awarded him a good deal of land when he was made Master of Horse, and he later acquired the Viazh region, which was as large as a duchy. Fedor assigned his brother-in-law an income of his own. In addition to quitrent from his Viazh and Dorogobuzh estates and numerous service-tenure lands in various parts of the country, Boris received revenues from villages controlled by the Master of Horse near Moscow and substantial cash receipts from Moscow (including revenues from the baths there), Riazan, Tver, Torzhok, and northern towns. No appanage prince enjoyed such a large income. The regent's fabulous wealth astounded contemporaries. In 1589 Horsey estimated the Godunov family's annual income at 175 thousand rubles and claimed it could field one hundred thousand armed men, and Fletcher, a more careful and cautious observer, calculated Boris' income was one hundred thousand rubles. These figures may be inflated, but the fact remains the same: in the course of a few years Boris, formerly a man of modest means, had become extremely wealthy.

Godunov acquired impressive titles, which in feudal society were badges of prestige, precisely defining the position their holder occupied in a hieratical order. Non-titled courtiers ought not to strive for higher rank, and so the nobility naturally opposed Boris' aspirations. Encountering thus insurmountable obstacles at home, Godunov sought to acquire distinction abroad and foreigners resident in Moscow helped him. Horsey, trying to impress the English court with Godunov's exceptional authority, showed the queen rescripts Boris had given him personally. In his translations the obliging Englishman designated Godunov as "by God's will regent of the famous realm of all Russia," or "lieutenant of all Russia and the kingdoms of Kazan and Astrakhan, and chief councillor" (rendered as "chancellor"). Shortly before her decisive battle with Spain, Queen Elizabeth sought an alliance with Russia and addressed Boris in a way designed to gratify the most soaring ambition, calling him "glorious prince and beloved cousin."[1]

Boris' secret initiatives met with as much success in Vienna as they had in London. His trusted emissary, Luca Pauli, helped him enter into correspondence with the Habsburgs and suggested the Austrians give him the title of regent. In their letters the emperor's brothers addressed him as "most lofty privy conciliar of the whole Russian land; most lofty and most radiant [sic—R.S.] marshal," and "our most honored and beloved."[2]

No matter how much foreign rulers exalted Boris, the ambassadorial chancellery had adhered strictly and undeviatingly to his official title. The expulsion of Godunov's chief opponents from the boyar council and Boris' considerable foreign-policy successes altered the situation. After the Tatars were defeated south of Moscow Boris was raised to the rank of crown servitor. Explaining the title abroad diplomats said: "This name is more honorable than all boyars and this name is conferred by the sovereign for great service."[3] The title of servitor, which had come down from appanage times, was indeed more highly regarded than other titles and very few members of the princely appanage aristocracy had borne it before Boris. Members of the nobly-born Vorotynskii family had been the last sixteenth-century servitors. Now for the first time since the formation of the Russian state a single individual had acquired the two highest titles—Boyar Master of Horse and Crown Servitor—but Boris' triumph was not complete as long as Andrei Shchelkalov, the powerful chancellor, enjoyed equal prominence. The time had passed since Shchelkalov was stronger in the government than Godunov, but as before he continued to direct the crown chancery apparatus and administer the ambassadorial chancellery.

A year after Dmitrii died, a daughter, Feodosiia, was born to Tsar Fedor. She had the best claim to the throne as the last lawful representative of the expiring dynasty, but the customs of the country would never allow a woman to rule in her own right. Feodosiia was no more than a year old when the Moscow authorities began planning to arrange a marriage for her, which might help the heiress become queen. In 1593 Shchelkalov held a secret discussion with Warkoch, the Austrian ambassador, in which he asked the latter to convey an unusual request to the emperor: he should send an Austrian prince fourteen to eighteen years of age to Moscow. The Muscovites would teach him Russian and familiarize him with the customs and habits of the country, and eventually he would marry Feodosiia and ascend the throne with her.

Platonov has argued that the secretary's participation in a pro-Habsburg intrigue compromised him in Boris' eyes and cost him his career, but in fact Shchelkalov was cooperating with Godunov in the negotiations with Austria, not working against him. In his discussion with the ambassador the chancellor emphasized he was fulfilling Boris' instructions, but he simultaneously tried to create the impression it was he, not Boris, who was the Austrian pretender's most determined champion. In the course of the negotiations he told the envoy: "For the good of the Christian world our two great sovereigns have begun to cultivate the pasture together. You, and I, and Boris Fedorovich are the toilers and sowers. If we work the land with a will God will help us, and what we have sown will take root and flourish. With God's help we, the workers, will all reap the fruits thereof, both in this world and the next."[4] By calling Boris the sort of toiler that he and the envoy, who came from the petty nobility, were, Shchelkalov showed what he thought of Boris' pretensions.

Boris and Shchelkalov both favored the plan to set Feodosiia and a Habsburg prince on the Muscovite throne. The former calculated he could play at his niece's court the same role he performed at his sister's court, while the latter assumed an Austrian tsar could not administer a strange country without his help. However, Feodosiia's death at the age of two rendered this scheme moot and Boris hastened to put distance between himself and the mighty head of the chancery apparatus. By June, 1594 Shchelkalov had resigned all his offices. Timofeev, who knew him afterwards, said that Boris, forgetting his oath, "chewed" Shchelkalov with his teeth "like a beast," and the latter died in dishonor.[5] Andrei ended his days within the confines of a Moscow church, but since the sentence of displeasure pertained to him alone his place as chief secretary and keeper of the royal seal immediately passed to his brother Vasilii.

The chancellor's fall at last allowed Godunov to concentrate the reins of power in his hands, and he soon assumed new titles. By 1595 his official title had become: "Brother-in-law of the tsar, Regent, Servitor, Boyar Master of Horse, Court Commander, and Upholder of the Kingdoms of Kazan and Astrakhan."[6] The traditional Muscovite hierarchy made no provision for the office of regent because it was incompatible with the official doctrine that Muscovite sovereigns were autocrats; even the distinguished Aleksei Adashev, who had possessed enormous influence while Ivan was young, had never aspired to it. Godunov had achieved an unprecedented victory. No Muscovite before him had ever borne so many impressive, sonorous titles. Everyone knew what they meant: Boris had proclaimed himself sole regent and even the tsar was now his obedient servant.

Fedor's relatives among the Romanov and Godunov families united around the throne survived the dynastic crisis by supporting Ivan's incompetent son and their alliance endured for ten years. Boris helped Fedor, Nikita Romanov's eldest son, to enjoy an outstanding career. While still a young man he became a main court commander and was considered one of the three leading figures in the tsar's intimate council. Fedor's cousins among the Romanov family were the most plausible contenders for the succession. The ten-year understanding between the two families constitutes strong proof that for a long time Boris had formed no direct aspirations to be tsar himself, but a break was inevitable as soon as the question of the succession became immediate. Precedence suits, which always harbingered the approach of political crises, indicate the time when the struggle for the throne made former friends enemies.

About a year before the tsar died Fedor Nikitich Romanov was named deputy commander of the right wing in a regiment, but although this was not a major assignment objections based on precedence at once flowed in from everywhere. Petitions opposing the appointment came from people like Petr Sheremetev, Prince Vasilii Cherkasskii, and Prince Fedor Nogotkov-Obolenskii, who possessed neither conciliar rank nor service. Nogotkov brazenly claimed in the tsar's presence that he was more eminent than Fedor Romanov, the latter's father, the famous Nikita Romanov, and his uncle, Daniil Romanov. Angered and offended, the gentle Fedor rebuked Nogotkov sharply: "Daniil and Nikita, my mother's brothers, were my uncles. They have been dead for many years; why do you insult my dead uncles?" Prince Nogotkov was held in prison in Moscow for five days but nevertheless prevailed. In spite of the autocrat's intervention, Fedor Romanov's appointment was not approved because, as the Military Records Office noted: "The sovereign searched the registers and found that Prince Fedor Nogotkov may not be lesser than Boyar Fedor Nikitich Romanov."[7] Fedor Romanov's humiliating defeat demonstrated that Boris had robbed the "great sovereign" of any influence he might previously have possessed. As a reward for his effrontery Fedor Nogotkov was advanced several steps and Stepan

Godunov took Fedor Romanov's place. These new appointments quickly showed that it was the Godunov family that had inspired the precedence intrigue against the Romanov family.

One after another Tsar Fedor's guardians, whom Tsar Ivan had named, had died. Only Bogdan Belskii was still alive, rusticating in exile, and Boris was in no hurry to restore him to state service. When Tsar Ivan's erstwhile favorite and head of Tsar Fedor's first administration turned up in Moscow Boris humiliated him by giving him a routine service position. In 1596 the Military Records Office dispatched the former armorer to superintend the pacification of the southern frontier. Belskii was a close relative and an old oprichnina comrade of Godunov and Boris might have found his friendship useful if the situation had been different, but the struggle for the throne was intensifying and his former patrons and friends, Shchelkalov, the Romanov family, and Belskii, were now his enemies.

Chapter Eight

FORBIDDEN AND FIXED YEARS

The formation of a unitary state in the fifteenth and sixteenth centuries created better conditions for economic and cultural development, but as the country grew more powerful the feudal landowners felt strong enough to introduce St. George's Day and restrict peasant movement. In the middle of the sixteenth century a peasant could leave his landlord during a two-week period after November 20 if he had previously paid him a special departure fee of one ruble for rent, a considerable sum at that time, but by the end of the century dramatic changes had taken place in the life of the Russian peasantry. They had lost the limited freedom St. George's Day had guaranteed them and the dark shadow of serfdom loomed over the land. What were the reasons and circumstances that brought serfdom into existence in the late sixteenth century? This is a question of fundamental significance for Russian history. The feudal archives have preserved many highly important statutes affecting the peasantry issued during the administrations of Ivan the Terrible, Boris Godunov, and the first Romanov tsars, but one remains missing—the most important one—the law that abolished St. George's Day and brought peasant freedom

to an end. Scholars have been trying to find solutions to the problem
of serfdom for more than two hundred years, and from their analyses
two basic views have emerged. One is the theory of juridical enserfment; the other, the theory of nonjuridical enserfment.

The well-known historian V.N. Tatishchev believed that in 1592
Godunov promulgated a special statute enserfing the peasantry, but
after the unlucky Boris' death the text of his law was lost so completely that it could never be found. The weakness of this juridical
theory is that it depends upon conjecture rather than facts subject to
strict verification. Recognizing this, Kliuchevskii termed the view
that Godunov created peasant servitude an historical fable. He claimed
it was the actual circumstances of life and peasant indebtedness, not
government statutes, that brought peasant movement to an end.
Kliuchevskii's skill won his formulation wide acceptance, but his concept was undermined when documents referring to forbidden years
were discovered in the archives.

The eminent French historiographer Charles Langlois[1] has observed that of necessity historians must work with data from which
any student of the natural sciences would turn away in scorn. The
scanty sources that refer to forbidden years constitute an excellent
illustration of the justice of this remark.

The word "forbidden" comprehended a mass of prohibitions in
Old Russia. The authorities might interdict trade in "forbidden"
goods or hunting in a "forbidden" forest. Certain charters found in
the archives show that in "forbidden years" the authorities would
return runaway peasants to their landlords. Analyzing these documents, historians have advanced the hypothesis that a specific law of
prohibition may well have cancelled the rights of St. George's Day,
and this inference has inevitably led to a reexamination of previous
views.

The new theory of enserfment acquired final shape and form in
the work of Academician B.D. Grekov, who set forth the history of
the peasantry in his remarkable study, *Peasants in Russia.* Along with
Academician Veselovskii, Grekov forcefully advanced the view that
Ivan IV had forbidden peasant movement three years before his
death. Veselovskii thought Ivan's order applied only to a few small
districts, but in Grekov's opinion the whole country came under the
serf system, and his view became highly influential.

In following years striking new archival finds were made. The Soviet scholar V.I. Koretskii was the first to discover a direct reference
to such a law, so diligently sought for two hundred years, not mere

tangential allusions to forbidden years. During Fedor's administration monks in a Novgorod monastery addressed the following words to the tsar: "Now, in accordance with your royal edict, peasants and laborers may not depart." If the long-sought serf law emanated from Fedor, in whose name Boris Godunov ruled, what becomes of the hypothesis concerning Ivan IV's statute of prohibition? The forbidden-years theory inevitably has undergone revision but not as a result of the new archival discoveries. The chronicle reference Koretskii found belongs to the seventeenth century, makes no allusion to forbidden years, and indicates the rights of St. George's Day were abrogated not by Fedor but by his father, "pious Tsar Ivan Vasilevich."[2] Unless the original text of the tsar's edict is found, opinions concerning it can never be more than hypotheses, and the scientific validity of each one depends upon how well it squares with known facts and sources.

When sources are flatly contradictory, the historian, working in a manner reminiscent of the laborious toil of a detective, must find the best way to interpret and explain them. Neither professional should take everything his witnesses say literally, for gullibility may easily lead him astray, but both should not become too skeptical, for this may lead the investigation down a blind alley. With this in mind I shall attempt again to examine the few surviving witnesses who refer to the introduction of serfdom in Russia. Their voices are indistinct and confusing, but they are all we have. The more striking the historical event the greater the likelihood it will be reflected in the sources and remain in the memory of contemporaries. The disappearance of the most significant piece of Ivan's legislation is surprising, but the absence of allusion to it in documents belonging to the last years of Ivan's reign is incomprehensible.

The first references to forbidden years occur in a few documents of Godunov's time consisting of charters granted to service-tenure landholders in what was called the Derev district near Novgorod. Five years after Ivan died three landholders went to law demanding runaway peasants be returned. Most of the peasants absconded in Fedor's time, but a few had fled during the last three years of Ivan's reign. In their suits the landholders called those years and the ones following forbidden. What motivated the landholders' suits besides greed? On what law did they base their contention? This source provides no data to resolve these questions. Time has spared only disjointed insignificant fragments of the cases from the Derev district involving peasants. The petitions filed by these members of the gentry are lost and so are the decisions rendered by the chancery court. Only the trial record remains, written testimony the judges required to substantiate the claims. Did the Derev landlords manage to get their peasants back? What rules did the court apply when deciding these cases? One can only guess.

Before it can be accepted that the allegations made by the three landholders constitute proof of anything at all, they must be subjected to close scrutiny. To sift the material needed for verification was a lengthy task, but the efforts to do so have been crowned with success. The archives have preserved descriptions of service-tenure estates in the Derev district compiled during the years later designated as forbidden, and their authenticity is beyond doubt. Sixteenth-century cadastral books belong to the group of basic documents that confirm the right of landholders to possess land and peasants.

The proprietor of one of the three estates in the Derev district was a lesser boyar, Ivan Nepeitsyn, who in 1588 agitated to recover two peasants, the Gavrilov brothers, who had fled, as he put it, in the forbidden years of 1581-1582 while he was "on government service at Lialitsa."[3] The battle with the Swedes in the village of Lialitsa was fought in February, 1582, so this is a clear indication of precisely when the Gavrilov brothers left their landlord's village of Krutsy. A few months later senior crown scribes came to the estate, described the general tillage, listed abandoned peasant homesteads, but said nothing about the Gavrilov brothers.[4] It seems as though the scribes did not realize they were making an inventory in a forbidden year; thus, it might be assumed Tsar Ivan promulgated his edict forbidding departure only shortly before the scribes began work, for otherwise they would surely have given at least the names of peasants who had boldly transgressed the ruler's recent statute by leaving Nepeitsyn's estate while officials were present on it. That they did not do so means the scribes had received no instructions about forbidden years affecting the Derev estates.

In an assessment of these two contradictory sets of evidence preference must be given to the cadastral books, which are earlier and more authoritative. Nepeitsyn's subsequent statements obviously reflected conditions in a later period; hence, it would be ill-advised to use them in order to describe the situation in Ivan's time. Defining areas where the idea of forbidden years first became operable, Veselovskii drew attention to the Derev district and also to the patrimonial estates belonging to the Joseph of Volokolamsk monastery.

The evidence concerning the Joseph of Volokolamsk peasants, which historians have uncovered in monastery income and expenditure records for the 1570s and 1580s, unquestionably merits attention. The earliest journals are full of lists of monastery peasants who departed; their numbers peaked around the spring of 1580, but from the fall of 1581 they completely disappear from the records. The question is not what the monks chose to record, but rather the actualities of life, on the basis of which one may conclude that starting with the 1580s the peasants of the Joseph of Volokolamsk monastery could no longer take advantage of St. George's Day. Can this new evidence be applied to the issue of forbidden years? If the monks were aware of the tsar's edict of prohibition, why did they not refer even once to forbidden years in their income journals or other monastery records?

In order to assess the validity of a witness' testimony it is first necessary to ascertain how much information he has been given. It is useless to ask him what he does not know. The monks used cadastral books that have not survived in order to compile records of the peasant population, and their income journals recorded financial transactions benefiting the monastery treasury, not peasant movement. For this reason their revenue office was interested only in peasants who paid the monastery the departure fee of one ruble for rent prescribed by law when they moved, so that the disappearance of lists of the departed from the income journals does not mean peasants had stopped moving; they merely indicated instances when payment of a departure fee ended a financial relationship.

Other documents support such a conclusion, as a glance at the Volokolamsk peasants' neighbors, who lived on estates of Khan Simeon Bekbulatovich, grand prince of Tver, reveals.[5] Alarmed by widespread peasant flight, in 1580 Simeon dispatched scribes to his patrimony to ascertain the cause. Their report disclosed some curious facts: out of two hundred missing peasants only a few had left their villages after paying the rent due on St. George's Day. The overwhelming majority had fled the estate during the hungry spring months without paying the fee. Many had gone to adjacent feudatories, who likewise were ignoring the rules of St. George's Day.

In the early 1580s a substantial proportion of the rural population had either fled or died and the countryside was like a desert. The peasants tilled no more than a small portion of the land previously required to maintain them. The extent of the disaster drastically affected the traditional right of movement on St. George's Day, and this state of affairs was reflected in documents mentioning the peasants of Volokolamsk and Tver, where no traces of legal abrogation of the rights of St. George's Day are to be found.

In 1607, during the reign of Tsar Vasilii Shuiskii, the land-tenure chancellery published a comprehensive enactment about peasants which contained a unique clause. The secretaries stated: "In the days of Tsar Ivan Vasilevich peasants enjoyed the right of free movement, but Tsar Fedor Ivanovich, ignoring the advice of his senior boyars, at the insistence of Boris Godunov interdicted peasant movement, and peasants were inscribed in ledgers wherever and with whomever they were."[6] The provenance of those who compiled this edict is unassailable. It emanated from the land-tenure chancellery that promulgated and preserved all laws pertaining to peasants. This source is of fundamental importance, for it disposes once and for all of the view that peasants lost the right of movement in Ivan's time. It has been contended that when introducing the prohibition Tsar Ivan made a census of the land in order to tie peasants to landlords, but this edict shows it was Fedor, not Ivan, who conducted the census. The facts fully support this view; in Ivan's day scribes were active only in Novgorod, and a general census was not held until after his death.

Earlier documents substantiate the 1607 pronouncement of the land-tenure chancellery, as Koretskii's discoveries show. In 1595 the elders of the Pantaleimonov monastery in the Derev district reminded Tsar Fedor that his royal edict had provided "peasants may not depart."[7] The land-tenure chancellery accepted their petition and did not object to the monks' statement, which it even cited in the court decision. The petition and the court decision have survived in their original form, which endows them with exceptional value. These authentic documents of 1595, fully supporting the 1607 statement made by the land-tenure chancellery, constitute irrefutable proof that Godunov, not Ivan, established serfdom.

Another document Koretskii found, a short chronicle stating that the "lawful and pious tsar" Ivan Vasilevich laid a "curse" on peasant movement but the usurper Boris, defying his wishes, reinstituted St. George's Day during the great famine of 1601-1603, must be explained. First it is necessary to determine the identity of the new witness who was decisively refuting the pronouncements of the land-tenure chancellery. Was he perhaps a contemporary of Ivan who had participated directly in events during those years? He was not. The chronicle entry, which appeared in the seventeenth century long after Ivan, Godunov and Shuiskii had disappeared from the scene, was composed by an anonymous provincial gentry serfowner who invoked the memory of the "pious tsar" to justify the existing system. There is nothing to indicate he had access to authentic documents about serfdom, and his observations are purely literary in nature.

The suits brought by the landholders in the Derev district and the lists drawn up by the monks of the Joseph of Volokolamsk monastery refer to forbidden years in an obscure manner. More information may be derived from a charter Andrei Shchelkalov, secretary of the land-tenure chancellery in 1590, composed for the town of Toropets. The town authorities received permission to bring back to the business section people paying state taxes, known as *tiaglo,* who had run away to landholders and monasteries "during forbidden years."[8] The To-ropets charter enhances our knowledge of forbidden years. Formal abolition of St. George's Day has been considered the main feature of the edict of prohibition, but the Toropets charter refers not to peasants but to townspeople, who had nothing to do with St. George's Day. Financial concerns motivated the restrictions on town dwellers. The treasury long had obtained the bulk of its cash revenues from urban taxpayers, but during the time of disaster[9] urban inhabitants had fled to the countryside and towns grew deserted. Using forbidden years the authorities forced townspeople to return to their homes in order to reconstitute urban communes able to pay taxes. The intro-duction of forbidden years in Toropets meant that taxpayers who had fled were temporarily attached to any taxpaying urban commune. The measures to reconstitute an urban tax system were dubbed "town edifice," of which more will be said later.

The government struggled to bring back taxpayers either from the towns or the countryside. To recover taxpaying peasants, in their depositions rural landlords tried to prove disputed peasants had aban-doned their tax-yielding plots, thereby diminishing treasury receipts. As another example, when administrators of the black or crown lands on the Dvina river complained that estate peasants were running away, in 1585 Shchelkalov ordered a search for these peasants con-ducted on lands belonging to a neighboring monastery. They were restored to the crown estates again to pay taxes.

The last charter referring to forbidden years, dated 1592, was issued to the Nikolskii monastery on the Dvina. The Nikolskii monks asked Moscow to help them bring back two peasants to their tax-yielding allotments. One had left the monastery estate; the other re-mained within its confines but had abandoned his allotment and gone to stay with his son-in-law. To reinforce their petition the monks carefully calculated how much the peasants' departure had cost the treasury. Secretary Shchelkalov, acting on the monks' suit, inserted in the text of the court decision a special section on crown lands sur-rounding the holdings of the Nikolskii monastery which enjoined

crown administrators from enticing peasants from the Nikolskii estate
"in forbidden years until we promulgate a statute."[10] The 1592
Dvina charter shows that a new plateau in the prohibition system
had been reached. To judge from the Toropets charter, the government regarded years prior to 1590 as forbidden, and the Dvina charter
implies that those who organized the new system intended to expand
prohibition to the foreseeable future, although they did not renounce
the view it was a temporary expedient a special crown ordinance
might someday abolish.

These reliable chancery sources for 1590-1592 reveal characteristic features of the prohibition system then in process of formation.
It focused on rural and urban taxpayers; it was initiated by individual
proprietors and feudal towns, and forbidden years were still temporary expedients. There is another oddity: most government decrees
returning taxpaying town dwellers and peasants to their former habi-
tations did not employ the phrase "forbidden years." It is not known
whether Nepeitsyn and the other two landlords won their suits, but
a year later their neighbor, Yazykov, prevailed in an analogous contest. The original materials in Yazykov's case have survived in their
entirety, including his petition and the chancery court's decision that
his peasants must be returned, but none of the documents alludes to
forbidden years.

The information the sources provide is unexpected. During Godunov's administration the contours of the serf system began to emerge,
but chancery officials, still hesitant to employ the term "forbidden
years," when deciding cases usually avoided reference to such a prohibition. This is conducive to the assumption that forbidden years
had not yet become a legal formula. If so, it follows that the use of
forbidden years arose not because they were law but from ongoing
decisions taken by the authorities. Financial concerns were the chief
spur stimulating growth of the system of prohibitions. At the close
of Ivan's reign, tax remittances to the treasury decreased sharply and
finances fell into disarray. In Fedor's time the authorities dealt with
the taxpaying elements among the population by implementing a
program primarily determined by the need to increase revenue. The
return of peasants and townspeople to their taxpaying units was initially caused not by formal abolition of St. George's Day but by a
shift in taxation policy that temporarily bound taxpayers to state
tax rolls. Prohibitions were considered a limited transitional expedient
to reinvigorate the parlous tax system. Such temporary measures,
which were dictated by immediate financial considerations, clearly

required no major legislative action, and at the outset virtually no one foresaw the consequences the new tax policy would produce.

The changes in the tax structure did not bring peasant departures to an end. Prohibition affected proprietors who paid imposts, not their brothers, children or nephews, and the device was not invoked until requirements of government service demanded it. In 1592 Shchelkalov circulated a rescript in the southern regions ordering inhabitants to serve as cossacks in recently constructed border forts; it involved only sons of peasants and poor laborers paying no taxes. Taxpaying peasants might also become cossacks and the very fact they could do so emphasizes how heavily financial considerations influenced the initial development of serfdom. Documents pertaining to the cossack levy paint a grim picture of the extent to which feudal landlords engaged in acts of rapine. They beat and tormented peasants to prevent them from entering state service, put them in chains, starved them to death, concealed peasant wives and children on their private plots, and filched livestock and equipment from peasant homesteads.[11]

The feudatories tried to make the courts restore runaway peasants. Their petitions could cite no law forbidding departure but they harped on the danger to the tax base. For their part peasants enrolled in government service sought to demonstrate they had found substitutes to work the allotments they had left and that their removal would not affect the treasury. Southern landlords literally deluged the land-tenure chancellery with petitions to bring their peasants back from the cossacks and Shchelkalov sent commanders new instructions sternly forbidding them to accept agricultural peasants as cossacks even if they had found a substitute. It can be seen the gentry was quick to appreciate the advantages inherent in the new financial policy, which its members sought to appropriate to their own interests. For all intents and purposes southern landlords were treating their peasants as though they were serfs.

Using the concept of forbidden years as a means to enserf the peasantry seemed insufficiently flexible. The number of forbidden years steadily increased, as did quarrels involving peasants. Landowners had to wait a long time for their cases to be decided and the tangle of lawsuits became horrendous. Discord within the feudal state intensified and the chancery apparatus was overworked. To put an end to the growing problem the authorities finally had to abandon the principle of unrestricted forbidden years and apply a statute of limitations to peasant suits.

On May 3, 1594 Shchelkalov decided a quarrel between Zinovev and Molevanov, two Novgorod landholders. Zinovev was trying to get back peasants Molevanov had taken from his estate in the last year of Ivan IV's life. Shchelkalov ruled in favor of Molevanov. Communicating his decision to Novgorod the secretary wrote that local judges should not decree the return of peasants who had fled more than five years ago: "In cases of peasant departure and matters of proprietorship occurring more than five years earlier petitioners may not file and if they do their petitions are to be rejected."[12] By a stroke of the pen the chief secretary had cancelled the old notion of forbidden years that had obtained in the 1580s.

The established custom of returning peasants to their original landlords gradually made temporary transient measures permanent and legal. Contemporaries immediately grasped the distinction. In 1595 Novgorod monks could write: "Now, in accordance with your royal edict peasants and poor laborers may not depart," but in order to interpret this source properly it is first necessary to understand the concepts underlying it. Here it is appropriate to recall that Godunov's contemporaries did not consider a tsar's rescript, or order, had the force of law. A personal decision, no more authoritative than its author, was enforced by the formula, "this is the sovereign's rescript." This means the Novgorod monks were referring to one of Fedor's rescripts and did not automatically assume it to be a comprehensive legal statute forbidding peasants to depart. Incidentally, their words little resembled an exact quotation from a legal text.

It is not strange that scholars have failed to find any law abrogating St. George's Day for most sixteenth-century archives have been lost, but one item is inexplicable. When the First False Dmitrii came to the throne (1605-1606) he ordered his predecessors' statutes collected and codified. Those executing his behest were secretaries who had served under Tsars Fedor Ivanovich and Boris Godunov and had access to the original archives, but they could find no rescript annulling St. George's Day to include in the compendium. There is only one explanation of this omission. The statute they sought seems never to have been promulgated.

Tsar Ivan the Terrible earned an unenviable reputation. He burdened the Russian people with taxes heavier than they had ever known before. Crown tax collectors ruined the peasants and extorted arrears from them. While the famine raged Ivan refused to open his bursting granaries to the starving populace, but his law code affirmed St. George's Day. The end of his reign coincided with the last decade peasants enjoyed freedom.

Boris Godunov stands convicted of a sinister role in enserfing the peasantry. The authors of the historic 1607 reference asserted the pious Fedor enserfed the peasants at Boris' insistence. In reality the situation was somewhat different. The basic conditions for enserfment were created in Shchelkalov's chancery, but after he eliminated the man who was in effect co-regent Boris in time appropriated the fruits of his endeavors. Three years after the secretary retired Godunov augmented Shchelkalov's advisories to the effect that peasants could not be forced to return after five years with the force of law. The edict promulgated in 1597 signified that the measures originally designed to regulate finances had been transformed into a system to tie the peasantry to the land. Such was the device that enserfed many millions of Russian peasants.

The serf law of 1597 was issued in the name of Tsar Fedor, but he was at the end of his days and contemporaries all knew who was responsible. His policy of enserfment won Boris broad support among the feudal gentry.

Chapter Nine

THE LAND ASSEMBLY OF 1598[1]

Tsar Fedor died on January 6, 1598. The ancient crown, the Cap of Monomakh, was donned by Boris Godunov, who emerged victorious from a power struggle. Many of his own and subsequent generations considered him an usurper, but Kliuchevskii has disposed effectively of this view. The eminent historian showed that Boris was elected by a lawful land assembly that included representatives of the gentry, clergy, and leading townspeople. Platonov supported Kliuchevskii. He wrote that Boris' enthronement was not the result of an intrigue; the land assembly deliberately chose him and knew better than one can today what its members were voting for.

Documents pertaining to Godunov's election have survived. Their authors studiously traced the course of Boris' elevation to the throne but could not avoid reservations and contradictions. Historians still cannot answer a simple question: how many participated in the assembly that elected Godunov. Karamzin estimated 500 electors; Soloviev thought there were 474; N.M. Kostomarov advanced the figure of 476; Kliuchevskii, 512, and a modern scholar, S.P. Mordovina, has assumed more than 600. The discrepancies are the more surprising because the scholars used the same sources in making their calculations. Here are the causes of the problem.

Two assembly decrees ratifying Boris' election as tsar have been preserved. If their dates are accepted both were composed almost simultaneously. The first was initialed in July, 1598; the second, composed during the same month, was completed by August 1, 1598. Their content differs markedly; they offer dissimilar interpretations of several important events in Boris' election campaign, and list a different component of electors. Furthermore, the names of the assembly members fail to correspond with the signatures affixed to both charters. When similar decrees are signed by different persons one is entitled to conclude the documents were promulgated at different times. This means the dates of the affirmatory charters must be subjected to comprehensive critical scrutiny.

Careful perusal of the July decree reveals that it is divided into two sections. The basic text ends abruptly when assembly members swear fealty to Godunov and curse the disobedient. There then follows a traditional terminating formula: "And to confirm this enabling charter sat . . ." followed by a list of members of the electoral assembly. The charter eventually was supplemented with an extensive appendix, which ended in exactly the same way as the basic text. Its compilers again swore fealty to Boris and cursed those who might refuse to do so. When dating the charter they noted it "was prepared and drawn up in the year 7106,[2] on the . . . (blank) . . . day of July." It may be assumed this date indicated when the appendix, not the original text, was composed. Its authors drew attention to the fact that the assembly list in the original text omitted the name of Hermogen, a leading church hierarch, and deemed it necessary to add that he "was at the time (*sic*—R.S.) in his metropolitanate, in the town of Kazan, for great church demands and other affairs."[3] These words leave no doubt that the original charter text was written considerably earlier than the appendix. A subsequent commentator, who detected omissions in the original text, explained them on the hypothesis that "the names in the affirmatory charter were written from memory . . . since at the time (*sic*—R.S.) there was no hurry to recruit persons of quality."

When was the original text of the decree electing Boris composed? The charter itself provides a precise answer. It states that on March 9, 1598 Patriarch Iov proposed the assembly should devise a charter confirming Boris as tsar: "And in future it will be immutable, for it will be enshrined in an enabling charter." On April 1 Boris took possession of the palace and then "This enabling charter, written over a short time, was brought to Iov."[4] This means the document was drawn up in March or early April, 1598, a date further supported by the fact that the assembly decree provided a daily journal of the electoral campaign from January to early April but says nothing about subsequent events. Herein lies the first forgery perpetrated in the literature pertaining to Godunov's election. Unlike the other precise indications they included, the editors of the primary text arbitrarily transferred the time of its composition from April to July and inserted the latter date into a supplement to the charter text.

The second decree concerning Boris' election is dated August 1. Unlike the first it is inscribed with signatures not only of churchmen but of secular figures who participated in the election. Kliuchevskii, who was the first to notice the discrepancy between the list of Godunov's electors and the signatures, attempted to explain it by assuming the list was compiled when the assembly met in February and March and the signatures were gathered when it concluded in August, but this hypothesis appears unconvincing. Careful comparison of the electoral list with the signatures gives grounds for assuming the charter was compiled at a different time. Early in September, after his coronation, Boris distributed rank to numerous noble courtiers who had played a part in his election. Although some discrepancies exist, both the electoral list and signatures assign these individuals the ranks they had been given in September-December, 1598. This means Boris' chancellery did not draw up the list in February, 1598, but almost a year later.

This new date explains why the lists found in the records of the spiritual assembly and the two enabling charters manifest wide discrepancies. A year, not just two or three weeks, separated the two charter redactions, during which time the heads of various monasteries changed. A new bishopric, first mentioned in the later redaction of the enabling charter, had been founded in Korela. This reveals the second forgery in Godunov's election literature, the purpose and motives of which are understandable. The new tsar's entourage was following the precedent provided by the election of Tsar Fedor. A land assembly had elected Ivan IV's feebleminded offspring to the throne exactly a month before his coronation, and Godunov's chancellery was endeavoring to prove that Boris too had been crowned a month after a land assembly had chosen him. It is now appropriate to investigate the land assembly of 1598 in detail.

Tsar Fedor left no will. It is unclear whether Boris prevented him from making one or whether he believed, in his piety, that he should not insist upon it. Divergent versions concerning his last wishes surfaced in the course of the election contest. Rumors abounded to the effect that Fedor had designated one of his Romanov cousins as his successor but this did not agree with the official position circulated by the Godunov interests. The earlier redaction of the enabling charter claimed Fedor had bestowed the throne upon his wife Irina and consigned the kingdom and his soul to Boris.[5] The final charter redaction proclaimed the tsar had left his wife in charge, naming Patriarch Iov and Boris Godunov as executors.[6] Reliable sources declare the patriarch kept reminding Fedor he should name a successor, but as was his custom the tsar remained silent, citing the will of God.[7] He was more concerned about his wife than the throne. Witnesses stated Fedor had told Irina to take the veil and live out her days in a nunnery.[8] Clearly Fedor, considered a noble holy fool, was acting fully in accordance with church prescriptions and traditional practice.

All the tsar's relatives had good reason to be dissatisfied with him and so Fedor died in neglect. When his grave was opened the corpse was found arrayed in a humble secular robe girt with a strap, and even the dish of myrrh set out for him was ordinary and unfit for royalty.[9] The saintly tsar who spent his life fasting and in prayer was not even allowed the honor of becoming a monk, although deathbed tonsure had been traditional for members of the Kalita clan since the time of Vasilii III and Ivan IV. Fedor was treated like a useless puppet even before he died.

Refusing to honor Fedor's wish for his widow to take the veil, Boris tried to take advantage of her in order to consolidate his position behind the throne. Immediately after her husband died Irina proclaimed a general and total amnesty and ordered disgraced traitors, thieves, robbers and other prisoners released at once. Devoted as he was to Boris, Iov issued instructions that all dioceses were to swear loyalty to the queen, but when read out in church his lengthy screed aroused great discontent. The people were told to swear fealty to Patriarch Iov and the Orthodox faith, Queen Irina, and Regent Boris and his children. Using the oath to church and queen as a pretext, the regent was actually requiring an oath to himself and his chosen successor. He had overestimated his strength seriously. Witnesses reported that in Moscow "the most important people refused to recognize Boris as grand prince;" similarly, not everyone in the provinces swore loyalty to the "new grand prince" (sic—R.S.), and people showed their dislike of "the Godunov gang."[10]

List of the Land Assembly of 1598 (excerpt)

While Fedor was alive Irina Godunova freely had been called great sovereign, but this mode of address did not imply she possessed a genuine regal title. Before and after the False Dmitrii, queens neither were crowned nor even permitted to participate in the coronation ceremony; Irina watched Fedor's coronation through an aperture in the women's quarters. Her subjects had not sworn an oath to her as a crowned head, and thus Irina could neither exercise royal power herself nor confer it upon her brother. From time immemorial the Orthodox had chanted "Long Life" for tsars and metropolitans in church, but Patriarch Iov did not scruple to set aside tradition and conduct a service to honor Fedor's widow. Chroniclers considered this an unprecedented occurrence and one wrote: "The first service was for her as sovereign; ere that no one had ever prayed to God for any queen or grand princess either during service or the invocation."[11] Iov was trying to instill the notion that Irina was lawfully entitled to wield autocratic power, but pious zealots, including Secretary Ivan Timofeev, pilloried his attempt as "a shameless attack on holy church."[12]

There are indications that during the interregnum the boyar council and other leading figures in Moscow seized the initiative and summoned an electoral assembly. After Fedor's death, wrote a Moscow chronicler, "the boyars of the city of Moscow, and all the soldiers, and from the entire Moscovite realm all the people in all the towns and villages chose men and sent them to Moscow to elect a tsar."[13] Other contemporary testimony supports this statement. A German agent noted that by the end of January prominent boyars and churchmen in Pskov, Novgorod and other towns had been ordered to proceed to Moscow at once to elect a tsar, but Boris' opposition prevented them from doing so. Many provincial commanders were avowed opponents of Boris and he had no wish to see them participating in the assembly. A witness in Pskov said Godunov had told his men to block the roads leading to Moscow and detain those who had been invited to come to the capital.[14] He had reason to be alarmed and anxious, for events had taken an unwanted turn. Foreign observers unanimously assert that because of the change in rulers Russia was a scene of great disturbance and confusion.

Queen Irina's independent administration had gone badly from the start. A week after her husband's death she stated her decision to enter a nunnery and a large crowd collected at the Kremlin on the day of her abdication. Official sources later pretended that the people, brimming with loyal sentiments, tearfully begged her to stay on the throne, but in reality the popular mood aroused great concern among the leaders. A Dutch observer, Isaac Massa, emphasized that Irina apparently was forced to abdicate: "The commons, which in that country is always prone to strife, thronged about the Kremlin in great numbers, shouted, and called for the queen, and in order to avoid great misfortune and revolt" Irina appeared on the Red Porch to announce her desire for tonsure.[15] She abdicated in favor of the boyar council, telling the people: "You have princes and boyars. Let them be leaders and rule over you."[16] Her words were just what the boyars wanted to hear; undoubtedly they had insisted she utter them. Fedor's widow then simply and without ceremony departed for the New Virgin convent, where she adopted the tranquil life of a nun. So ran the official legend. Reality was otherwise.

After her tonsure Elder Aleksandra Fedorovna did not abandon secular life and tried to rule from her nunnery, signing decrees in her own name and circulating them to the towns. Behind her stood her brother, Boris Godunov, who had been unable to prevent Irina's tonsure but had no intention of giving up his position. On the memorable day the queen was summoned to the square Godunov appeared beside her on the Red Porch and tried to convince the people that everything in Moscovy was as it had been. Speaking after his sister, Godunov declared he would administer the realm with the help of the princes and boyars. This is how an Austrian envoy, Michael Schiele, puts it and the accuracy of his information is borne out by the text of the April charter, which has Boris affirming he would be "happy to advise and consult with the boyars not only as before but even more than before." Those who compiled the final charter redaction rendered Boris' speech quite differently: he purportedly said he would lay aside the conduct of affairs and the patriarch would rule the country. His chancellery tried to obfuscate this inexplicable contradiction. At first Boris was to rule the realm and sought to bind everyone with an oath to that effect, but then he was going to lay aside affairs of state. What was the reason? Was he motivated by magnanimity, as the final charter editor contended, or compelled by circumstance?

During Fedor's lifetime Boris Godunov had been able to make the great nobles obey him but after the tsar died the boyars no longer troubled to conceal the animosity they harbored against the favorite. The aristocracy simply refused to consider conferring the crown upon him and their stubborn attitude was bolstered by hallowed tradition. The feudal mind could not accept the idea of making a minor

member of the gentry tsar and everyone was convinced that only a
man proceeding from "the tsaric root" should occupy the throne.
The closest relatives of the Muscovite royal house were the princes
descended from Rurik, among whom the Shuiskii princes of the blood
were preeminent. Kalita traced his descent from Aleksandr Nevskii;
the Shuiskii princes from Nevskii's older brother, and the nobility
recalled this even in Ivan's time. Some accounts claim that the Shuiskii
princes, hoping to ascend the vacant throne, intrigued incessantly
against Boris. The New Chronicler alleges that after Fedor's death
the patriarch and the government "took counsel with the entire land"
and decided to place Boris on the throne; "only the Shuiskii princes
did not want him to be ruler."[17] Since the New Chronicler flourished
in the circle around Filaret Romanov, in Platonov's neat phrase the
name "Shuiskii" was inserted in his chronicle in order to draw attention away from the fact that Godunov's principal opponent was not
the Shuiskii but the Romanov family. The noble Shuiskii princes
had been forced to endure the oprichnina terror and Godunov's persecution completed the process. They dared not make an open claim
to the throne and preferred to bide their time.

By January, 1598 it was reported in Lithuania that there were
four likely aspirants to the Muscovite throne. The two leading contenders were the Romanov brothers, Fedor and Aleksandr, sons of
Nikita, whose chances appeared excellent. In February news circulated abroad that the boyars had chosen the older Romanov brother
and murdered Godunov. The Lithuanian secret service soon became
convinced these rumors were groundless but spies kept insisting the
boyars and commanders had agreed to pick Romanov because of his
kinship with the previous tsar. Mstislavskii and Godunov were considered minor candidates. Mstislavskii had royal blood; the great-
great-grandson of Ivan III, he was president of the boyar council, but
the Mstislavskii princes, who originally had come from Lithuania,
lacked authority among the indigenous Russian nobles. The Lithuanians gave Boris little chance. He had no formal right to the throne because he was not of royal blood and before he died Fedor was rumored
to have been hostile to Boris' candidacy because of his non-noble
origin. The spies also reported that Boris drew his support from minor
boyars, fusiliers, and virtually the entire commons. However, feudal
practice denied fusiliers and the people a decisive voice in so important a matter as the election of a tsar.

The power struggle split the boyar council. In February it leaked
abroad that the Moscow boyars "could not make peace amongst

themselves and great dissension and ill-feeling existed among them."[18]
The Romanov forces considered their position so strong that they
could indulge in sharp attacks on Godunov. Their hostility was so
palpable that Boris ceased to attend meetings of the boyar council
and withdrew to his residence. At first he tried to direct affairs from
the confines of his home, and his wife's cousin, Boyar Shuiskii, tried
to help him. The Lithuanian spy network reported that Shuiskii had
tried to convince the boyars not to initiate action without Boris'
knowledge[19] but that his intervention was unsuccessful. The factionalism in the council reached such heights that Boris was obliged to
abandon his residence in the Kremlin and retire from the city, en-
sconcing himself behind the walls of the well-fortified New Virgin
monastery.

On departing the Kremlin, Boris left Iov behind as his trusted
representative. The patriarch's exertions on Boris' behalf were valuable
but they could not determine the outcome of the election, for Iov
possessed neither strong character nor adequate authority. His unceremonious interference in the political struggle brought down the
nobility's wrath upon him and Iov never spoke of the period prior to
Boris' election save with pain. In those days, the patriarch recalled,
he fell "into great sorrow and sadness," and he was the target of
"spite, slander, insults; sobs and tears; all such was the lot of my
humble self."[20] Iov may have been exaggerating, but not a great deal.

The noble boyars denied the patriarch had any right to conduct
affairs and held their own views about the succession. The contending
factions did everything in their power to win over the people of
Moscow,[21] which became a center of frenzied agitation against Boris.
Rumors spread from one person to another that he personally had
poisoned pious Tsar Fedor in order to acquire the crown. This frightful crime was an object of discussion both during the first weeks of
the interregnum and for many years afterwards. A charge more serious
than regicide could not be conceived, nor a better way found to
arouse the lower townspeople against Boris. Their discontent constantly sought outlet and their volatile mood could shift instantly.
Ivan Timofeev, who saw and participated in the events of this time,
stated categorically it was fear alone that drove Boris from Moscow.
He believed Godunov was deathly afraid of a sudden popular revolt,
when the people would attack the tsar's murderer in order to avenge
his death.[22] The facts reveal the mendacity of the official version
that Boris quitted the city of his own volition. His flight from the
Kremlin proved he had suffered a defeat during the first stage of the

election contest that might well lead to his removal from the office of regent.

On February 17 the period of mourning for Fedor expired and Moscow set about the task of electing a new tsar. The patriarch called a meeting at his palace, in which it was decided to elect Boris. Each edition of the affirmatory charter emphasizes that clergy, boyars, courtiers, lesser boyars, chancery people and men of all ranks in Moscow and the rest of the Russian land participated in it, but both variants bear obvious traces of editorial revision. The April charter states that a host of people assembled in the patriarch's court: "Every age of the innumerable clans of the Russian realm." The editor of the 1599 redaction considered the allusion to every age improper, struck it out, and substituted a roster of the assembly's complement, mentioning Moscow merchants and traders first and introducing the word "assembly" into the text for the first time.

According to the earlier redaction Iov proposed Boris' candidacy in the name of the few ecclesiastics who had witnessed Tsar Fedor's death in Moscow. This failed to satisfy the later editor, who simplified the procedure of nominating Boris in the new edition. The patriarch was supposed to have advanced him in the name of all secular and ecclesiastical ranks: boyars, courtiers, chancery people, merchants, and "all Christians."[23] A closer determination of the actual complement of the first land assembly cannot be made. Without doubt its participants included boyars from the Godunov family, their relatives in the Saburov and Veliaminov families, junior council members such as, presumably, Boyar Prince Khvorostinin, Associate Boyar Prince Gagin, and conciliar courtiers like Princes Buinosov and Tatishchev. Of course none of Boris' enemies were members.

The affirmatory charter mentions that certain boyars taking part in the assembly presented written testimony in support of Boris. This detail is confirmed by Timofeev, who was directly involved in Boris' election. Since he was not one of Godunov's unqualified supporters his memoirs may be used to counterbalance the official sources. The well-informed secretary wrote that Godunov's most committed partisans took matters into their own hands and approached the patriarch with a written interpolation.[24] It is noteworthy that Boris' supporters valued the interpolation so highly they included it, apparently without change, in the April enabling charter.

Composed in the heat of the election campaign the interpolation constitutes an outstanding example of preelection literature. It sets forth the candidate's biography in a most flattering manner, omitting no detail that might advance his aspirations. Its authors stressed that Boris had been raised in the royal palace; Tsar Ivan had visited him at home while he was ill and lifted three fingers to indicate that Fedor, Irina and Boris were equal in his eyes. Ivan had commended his son Fedor and entrusted his entire realm to Boris, and Boris had received Fedor's blessing.

Details in the narrative reveal its authorship. Recalling Ivan's visit to Godunov's home the compilers state: "And we, his slaves, were with him" (the tsar—R.S.). The visit was unofficial and only those closest to Ivan accompanied him. By 1598 most of these individuals were either dead or included among Boris' enemies, with the exception of Dmitrii Godunov, Ivan's old chamberlain, who was clearly the principal instigator of this move to help Boris and willing to lie in order to further his nephew's pretensions. The bulk of his presentation is anecdotal, but this caused Iov and his circle no embarrassment.

The patriarch listened with approval to what was termed the wise speech of the boyars and together with the rest of the assembly participants ordained they should meet the following day in the cathedral of the Dormition to arrange a procession to New Virgin monastery. Participants were under strict orders as to the line of march they were to follow. They devised a scenario calling for courtiers to take their places by Queen Irina's cell, with a huge crowd at the nunnery and behind the convent in a field, and "all in unison, with great urgency and unquenchable wailing," were to beseech Boris to assume the throne.

Official documents have painted an idyllic portrait of the unanimous election of Godunov, but reality was vastly different from the idyll. The composers of the enabling charter described what occurred in the patriarch's residence, but said nothing about the more important events unfolding in the Kremlin palace where the boyar council met. Michael Schiele's report helps to fill this gap in the official sources. He recounts that as soon as the period of mourning came to an end the boyars assembled in the palace and after protracted debate approached the people with a special appeal. They appeared twice on the Red Porch and urged the populace to take an oath to the council. Its finest speaker, Chancellor Vasilii Shchelkalov, earnestly tried to convince the crowd that an oath to a nun was no longer binding and the only solution was to swear loyalty to the boyars.[25]

A letter from an unknown Pole, dated July, 1598, confirms Schiele's report. Citing the narrative of a Polish courier in Moscow, the author of the letter noted: "The wife of the deceased grand prince (in Moscow—R.S.) has set her brother Boris at the helm of the principality until a genuine prince is crowned, but the chancellor has proclaimed to the estates that Boris has not been confirmed as grand prince; noble Muscovites oppose him and a few are openly calling for his assassination."[26]

The major difficulty confronting the council was that although the great boyars had rejected decisively Boris' claim to the throne they could not compose their own disagreements. The Romanov brothers had inherited their father's popularity but they lacked the resourcefulness and experience needed to unite Boris' enemies. The Romanov family was far higher born than the Godunov family, but it too was connected with the royal family only through the female line. Princes of the blood and great boyars refused to give up their rights to the throne to them. The decision taken by the boyar council shows that neither the Romanov nor the Mstislavskii families could muster enough council votes, and the refusal of popular men to become candidates as well as other differences paralyzed the council.

The electoral contest had entered a critical phase. The land assembly's decision in favor of Boris Godunov could not be regarded as legal because the boyar council, the highest organ of state, had rejected his candidacy out of hand, but the council proposal to make the people swear fealty to the boyars and establish a boyar regime was likewise unacceptable. The split at the center transferred the question of the succession from the council and the patriarch's residence to the streets and the contending factions resorted to agitation, bribery, and other similar activities.

The land assembly proved more efficient, managing on February 20 to organize a procession to New Virgin monastery. Boris listened graciously to speeches by assembly members but refused to respond to their entreaties. Appearing before the crowd with tears in his eyes, he swore he had no intention of aspiring to the lofty dignity of tsar. It is not hard to divine the motive behind Godunov's refusal. He was clearly disappointed the crowd was small and wanted to scotch slanderous rumors he had murdered the tsar. To achieve these aims effectively he let it be known he would soon become a monk, and influenced by this ingenious gambit the mood in Moscow began to change.

The patriarch and assembly members, seeking to capitalize upon the success they scented, redoubled their efforts to elicit a new manifestation of support. The church invoked its authority. The patriarch decided to keep Moscow churches open to parishioners from the

evening of February 20 to the following morning and his calculations
proved justified when the nocturnal service attracted a host of people.
Next morning the clergy brought the most holy icons out of their
shrines and in all sanctity set out in religious procession to New Virgin monastery. By this means the leaders of the land assembly managed
to attract a large crowd.

The senior assembly members negotiated with Queen Irina and
her brother in the name of the people. In an effort to persuade Boris
to accept the crown churchmen threatened to close churches and lay
down their badges of office if he rejected their representations. Boyars
next appeared, who said: "And we shall stop calling ourselves boyars,"
by which they meant they would not administer the country if Boris
refused to mount the throne. Lastly, as befitted its status, the gentry
expressed its views.

The gentry unquestionably had considerable influence on the outcome of the electoral contest in Moscow. There were many indications
that its members favored Boris. By early February Lithuanian spies
were reporting that minor boyars supported Godunov and the chronicles stated that the crowd in the field at New Virgin monastery contained numerous serving-men, who expressed their opinions, declaring
that if Boris refused the crown they would cease to serve and fight
the enemy and "there will be bloodshed in the land."[27]

After his death his opponents asserted Godunov's administration
forced people to come to New Virgin monastery by threatening to
fine them. Special escorts saw to it that everyone would shout and
weep loudly and lustily, and those who refused were beaten about
the neck. These measures, in the words of a later chronicler, were designed solely to influence righteous Elder Aleksandra, who is supposed
to have refused to give her brother her blessing.[28] This piece of information displays little knowledge and shows total contempt for
the truth on the part of an author of a scurrilous pamphlet attacking
Boris.

Timofeev, who actually witnessed these events and was not an
admirer of Boris, says nothing about fines and escorts. He saw Boris
appear on a balcony and wrap his neck in a silk handkerchief, meaning he preferred to strangle himself rather than accept the crown, a
gesture that made a strong impression on the crowd. All his life
Timofeev remembered the deafening shouts of the people hailing
Boris. He noted particularly how ordinary people and the commons
shouted "awkwardly, with loud cries . . . as individuals," which made
their faces red and their bellies swell.[29] Boris was finally able to taste

victory after his long struggle. The general outcry made it seem he
had been popularly elected, and cleverly waiting for the right moment
he generously announced to the crowd he would accept the crown.
The patriarch immediately conducted him to the nearest church in
the monastery confines and proclaimed him tsar.

The events of February 21 were important in the electoral contest. The danger of a boyar regime diminished and the position of
Boris' partisans improved. To defeat the nobility Godunov had to
look for support among the townspeople of Moscow but the power
structure at the time was such that no popular election was valid
without the approval of the highest state office, the boyar council.
After the election nothing prevented Boris from returning to Moscow
and taking the crown, but he procrastinated and remained in his cell
at New Virgin monastery another five days. The reason for his strange
inactivity is easy to understand. He was waiting for boyar council
approval, but by all accounts failed to obtain it.

Boris did not leave his refuge and return to Moscow until February 26. His supporters had done everything they could to prepare the
capital to offer a triumphant welcome to the new tsar. The people
greeted Boris in a field outside the city walls. The poor brought bread
and salt and boyars and merchants brought gold pitchers, furs, and
other rich gifts appropriate for a ruler. Boris refused all gifts except
the bread and salt and graciously invited everyone to a royal feast.
In the Kremlin the patriarch escorted Boris to the cathedral of the
Annunciation, where he blessed him as tsar a second time, and those
present cheered him when he took up the sceptre.[30] The leaders of
the land assembly had assumed that the service in the cathedral of
the Annunciation, where sovereigns were traditionally crowned,
would definitively confirm Boris on the throne but by the end of the
day everyone knew the solemn ceremony had failed to achieve its
purpose. After a time in the Kremlin Godunov conferred privately
and at length with the patriarch and announced he intended to give
up his post and return to New Virgin monastery on the pretext his
sister was seriously ill. Godunov could not accept the crown unless
the boyar council swore an oath to him and senior boyars were in no
hurry to express sentiments of loyalty. This was the circumstance
that forced Boris to leave Moscow again and return to New Virgin
monastery, some distance away, but he was not discouraged and the
number of his supporters was growing daily.

Early in March, 1598 the patriarch once more summoned the
members of the assembly. The April charter states that at the March

session Iov made a speech to "boyars, courtiers and chancery people," and then addressed "the whole senate, boyars, associate boyars, princes, commanders, courtiers, and senior provincial lesser boyars." The later editor supplemented the text by saying that the patriarch had spoken to "all boyars, courtiers, chancery people, serving-men, and merchants." The editor of the 1599 version included representatives of the third estate, the Moscow merchants, among those present at the March session. This interpolation constitutes a good example of the editors' partisanship; they were trying to prove a representative assembly elected Godunov.

It would be necessary for everyone to take an oath to Boris before he could be crowned; thus, the March meeting devoted the bulk of its time to debating how to accomplish it. In his speech the patriarch asked those present to serve Boris loyally and honorably, "as you have kissed the cross," and "as is written in the oath rosters." Iov's words lead to the conclusion that the assembly inserted the text of the new oath into its decree. This document apparently has survived. When publishing it the archeographical commission entitled it: "The assembly decree on the election of Boris." The actual meaning of the word "decree" was expressed as follows: "And thereto, unto him, our sovereign (the Godunov family—R.S.) we give our souls and all of us kiss the cross to him, from the humblest to the mightiest."[31] The March oath reiterated several items found in a statement certain boyars had presented to the land assembly on February 17. The chief one, included in the affirmation charter, was that both Ivan and Fedor were purported to have blessed Boris as tsar.

After the meeting the patriarch instructed provincial bishops to summon the laity and clergy to the main churches, read them the charter affirming Boris' election, and sing "Long Life" to the widowed queen and her brother for three days while bells rang. Afterwards Boris' emissaries went to the provinces: Conciliar Courtier Prince Petr Buinosov to Novgorod, Associate Boyar Prince Ivan Gagin to Pskov, and Associate Boyar Semen Saburov to Smolensk. Godunov was worried about the Kazan region, the abode of his longtime foes Commander Ivan Vorotynskii and Metropolitan Hermogen, and sent Boyar Prince Fedor Khvorostinin to administer the oath to the gentry and population there and overcome his enemies' opposition. Boris' legates occupied modest positions among men of conciliar rank and the boyar council had not given them a grant of authority, but they did not go to the provinces empty-handed. Money distributed among the gentry formed a persuasive argument in the election contest. There is no reason to doubt an oath was administered in the spring of 1598 but whether Godunov managed to invest it with universal significance is another matter. In most areas the government's action apparently encountered little opposition, for the provinces were not accustomed to resisting decrees emanating from the center but their influence on the election was small. The fate of the crown was not decided in the provinces but in Moscow.

Boris remained at New Virgin monastery through March and rarely appeared in the capital. Whenever he did so he would "confer with his boyars about the country's affairs and about military matters, displaying very great diligence."[32] On March 19 for the first time Boris summoned the boyar council to decide a spate of pressing precedence suits.[33] Although Godunov was now starting to act like a ruler he was in no hurry to leave his residence outside the city and long delayed his move to the palace for fear of provoking the opposition to take overt steps.

To facilitate his return to the Kremlin Boris' supporters organized yet another (the third) procession to New Virgin monastery. Iov and loyal boyars begged Boris to come back at once to the city and occupy his kingdom. To show their submission the petitioners fell to their knees before him and bowed their heads to the ground. Godunov unexpectedly replied that he would renounce the throne, saying: "The tsaric power again I abjure with tears and I do not wish to sit upon the throne." Boris' abdication is inexplicable if the boyar council had taken an oath to him. The royal chancellery deliberately deleted this episode from the text of the affirmatory charter it edited in 1599.

Boris' abdication impelled the patriarch to ask Irina for another decree. Elder Aleksandra ordered her brother to proceed immediately to the Kremlin to be crowned. The former queen's instructions were explicit. She said to Boris: "The time has come for you to don the royal purple." Godunov's faction had made a shrewd move. The patriarch could not crown a candidate without a council decree and council leaders remained recalcitrant; thus, an edict issued by Irina was substituted for the requisite council resolution.

On April 1 Godunov made a second triumphal entrance into Moscow. The ceremony was repeated in detail. The clergy and people awaited Boris on the far side of the Neglinnaia river. After attending service in the cathedral of the Annunciation he proceeded to the palace where, as the official account states, he "sat on his tsaric throne." Later the patriarch had the spiritual assembly listen to the charter affirming Boris' election. It declared that a legal election and

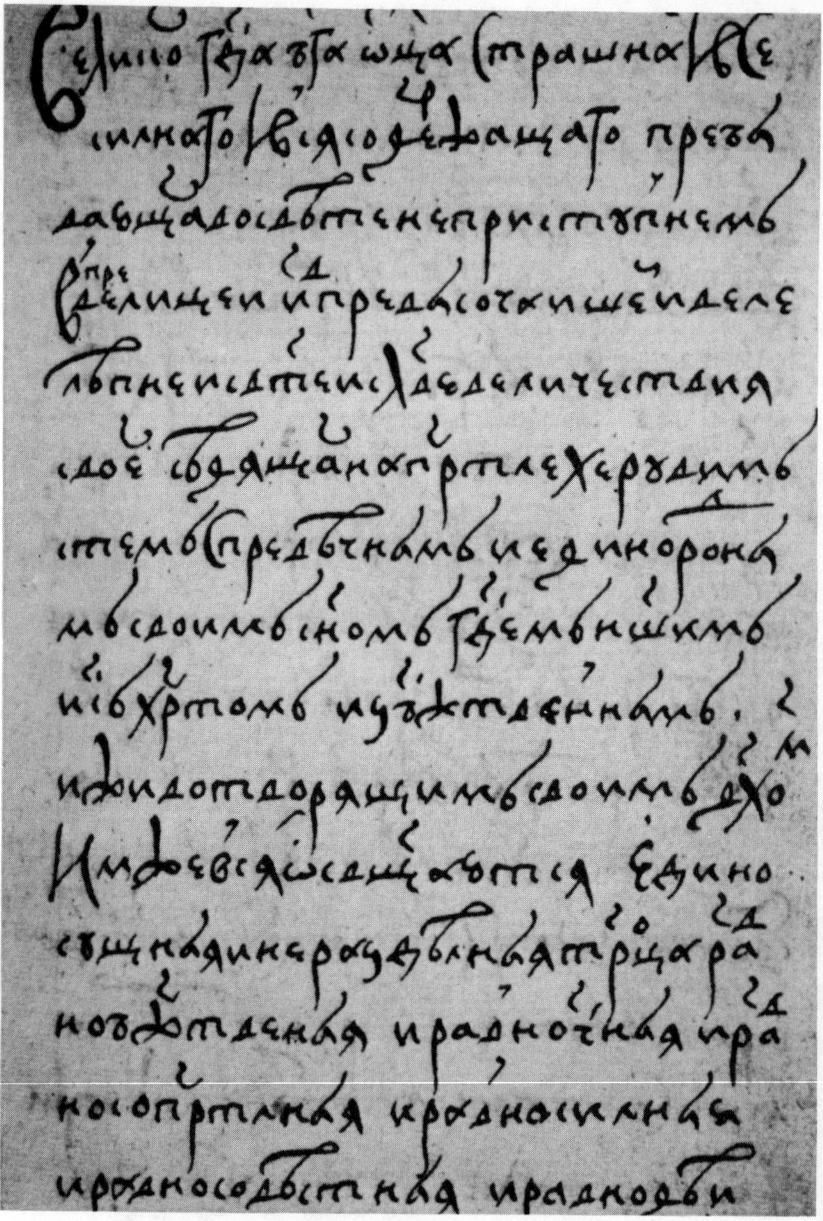

The Charter of Affirmation (excerpt)

the patriarch's blessing had placed him on the throne. The charter carefully described the ceremony held on April 1 in the cathedral of the Annunciation, with special reference to the moment when the patriarch laid upon Boris the cross of Peter the Wonder-Worker, "which is the beginning of the tsaric sovereign investiture and sceptre-bearing." Clearly the authors of the document wanted to portray Boris' elevation to the throne as an accomplished fact.

The earlier version of the election charter ended with a reference to the fact that the patriarch and other churchmen had attested the document with their hands and seals, "and boyars, associate boyars, courtiers, and conciliar secretaries also have laid on their hands . . ."[34] These lines point to one of the most puzzling issues in Boris' election campaign. Why did the leaders of the land assembly attest its measure with only the signatures of men of conciliar rank like boyars and conciliar secretaries? Why did they not ask other participants such as gentry, chancery people and merchants to sign the document? An affirmatory charter so constructed less resembled a land assembly decree than an official enactment of the boyar council and clergy, but a plan to have the boyar council sign the charter soon collapsed. The patriarch's chancellery could not find a quorum of men holding conciliar rank to attest it and only clergy figured in the roster and among the signatories of the April charter.[35]

Godunov's move to the palace and the efforts to force the affirmatory charter on the council aroused the opposition. Leading boyars finally saw that further delay would rob them of their last chance to establish a boyar regime. The council had long been paralyzed by internal dissension. Shchelkalov had managed to control it for a brief period and when he was compelled to retire Bogdan Belskii took his place. Ivan the Terrible's notorious favorite was a well-seasoned political intriguer and possessed huge financial resources. He brought in large numbers of armed retainers from his estates to Moscow in the hope of exercising decisive influence on the election. Ivan's last legal executor thought his time had come and he enjoyed initial success, reports about which made their way to Lithuania. Spies said that in April "some princes and conciliar boyars, particularly Prince Belskii, their leader, Fedor Nikitich and his brother, and a number of others, though not all, have begun to take counsel among themselves, for they refuse to recognize Boris as grand prince and want to choose a certain Simeon."[36] This shows Belskii had managed to reconcile the contenders for the throne and had persuaded them to act in concert. The Romanov faction temporarily gave up its claims in favor of

Simeon because the nobility did not support it, and Mstislavskii came out for Simeon because the latter was his brother-in-law.

Ivan's caprice had set the baptized Tatar khan Simeon on the Muscovite throne for a time and afterwards he became grand prince of Tver. Godunov had removed him from his Tver principality and he had been living entirely forgotten in a remote place, even though royal blood and Tsar Ivan's blessing made Simeon more prominent than the lowborn Boris. The boyars needed him to thwart Boris' coronation and they expected he would prove a pliant tool in their hands. Their chief goal was still to establish a boyar regime but this time they would use a figurehead. When his opponents combined, all Boris' striving was threatened with disaster.

He was afraid to attack the council directly but tried to inhibit its activity by alleging a Tatar invasion was imminent. Moscow had an excellent espionage network in the Crimea and unquestionably knew the khan was preparing a campaign against Hungary, but the military department early in March assiduously spread rumors that the enemy would soon invade. On April 1 the Military Records office announced the Crimean horde already was moving against Russia. It is not hard to guess who was responsible for this false information. That was the day Godunov was preparing to enter the palace and, fearing protest from the boyar opposition, he wanted to divert attention to a threatened danger from abroad. If a military alert existed he could pose as the country's savior and make the boyars obey.

For a long time Boris had been unable to persuade leading boyars to take up stations on the Tatar frontier, but after April 20 he announced he would personally conduct a campaign against the Tatars. By early May regiments were mustered and the boyars were faced with the choice of either assuming high commands in the army or refusing to defend the frontier at the risk of a charge of treason. Under the circumstances council leaders preferred to yield temporarily. Boris had achieved his goal and was entitled to gloat.

After ordering the gentry contingents to assembly below Moscow Godunov joined the forces positioned along the Oka early in May. Arriving at headquarters he bestowed signal honor on the army by inquiring about the health of gentry, fusiliers, cossacks and all other soldiers. There was no enemy attack for the ruler to repel but Boris spent two months on the Oka with architects and builders he had called from Moscow, who erected a veritable town of pure white tents, extraordinary towers, and a gate on the river bank. There Boris arranged for a lavish entertainment in order to celebrate the felicitous outcome of his enterprise.

Godunov achieved a diplomatic triumph in Serpukhov. Crimean envoys, who came there with a peace proposal, recognized him as tsar, and the queen of England officially congratulated him on his accession to the throne. The Serpukhov affair marked a decisive stage in Boris Godunov's election campaign. The din of military activity drowned out opponents' voices, and once they had knuckled under to Boris the boyars turned to him to decide precedence suits, thereby acknowledging his superior authority, while for his part Boris aimed to satisfy the ambitions of his principal foes by awarding them army commands.

Godunov made every effort to win over provincial gentry and soldiers, entertaining them generously at a royal feast and ordering a disbursement of money. He was endorsed by the gentry forces because his policy of enserfing the peasantry and freeing their tillage from crown taxes corresponded with the general needs and aspirations of this stratum of feudal society. The enthusiasm displayed by the petty provincial serving-men helped Boris overcome the vacillating Moscow gentry, but when the provincials had done their duty it was time for them to retire. At the end of the Serpukhov campaign Boris dispersed "the lesser boyars of all the towns of Muscovy" and the soldiers, and told those from Moscow, "boyars, associate boyars, chancery people, cupbearers, senior courtiers, junior courtiers, major gentry, and all gentry from the towns" to proceed to the capital.[37] The members of this group, which included the town levy, so called because the authorities from time to time mustered a picked detachment of senior provincial gentry, were stationed in Moscow, and this was why they too were summoned there. The leading gentry's return to Moscow made it possible for the representative land assembly to resume its work, but it is difficult to say to what extent the authorities took advantage of the situation. It has been argued that in summer, 1598 the electoral assembly was engaged in decisive activity but this contention essentially depends on the date of August 1 given in the later edition of the charter of affirmation and it has already been demonstrated this date is incorrect.

Patriarch Iov was waiting for Godunov to return from the Serpukhov campaign and carefully preparing for this triumphal moment. By July his chancellery had finished collecting signatures for the text of the April charter of affirmation. The register of the spiritual assembly drawn up in April, 1598 contained 115 names but by summer the charter had been signed by 126 ecclesiastics, many of whose names had not appeared in the original register. Two different abbots of the Snetogorskii monastery signed the same document, as did two abbots of the Viazhnetskii monastery, and there were other similar examples. It is obvious that neither the roster nor the signatures on the charter of affirmation reflected the assembly's actual complement at any point in time. Provincial churchmen signed the charter whenever they came to the capital but the situation touching the Moscow clergy was different.

A count shows that nineteen elders from Moscow churches and monasteries were involved with the charter of affirmation. Nothing prevented the authorities from obtaining the signatures of these persons, most of whom were domiciled in the Kremlin, yet six failed to sign. The charter lacks the signature of the protopope of the cathedral of the Annunciation, who had been the tsar's confessor. Perhaps he refused to attest a document confirming Boris' election or it may be he was not invited to attend the patriarch's assembly. These indications point indirectly to the fact that the patriarch could not fully control even the Kremlin clergy.

To attest the April charter the patriarch summoned princes of the church, heads of leading monasteries, and a number of monks and priests who never before had been part of a spiritual assembly. Although many minor figures participated in the electoral assembly some highly distinguished and influential prelates were absent. In July the patriarchal chancellery offered an explanation, saying that its scribes had compiled the list from memory, not from the book of degrees,[38] which they had been too rushed to find. Such naivete convinced no one. The authorities could not have forgotten Hermogen, metropolitan of Kazan, and his archimandrites, for in official rank Hermogen came third after the patriarch. He was not allowed to journey to Moscow because he refused to be loyal to Godunov. In July Iov vaguely promised that Hermogen and his associates might sign the affirmatory charter when Tsar Boris saw fit to invite them. This was the composition and such was the activity of the spiritual assembly, which was one of the leading components in the land assembly that elected Boris Godunov.

In July the patriarchal chancellery supplemented the charter of affirmation with a statement to the effect that besides the patriarch there had sat in the electoral assembly "Boyar Prince Fedor Ivanovich Mstislavskii, all . . . boyars, associate boyars, gentry, secretaries, merchants, and leaders of the traders from the whole land of the Russian realm."[39] These words might constitute definitive proof that in July the assembly took up its tasks again and Mstislavskii, president of the boyar council, joined in its work for the first time, thereby transforming this meeting into a regular assembly with full powers, but it is not entirely clear whether the statement made in the July supplement to the text of the charter of affirmation is reliable. It may have reflected the facts of the case or have been merely the hopes and dreams of the patriarchal chancellery. If Mstislavskii and his comrades had attested the document there would have been no doubt, but, unfortunately, the April charter's text contains no boyar signatures, and this is the more surprising because the supplement to the text implies the chancellery planned to transmit the document for gentry and chancery people to sign,[40] an intention that likewise failed of realization. It is also noteworthy that even in July the patriarchal chancellery did not deem it necessary to invite humbler participants in the land assembly, such as lesser boyars and representatives of the commons like traders and townspeople, to sign the charter of affirmation.

The patriarch already had devised the scheme of drawing up a charter of affirmation when his dispute with the leaders of the boyar council broke out. A signed charter might well have superseded the swearing of an oath in council but the pressure to obtain it diminished after Godunov made the boyars obey him. The charter finally was deposited in the archives in July. The Serpukhov campaign had cleared away the last barriers preventing the people from taking the oath. Ancient custom decreed the oath should be sworn in the chambers of the boyar council, the highest state institution, a ceremony over which only senior boyars could preside. The council was determined to follow traditional custom but Boris, ignoring it, ordered the oath administered in church, which the devoted Iov controlled, not in the council, where the ruler had many enemies.

Moscow took the oath to the tsar at harvest time, in late July and August. Timofeev, who participated in the ceremony, narrates that the people assembled in the cathedral of the Annunciation chanted it so loudly as to drown out prayers and forced everyone to hold his ears and he also stated the people came to the church because they feared to disobey a threatening decree. The text of the oath administered in summer differed markedly from the one in March. In spring the authorities had written at length in order to convince everyone Boris' election was legal but now they merely formulated in general terms what his subjects' responsibilities were to a tsar chosen by God. The citizenry promised "not to think, plot, associate with, be friendly to, nor concert with Emir Simeon," and immediately to hand over to Boris anyone who might try "to set Simeon on the Muscovite throne."

This item, which had not appeared in the March text, revealed the basic political thrust of the new measure. At last Boris had thwarted ingeniously the schemes of the opposition, which had planned to hand the throne to Simeon. The oath sworn that summer annulled a boyar council decree electing the Tatar to the throne. Other new clauses in the oath were designed to persuade that Godunov was determined to establish order and justice in the country and officials had to swear they would render righteous judgments without fear or favor.

On ascending the throne Boris was greatly afraid the boyars and his other foes might engage in secret machinations against him. Everyone had to swear not to harm the royal family. It almost seems as though Godunov anticipated future dangers and was trying to protect himself and his family. Those taking the oath bound themselves "not to combine for any kind of evil or wickedness or conspiracy" (against the Godunov family—R.S.).[41]

Preparing for the coronation on September 1, the authorities organized a fourth triumphal procession to New Virgin monastery in which boyars, clergy, merchants, chancery people, and the Moscow populace took part. Responding to this further appeal, Boris, who had arrived at the monastery earlier, graciously consented to be crowned in accordance with ancient custom. Two days later he finally was crowned in the cathedral of the Annunciation, and in honor of the event he conferred senior boyar and conciliar rank upon many noblemen, singling out members of the Romanov family and Belskii. The boyars were guaranteed there would be no more executions and the sovereign pledged secretly not to shed blood for five years, although he saw to it that his promise did not remain secret.

However, even after his coronation Godunov's position still remained somewhat precarious and, as expected, persistent rumors circulated in Poland and Livonia in early January, 1599 that his subjects had assassinated him. King Sigismund received three simultaneous reports to this effect: from Orsha he learned that "a certain princeling" had cut Godunov down. Vilna claimed that during an audience in the Kremlin palace Boris struck one of the Romanov family with his staff, in requital for which the latter stabbed him.[42] These reports, though untrue, showed that the Godunov faction and the nobility were still at loggerheads.

Since the political situation in Moscow remained unstable Kremlin leaders again bethought themselves of the charter of affirmation. After the coronation the April text, which had functioned as a pre-election pamphlet, was hopelessly outmoded. Boris' chancellery went to considerable lengths to compose a new text, radically different from the old one. The tsar told his scribes to rewrite his election charter in two display copies. The first, affixed with gold and silver seals, was placed in the treasury for safekeeping and the other was sent to the patriarchal vestry in the cathedral of the Annunciation, where in his zeal Iov had the tomb of Peter the Wonder-Worker opened and deposited his copy in it.

In late 1598 and early 1599 the authorities convoked a land assembly in Moscow and charged it to examine the new charter. The new assembly's legality was never questioned. In conformity with sixteenth-century practice the government designated its members, and as a fully representative body it contained both partisans and former opponents of Godunov. The new assembly's complement reflected these changes; the general assembly that had functioned prior to the coronation was dissolved to make way for a traditional spiritual assembly. Churchmen who had not been members of the earlier one were omitted from the list of those subscribing the charter of affirmation and only an exceptional few were now allowed to sign it. Only a few boyars, mostly Boris' relatives, had taken part in the first electoral assemblies, but almost the entire boyar council was represented in the 1599 assembly, although the signatories of the 1599 affirmatory charter did not include such influential boyars as members of the Golitsyn and Kurakin families, Ivan Shuiskii, Shestunov, and Sitskii. Except for the last two all the others eventually signed, but clearly it took some boyars a long time to subscribe the document.

In addition to council members, the government brought much of Moscow's gentry, prominent courtiers, cupbearers, senior court attendants, junior court attendants, chancery bureaucrats, and fusilier captains into the new assembly. The flower of Moscow's nobility and senior serving-men was fully represented and decisively predominated among the service groups. The provincial gentry was represented by the town levy, although only half of the members of the levy who were in Moscow attended. A few lesser boyars not in service from Novgorod, Rzhev and Belaia also signed the charter, but their signatures were buried among those of merchants and town elders. There had been no previous plan for men from Novgorod to participate in the assembly and their names are not conspicuous in the roster. Unlike the rest of the gentry, provincial lesser boyars signed for themselves and the districts they represented. The signatures of two Novgorod landholders prove that serving-men from that city took part in electing the tsar.

After the coronation the authorities were less anxious to cultivate broad popular support but they invited many rich merchants and leaders of the Moscow commercial community to the assembly, and on its roster appear the names of twenty-two merchants, two merchant elders, and fourteen hundredmen, who headed taxpaying communities in Moscow. The merchants signed the charter and ordinary householders signed for several of the hundredmen. The presence of persons from taxpaying household units imparted a genuinely representative character to the assembly.[43]

Since the members of the final land assembly signed the charter of affirmation after Boris was already secure on the throne they could not discuss whom to elect because no choice remained to them. The assembly's task was apparently merely to have its participants listen to the text of the charter and affix their signatures to the document, which deliberately distorted the story of Godunov's coronation. Signing the charter consumed much time, but even so the authorities were unable to correlate the roster with the signatures of assembly members. In the last analysis those who actually participated in the assembly and those who signed the decree later cannot be determined. The 1599 charter of affirmation also constituted a kind of pledge, for its roster clearly indicated the individuals from whom Boris was demanding special proofs of loyalty, including boyars, Moscow officials and nobles, the upper church hierarchy, and leading townspeople.

Critical examination of the sources leads to the conclusion that Godunov's electoral assembly changed its shape and complement frequently during the political struggle. The early convocations, which drew from the town populace, yielded to a traditional land assembly headed by the boyar council and nobility. The elections of 1598 and 1599 were important in the development of institutions representing the estates in Russia.

The boyar aristocracy during the centuries it had held power had determined Russia's political structure. Tradition posed overwhelming obstacles to Boris' rise to power and the interregnum threatened to end in revolt at any moment, but Godunov succeeded in avoiding all pitfalls without once resorting to force. He had no peer in the art of forming political combinations. In winning the support of the mass of the gentry and the populace of Moscow he overcame the nobility's opposition to become the first elected tsar.

Chapter Ten

ILLNESS

The object lessons Boris learned during the electoral contest were not lost upon him. Keenly aware that his dynasty depended upon the nobility, he tried to win boyar support. His generous grants of high conciliar rank may be seen as a sign of this, for through them the princely aristocracy apparently regained the influence in the boyar council it had enjoyed prior to the oprichnina. Boris kept appanage Prince Fedor Mstislavskii as president of the council and next to him stood Boyar Princes Vasilii, Dmitrii, Aleksandr, and Ivan Shuiskii. After the oprichnina the Rostovskii princes had been without boyar rank for thirty years, but Boris awarded high conciliar office to Mikhail Katyrev-Rostovskii and Petr Buinosov-Rostovskii. After their long years of humiliation the Rostovskii princes made an attempt to unseat the Mstislavskii and Shuiskii princes and recover their primacy in the council. The Starodub princes, who had also been expelled, returned to the council and Vasilii Khilkov was made an associate boyar. The oprichnina had ruined the Obolenskii princes, but Boris made Fedor Nogotkov-Obolenskii a boyar and used his illustrious pedigree to prevent the Romanov family from advancing its interests by means of precedence suits. Prince Andrei Kurakin had done Boris considerable harm during the early years he was regent, which he requited by long exile, but after the coronation Kurakin again sat in council with boyar rank. Although Boris did not trust the Golitsyn princes he granted high rank to Vasilii Golitsyn.

Boris was less generous to members of the old Moscow nobility such as the Morozov, Saltykov, Shein, Romanov, Sheremetev and Buturlin families, but he made an exception for his own numerous clan. It may be recalled that the Saburov and Veliaminov families followed the Godunov family into the council but in spite of their connection with the tsar his young cousins held comparatively minor posts. In this way Godunov showed he respected the privileged aristocracy.

Having won supreme power Boris did not restore to conciliar courtiers the authority they had possessed in Ivan's time. During his administration their number remained small and their influence insignificant. Godunov's former oprichnina associates expected his

Goldsmiths and Scribes

elevation would change the existing system of precedence relation-
ships completely but they were disappointed in their calculations.
When members of the Polev and Pushkin families boldly filed precedence suits against the great Saltykov family they were rebuffed immediately and punished as an example.

After fifteen years as regent Godunov was not afraid of open
challenges and was prepared to use force to repress them, but being a
superstitious man he felt helpless against hidden intrigue. To save
himself from harm Boris made his subjects swear "not to damage the
tsar, the queen, or their children with any magic spells and not to use
sorcery to waft any evil on the wind," and "not to send sorcerers
with evil potions and herbs or let witches or warlocks cause evil to
the sovereign."[1] During the first years of Boris' reign several warlocks
were tried in Moscow. One was Boyar Shuiskii, who was suspected
of breaking his oath. The archives have preserved "A preliminary inquiry concerning Prince Ivan Ivanovich Shuiskii's men, Yanko Ivanovich Markov and his brother Poluekhto, who used herbs and spells on
behalf of Prince Ivan Ivanovich Shuiskii." The Markov brothers were
prominent courtiers in the Shuiskii family's service and the authorities proceeded to trial. Boris had a chance to dispose of the entire
Shuiskii clan, but he preferred leniency. Ivan Shuiskii escaped disgrace and was not even forced to retire from service. He was saved
because, although he belonged to the highest titled nobility, he had
not opposed Boris during the interregnum.

At his coronation Boris promised to rule mercifully and execute
no one, but his good intentions failed of realization. Bogdan Belskii,
the new tsar's close relative, was the principal figure in the first political trial. In summer, 1599 Belskii led an expedition to the northern
Donets river; he was charged with building a new fortress near Azov,
which received the grandiose name of Tsarev-Borisov. Belskii set out
attended by a large retinue and with huge supplies of provisions drawn
from his own estates. Under his command were 3,000 gentry, fusiliers and cossacks, whom he generously rewarded with money and
clothing and to whom he gave food and drink from his stores. This
won him popularity and he achieved his purpose. Rumors of his
prodigality spread through Moscow and everywhere soldiers sang his
praises. Throwing caution to the winds Belskii made disrespectful
remarks about Boris, saying, among other things: "Let Boris Fedorovich lord it over Moscow; I am tsar in Tsarev-Borisov." Foreigners in
his service hastened to report his provocative statements. Growing
alarmed, the government recalled Belskii and put him on trial. Witnesses were interrogated and a court found the commander guilty.

Belskii escaped prison and execution, but an unusual punishment was devised for him. He was tied to a pillar of shame; deprived of office, and his long beard was plucked out hair by hair. He lost his conciliar rank and was exiled to Nizhnii Novgorod. The nobility was delighted when the former oprichnina favorite was humiliated.

By 1600 Vasilii Shchelkalov, the chief council secretary, had ceased to be keeper of the royal seal; Godunov replaced him with his old associate Ignatii Tatishchev, and after 1601 Shchelkalov was removed completely from the conduct of affairs. Contemporaries declared he also had lost his conciliar rank and all his property but they were apparently mistaken, for three years later Shchelkalov took the field against the False Dmitrii as a conciliar secretary with fifty armed men from his extensive estates. This shows that by then he had earned forgiveness.

The harshest persecution was directed against the Romanov family, whose case began in the same way as had that of Ivan Shuiskii. Vtoroi Bartenev, a courtier serving as one of Aleksandr Romanov's treasurers, laid information against his master, charging him with keeping magic herbs in his treasury for the purpose of harming the royal family. The original documents decreeing that the Romanov family should be exiled acknowledge its members were victims of a trial for witchcraft. They preserve the words of an escort attacking Aleksandr after he was arrested: "Wicked traitor, you tried to acquire dominion through sorcery and herbs."[2] Konrad Bussow, a member of Boris' bodyguard, also noted the members of the disgraced Romanov family were charged with desiring to eliminate the royal family.

Russian sources provide only an approximate date for the fall of the Romanov family but a newly discovered source, the journal of a Polish delegation in Moscow, can now fill the gap. The full text of the journal has apparently been lost but the manuscript section of the M.E. Saltykov-Shchedrin State Public Library in Leningrad has preserved a fragmentary German copy. An entry for October 26, 1600 is most interesting. A member of the delegation wrote: "That night his excellency the chancellor heard, and in our residence we saw, several hundred fusiliers issue at night from the fortress (the Kremlin—R.S.) with blazing torches, and we heard them open fire, which frightened us." The Polish envoys witnessed government troops attacking the Romanov residence: "The house in which the Romanov family lived burned down; several (of the disgraced—R.S.) were killed by him (Boris—R.S.), others arrested and taken away . . . ."[3]

The envoys had not been accurately informed about the fate of Aleksandr Romanov, who supposedly was executed ten days later.

He was actually the main defendant in a trial for sorcery the authorities initiated. The tsar ordered a special boyar commission headed by Mikhail Saltykov to conduct an investigation on the premises the fusiliers had seized; it discovered Aleksandr's treasury contained magic herbs. This evidence was conveyed to the patriarch's palace, where the boyar council and higher clergy had assembled. In their presence the tsar ordered Saltykov to open the bags he had brought and "dump the herbs out of the bags onto the table."

The boyar council included many opponents of the Romanov family. Associate Boyar Saltykov took a direct part in investigating their treachery. Boyar Prince Petr Buinosov-Rostovskii supervised the residence Fedor Romanov forfeited after his arrest. As those close to the Romanov interest expressed it, during the trial in council boyars "raged and shouted like beasts" and in exile Fedor Romanov angrily declared: "The boyars are my great enemies; they have sought our heads and now they incite our retainers to speak against us, as I myself have seen more than once."[4] The Romanov family had good reason to complain of the nobles sitting in council. The princely aristocracy long ago had indicated its distaste for the exaltation of the members of the Romanov family and was glad to help Boris get rid of them.

The Romanov brothers were charged with the most serious crime, an attempt on the tsar's life, for which the penalty could only be death. Boris hesitated for a long time, since he was unsure how to deal with the sons of Nikita Romanov. The disgraced men remained in Moscow for several months until their fate was finally decided. Fedor Romanov was tonsured and immured in a remote northern monastery and his younger brothers were banished. Aleksandr, Mikhail and Vasilii Romanov died in exile and their deaths were at once attributed to secret orders from the tsar. Actually, the fact they died was not as surprising as that any of them managed to survive. The condemned were given little food and transported in chains, often in bitter cold, more than 600 miles to Siberia or the shores of the Arctic ocean where no roads existed.

Fedor Romanov's fate disproves the claim that Boris deliberately used banishment quietly to eliminate his foes. Nikita Romanov's eldest son was the chief contender for the throne but Godunov sent him to a monastery instead of exiling him. Tonsure saved Fedor Nikitich although it denied him any chance to win the crown, for a monk could not be a tsar. Boris was content with this. He purged the Romanov faction in council. The first to suffer was Boyar Prince Fedor Shestunov, whose servant laid information that he harbored evil intentions. The tsar liberally rewarded the informer but did not punish the aged boyar. Shestunov died in house arrest and his death occurred before the Romanov brothers were disgraced. If he had ended his life in prison or in exile another murder would inevitably have been laid at Boris' door. Fedor Nikitich's son-in-law, Boyar Prince Boris Cherkasskii, who had long been ill, was imprisoned in Beloozero, where he soon died. Another Romanov son-in-law, Ivan Sitskii, was packed off to a monastery and Prince Aleksandr Repnin and the Karpov courtiers were disgraced.

After the Romanov family came to power chroniclers went to extraordinary lengths to portray Boris as a villain and to surround the members of the once-disgraced family with the halo of martyrs. These dramatic episodes made their way from chronicles to historical and literary works. One of the heroes in Pushkin's tragedy, *Boris Godunov,* condemned Boris' whole administration and style of governance in the words:

> "He rules us . . .
> Like Tsar Ivan (think not of him at night).
> What good to us that open executions have ceased . . .
> Are we not convinced our life is sad?
> Over us each day disgrace hovers,
> Prison, Siberia, the cowl, or irons,
> and there—in the wilderness, starvation, death or the noose."[5]

Godunov's mode of governing actually had little in common with the techniques Tsar Ivan had employed. Even in times of great danger Boris never unleashed a reign of terror, bloodshed and slaughter and the periods of time disgraced persons spent in exile were remarkably short. The Romanov brothers' fate is illustrative. A few months after their trial Boris improved the conditions of their imprisonment, brought Ivan Romanov back from banishment and investigated the cruelty with which his escorts had treated Vasilii Romanov when he was ill. Fedor Nikitich's children and Aleksandr's widow were allowed to leave their places of exile in Beloozero and retire to one of their estates. Prince Ivan Cherkasskii and the Sitskii family were granted a full pardon, whereupon they reentered service. The tsar ordered Filaret (Fedor's church name—ed.) made comfortable in the Antoniev-Siiskii monastery.

Boris was constantly accused of perfidy, but on assuming the throne he showered favors on his most potent rivals: Aleksandr Romanov was made a boyar and Bogdan Belskii and Mikhail Romanov became associate boyars. Did Boris plan to lull his enemies' suspicions in order to visit unexpected vengeance upon them later? Such an assumption may appear plausible but it does not square with the facts. Scholars are still unaware of a circumstance that strongly affected the political struggle during Godunov's years; namely, the state of the ruler's health. Even prior to the coronation stories circulated abroad about how poor his condition was. A contemporary observed that for six years he ruled "not like a tsar but always like a sick man." When doctors proved powerless to cure his malady the tsar sought salvation in prayer and pilgrimages. When late in 1599 he could not undertake a pilgrimage to the Trinity-St. Sergius monastery at the proper time his son personally informed the monks his father's indisposition was the reason for postponement. In the autumn of 1600 Boris' health grew worse. A member of a Polish delegation, who wrote a poem about his journey to Moscow, noted that the failure of the authorities to conceal the tsar's illness had caused great alarm in the capital. After the issue came before the boyar council Boris at his own request was carried on a stretcher from his palace to a church to show that he was still alive. Tales to the effect that Boris would die soon created an artificial dynastic crisis. Preparing for a *coup* the opposition spread rumors at home and abroad that Boris' son Fedor, destined to succeed him, was sickly and feebleminded. The Polish envoys in Moscow believed Godunov had many enemies among his subjects, against whom he was daily stepping up attacks, although his efforts would not retrieve his position. They wrote: "No doubt any day now a rising is bound to occur."[6]

These circumstances explain why the government showed such concern about the activities of the Romanov family and Belskii. The latter clearly was striving to win popularity among the soldiers, while the former had assembled a large armed entourage in Moscow. The Polish envoys expended considerable effort to learn why the Romanov brothers had been disgraced. The information they collected is particularly interesting because it emanates from Muscovites sympathetic to Tsar Fedor's relatives. The Polish journal reads: "We have managed to find out that the present grand prince (Boris—R.S.) used violence to seize the office he snatched from the legitimate relatives of the deceased grand prince belonging to the Nikitich-Romanov line. These aforementioned Nikitich-Romanov people struggled, and, it seems, again made an effort to take power into their hands. This was right, and they had sufficient supporters, but that one night the grand prince [Boris] attacked them."

The journal shows the real reason why Tsar Fedor's cousins were harassed. Godunov's severe protracted illness inspired the Romanov brothers to hope they might soon renew the contest for the crown. Boris' minor successor had virtually no chance of retaining power if his father died. The new dynasty was not firmly established and the sick tsar was the only person capable of preserving it. It was his desire to eliminate contenders for the throne that led him to issue orders to storm the Romanov residence. By so doing Boris managed to quell the political conflict that had flared up briefly and to stabilize the situation.

In foreign affairs Godunov tried to obtain a long, peaceful breathing space in which to expand the country's eastern frontiers. The Siberian khan Kuchum, after sustaining several defeats at the hands of the tsar's commanders, withdrew from the Irtysh river to the Barabinskii steppe. In 1598 the commanders of the new fort of Tara pursued Kuchum deep into the steppe, destroyed his headquarters, and captured his family and many of his servitors, who were sent to Moscow. The Siberian khanate ceased to exist. Nothing prevented the Russians from moving rapidly east, and proceeding from the Irtysh and Ob rivers they determinedly advanced to the mouth of the Enisei. Units dispatched to reconnoitre the Mangazi region subdued local tribes and in 1600 remitted the first tribute such people ever paid to Moscow.

Boris hoped for peaceful relations with the Crimea and Turkey and sought to maintain peace with the Rzeczpospolita. The quarrel over Livonia heightened contradictions between Poland and Sweden and prevented them from forging a strong anti-Russian coalition. Russia concluded a twenty-year truce with the Rzeczpospolita in 1601. Realizing it was essential to maintain close economic and cultural ties with the rest of Europe, Godunov took vigorous measures to expand trade with the West. Supported by the Hansa town of Lübeck he had hoped to stimulate maritime communication through Ivangorod, the Russian town on the Narova river, but Sweden, possessing a first-class fleet, frustrated his plans. Invoking the treaty of Tiavzin, Sweden instituted a naval blockade of Ivangorod.

To increase trade with the West Boris granted concessions to German merchants brought to Russia from Livonia. The treasury gave them generous loans and permission to move freely inside the country and elsewhere. These Livonians, who were obliged to swear fealty to the tsar, henceforth were employed for both mercantile and political purposes; the inhabitants of the German suburb were once more in favor. Boris manifested keen interest in education, culture, and the achievements of western civilization. In his time more foreigners

were in Moscow than ever had been before. Boris delighted in the
society of foreign physicians in residence at court and questioned
them at length about European practices and customs. The new tsar
broke with tradition by forming a bodyguard of German mercenaries.
Godunov was the first Russian ruler to send young noblemen abroad
to study other languages and acquire culture. In his time the authorities showed interest in publishing books and established printing
presses in numerous towns. Boris dreamed of opening schools and
even a university on the European model in Russia.

Godunov was determined to make Moscow a showplace, build
new frontier towns, and strengthen existing ones. In his time amazing
technical innovations were introduced into Moscow. Russian craftsmen constructed an aqueduct with a powerful pump to supply the
Kremlin with water from the Moscow river, which was raised "by
great cunning" to flow through an underground conduit to the Stable
Palace. Benefiting from Pskov's experience Boris built Moscow's first
almshouses. He also built substantial edifices to house the military
chanceries near the cathedral of the Archangel in the Kremlin, and
replaced rows of shops that had burned down in Kitaigorod with
stone structures. Artisans rebuilt the dilapidated old bridge over the
Neglinnaia river. The wide new bridge had buildings for merchants
located at each end of it. A new stone podium embellished with carv-
ings and a lattice door, from which the tsar and his officials might
proclaim policy, arose on Red Square.

Boris developed a veritable passion for building. He ordered craftsmen to raise a pillar in the belfry of the church of Ivan the Great and
planned to erect a splendid shrine to the Holy of Holies to adorn the
central Kremlin square. The architectural model was finished and
building materials had been delivered but Boris' death prevented com-
pletion of the design. Boris sponsored the remarkably talented Russian architect, Fedor Kon, who supervised the Russian builders sur-
rounding Kitaigorod with heavy fortifications. A second, broken wall
followed the moat near the old Kremlin wall on Red Square. Fedor
Kon oversaw the erection of a stone fortress in Astrakhan and massive
fortifications in Smolensk, of which Boris himself laid the corner-
stone. "All the towns of the Muscovite realm" took part in building
this fortress, which was equipped with 38 towers and became Russia's strongest defense post on the western frontier.

A true man of his era, Boris combined interest in education with
a belief in miracles, which of course was characteristic not only of
Russia but of Western Europe as well at the time. Doubting the skill

of physicians, Boris sought the aid of magicians and sorcerers and even more often had recourse to the device upon which pious people in Old Russia invariably relied—he prayed earnestly and went on pilgrimages to holy places. His piety produced a poor return. Once, in despair he had his son who was ill given holy water to drink and conveyed to the shrine of the Blessed Vasilii when it was very cold, thereby causing the death of his eldest son, who might have inherited the throne.

The affair involving Duke Hans of Denmark, who was betrothed to Boris' daughter, Kseniia, supplies quaint details pertaining to Godunov's life. The duke was taken seriously ill when he came to Moscow in 1602. In alarm Boris assigned all his doctors to attend the sick man but four days later suddenly forbade them to visit him and cancelled the treatment they had prescribed for him. His action has led chroniclers to consider Boris responsible for the duke's death, but their story contains numerous incongruities. Boris was supposed to have formed evil designs when he learned that the people of Muscovy had grown fond of Hans. In fact, the young Lutheran, who did not know the language, spent but a month in Moscow, met virtually no one, and thus was in no position to acquire popularity among the Muscovites, and the tsar damaged his reputation considerably by befriending someone of a different faith. Godunov's decisions how best to cure Hans are easily explained. Seeing the doctors were powerless to deal with the duke's mysterious stomach ailment Boris put his trust in the Orthodox God and lavished alms upon the poor. Next he visited his destined son-in-law and said at his bedside: "Yes, my physicians understand little about this malady." He threatened the doctors would suffer and the interpreter would be impaled on a stake if the duke were to die. Whenever the tsar visited the sick man he would sob; the boyars would moan and cry, and the sickroom became unbearably noisy. A member of the Danish delegation listened to the tsar's lamentations and wrote them down: "Would not the very stones weep over the death of such a man, from whom I expected great solace," Boris exclaimed. "My heart bursts from my bosom in sadness."

Contemporaries declared Boris was a remarkable orator; those who knew him praised his speeches and Horsey wrote that he was endowed with a naturally resonant voice and a gift of elegant expression. Semen Shakhovskoi, a younger contemporary, called Boris a man able to speak "most sweetly." These writers have left good descriptions of Godunov. Horsey mentioned his fine manners, his handsome face, and his invariably polite address. Shakhovskoi felt Boris radiated grandeur and "his appearance surpassed that of many." Although possessed of indomitable will Godunov conveyed an impression of gentleness and he would weep whenever he was distressed. Boris impressed contemporaries with his constancy in family life and devotion to his children. When enumerating the tsar's good qualities Russian writers would stress his dislike of the "God-loathed" practice of drinking wine.

Even his enemies gave Godunov his due and believed he might have accomplished many splendid things if adverse circumstances had not prevented him, a view expressed by foreigners and natives alike. Of course, the sources that sang Boris' praises must be properly identified; those who extolled Godunov were members of the gentry, who greatly admired his generosity to serving-men.

Russians failed fully to appreciate Boris' worth until after the Time of Troubles, when the throne was occupied by worthless successors. Timofeev diplomatically observed that other capable tsars followed Boris but their intelligence was vastly inferior to his.

By winning the crown Boris aroused the disaffected nobility against him, although his shrewd policies enabled him to unite the upper levels of society to support him. What ruined the Godunov dynasty was the hatred of the commons. The throne on which Boris sat was a volcano.

Chapter Eleven

THE GREAT FAMINE

The beginning of Boris' reign seemed extraordinarily auspicious but appearances were deceptive. His attempts to enforce serfdom provoked the masses to determined opposition, which grew stronger every year. Signs of disaffection multiplied in the countryside and in the towns.

Taxes and lack of freedom drove peasants from the old feudal centers to the periphery. Cossack communes formed deep in the Wild Field, far beyond Russia's defense perimeter, and attracted peasants like magnets. Beating back frequent attacks by the steppe nomads the Don cossacks pushed to the mouth of the Northern Donets river, where they established their capital of Razdory. Cossack successes greatly alarmed the government in Moscow, for as long as the quiet Don[1] served as a haven for runaway peasants the serf system could never prevail in the center. Boris well understood this and his policy towards the periphery was decisive and merciless.

Government troops closely followed the cossacks into the Wild Field, building settlements and fortresses. The commanders pressed colonists into service and made them farm state lands. It will be recalled that the year after his coronation Boris had dispatched substantial military forces deep into cossack land to found the town of Tsarev-Borisov. The new fortress, more than 60 miles beyond the original Russian frontier, offered the quickest route to Razdory. The contrast between the fortress named for the tsar and the cossack capital was symbolic;[2] the name Boris gave to the former shows that he considered his relations with the cossacks not merely a continuing source of concern but a matter of prestige.

The cossack army could not survive without military supplies and equipment from Russia. Seeking to subdue the communes Godunov interdicted the sale of powder and weapons to the Don cossacks and prosecuted those who violated his stern edict. He realized how dangerous the turbulent periphery was to him, but his efforts to repress the communes redounded upon his own head. Open revolt by the cossacks precipitated a peasant war.

Urban disturbances, which had been frequent in the 1580s, later subsided as Boris did everything in his power to win over leaders of the town communes. At his coronation he granted Moscow's townspeople substantial privileges. The merchants controlling the eastern trade that moved through Astrakhan were granted a two-year exemption from transit duties; the inhabitants of the capital were freed from imposts, and money, clothing and goods were distributed to needy widows and orphans. Novgorod, with its second largest concentration of townspeople, was treated with equal generosity. Boris temporarily bestowed immunities on what he termed his patrimony, "the great state of Great Novgorod," and abolished the financial levies exacted from homes, small businesses and mercantile enterprises. Novgorod merchants were granted the right of free trade in Moscow and the towns of Livonia, and the authorities exempted the townspeople from paying taxes to the treasury when trading in wine and closed crown taverns in the city. Godunov promised to ensure that "all townspeople will live tranquil, peaceful and prosperous lives; you will not be constrained, and no one will make you endure losses or confiscations." These policies were implemented because during the time the country lay in ruins towns had declined and become depopulated. In order to revive urban life the authorities had to adopt these exceptional measures, which were collectively called "the town edifice."

The town edifice, like many other of Godunov's innovations, finds no reflection in the legal documents and thus is difficult to assess. Isolated data concerning various towns do no more than indicate the general thrust of Boris' policy: in Bolkhov, Korela and Rostov the authorities made efforts to bring back to their town units former tax-payers who had fled to landlords' estates or moved into the town residences of feudatories, and who had, in the term used then, pledged themselves to gentry. In Kazan and Zaraisk the administration confiscated several monastery villages and placed them on the tax rolls; in Vladimir they augmented the town population with peasants drawn from a village belonging to the patriarch, and in Kaluga they settled peasants from monastery and gentry estates, who paid quitrent, in the town.

To increase the number of urban taxpaying units corresponded with the interests of the treasury and also satisfied the influential chief merchants. The authorities had not forgotten the disturbances that had occurred in Moscow during the first years of Fedor's reign, and in making concessions hoped to prevent repetition of them. Those paying taxes in the towns had been suffering substantial losses due to competition from country people living on land in the towns that belonged to feudatories and thus enjoying tax advantages. To offset this, town units paying taxes were given the exclusive right to engage in trade and industry. On occasion the government hearkened to townspeople: in Rostov traders employed by the metropolitan, monasteries and the upper classes were placed on the tax rolls, thereby effectively ending the competition from these tax-privileged town dwellers.

Godunov's policy was a clear blueprint for the "town edifice" of the mid-seventeenth century and served as a harbinger of the future. Towns were centers of progress and their recovery corresponded with the state's basic economic interests. Boris' policy encouraged development of town estates, but it was pursued inconsistently. It was not enacted into law and apparently was carried out only in individual places. Since Moscow still had the largest concentration of townspeople and contained a substantial proportion of Russia's urban population the need for a town edifice there became steadily more

Milling Grain

pressing, but the tsar hesitated to quarrel with the powerful Moscow nobility and clergy to advance the interests of townspeople and so the reforms made there were insignificant.

Godunov's urban reform was highly complex. The crown was attempting to revive the towns while tying members of town communes to the tax rolls. Taking the towns under his patronage the ruler was forcing them to develop along feudal lines. In carrying out the "town edifice" the authorities sharply differentiated between gentry, whose members were designated a hereditary estate of serving-men, and the rest of the soldiers, who were called men of the levy and recruited from the urban population. Those not members of the feudal estate were taxed like townspeople. In Pereiaslavl and Zaraisk those erecting Boris' "edifice" were known to tax city cannoneers and others whom the levy had pressed into service. The differences among the estates constantly accentuated the cleavages in urban society. Once part of the taxpaying estate, petty serving-men, now experienced the full force of the serf system. The "town edifice," wherever it was implemented, intensified social contradictions.

Townspeople constituted a small part, no more than two percent, of the country's population. The rest lived in tiny villages scattered throughout the vast expanse of the eastern European plain. Godunov's policy towards the peasantry smacked strongly of serfdom. Abolition of St. George's Day and implementation of the edict authorizing recovery of runaway peasants enormously increased the power feudal landowners exercised over the rural population. Members of the gentry were steadily introducing a system of forced labor on their holdings and raising quitrent, and peasants found it hard to adapt to the new order. They could accept temporary abrogation of St. George's Day as long as they were promised the crown would soon approve departure years, but as time went on the people grew convinced they had been brutally deceived. Peasants protested the tightening noose of serfdom any way they could. This usually took the form of flight from landlords, but more menacing signs appeared. The country was agitated by increasing reports of murder of landlords and the authorities were forced to ponder ways to pacify the countryside.

On ascending the throne Boris pledged that both gentry and peasantry would prosper. The heads of the ambassadorial chancellery claimed the new tsar had calmed the Russian land and arranged for the country to live in tranquility, peace and prosperity. The official version impressed foreigners deeply. One of them, Michael Schiele, an Austrian courier in Moscow, wrote that although Russian peasants were slaves to the gentry Boris was determined to define strictly the duties and payments for which each peasant household was responsible. Such a measure might have limited increases in quitrent and the expansion of forced labor, but it is not known whether the plan was ever implemented.

At the coronation the authorities announced taxes would be lowered. Konrad Bussow, a foreigner in the service, wrote that the tsar was supposed to have freed the entire country from taxation for a year, but he was merely reporting what others had told him and it is impossible to believe such a story. In fact, the government followed different policies when dealing with different entities among tax-paying groups. The large rural population enjoyed far fewer tax reductions than the small urban populace, although areas in greatest need were given preference: the ruined district of Korela, which Russia recently had recovered from Sweden, was exempted from taxes for ten years. For a long time the Voguls of Siberia had been requesting relief and Boris ordered them exempted from tribute for a year and future imposts equalized in such a way that "henceforth each can pay without privation, so that in future matters may stand on a firm comprehensive basis without privation." Among the Siberian Tatars and Ostiaks tribute was reduced only for the old and impoverished. These concessions granted specific regions were of short duration; peasants groaned under the burden of taxation, and fiscal oppression was ruining the countryside.

In the early seventeenth century natural disasters destroyed Russian agriculture. In this agrarian land production was extraordinarily unstable and depended extensively upon the weather. Students of climatic change have come to the conclusion that during the last thousand years the most severe cold trend occurred in the second half of the sixteenth and early seventeenth centuries. Throughout Europe from France to Russia tillers of the soil had to contend with manifestations of the same problems: short warm summers, exceptional cold, and heavy snow. The climatic changes were not so severe as to induce an overall decline in production but certain parts of Europe at this time experienced agrarian catastrophe. In many countries deteriorating weather conditions were attended by disruption of the climatic cycles. Each decade usually included one or two poor years and one very bad one, but poor years normally alternated with good ones so that peasants could recoup their losses in succeeding harvests, but when disaster struck two years in a row small peasant production suffered ruin.

In the early seventeenth century Russia felt the impact of the general cooling trend and disruption of the weather cycle. Extensive rain hampered the harvest in the chill summer of 1601 and premature frosts completed the havoc. The peasants had to use frozen immature seeds to sow the winter crop and the winter wheat either failed to grow or grew feebly. The frosts of 1602 destroyed the crop on which tillers of the soil depended and by 1603 villages had nothing to sow. Frightful famine ensued. Prices usually rose in the spring; thus, it is not surprising that bread was expensive as early as the spring of 1601, but in less than a year rye sold at six times its original cost and its price later increased again at least three times. Smallholders and now the middle level of the population were unable to afford bread at such prices.

Having exhausted their food reserves the famished people ate cats and dogs and then devoured grass, bark, and finally corpses. People starved to death everywhere. Bodies were heaped along roads and in the towns men could barely manage to transport bodies out into fields for burial in big pits. During the famine in Moscow alone the authorities buried 120,000 persons in three large common graves. Both foreigners like Jacques Margeret and Russian writers like Avraamii Palitsyn cite this figure. Contemporaries estimated a third of the population of Muscovy perished during the famine years.

To its credit Godunov's administration immediately apprehended the danger and did everything possible to forestall mass starvation. Townspeople were its primary concern. In Solvychegodsk the authorities issued a special edict imposing a uniform fixed price for bread twice as low as the one prevailing in the market and the town commune was allowed to requisition grain from suppliers at this fixed price. Hoarders were to be beaten with a knout and a second offense meant imprisonment. Measures to check grain speculation in urban markets, apparently applied generally, were introduced in November, 1601, while the people still had some supplies.

It is not hard to explain why the authorities made haste. Godunov's generation had endured a famine lasting two years during the oprichnina and even by the end of the sixteenth century the country had not fully recovered from that disaster. The new tsar's manifestos used language no previous ruler had ever employed to the people. They tried to convince that Boris was ruling justly, "bringing tranquility, peace and prosperity to all; in my mercy I am protecting you in every way and seeking what is beneficial to the entire people, so that every region may have an abundance of bread, a life free from disturbance, and uninfringed peace for everyone alike."[3]

The government spared no efforts in its struggle with the famine. Once Godunov sent 20,000 rubles to the people of Smolensk; he ordered even larger amounts distributed among the needy in Moscow, and organized mutual assistance leagues to feed the people, but cash disbursements failed to achieve their purpose because money was daily losing its value; units of the official currency no longer could maintain a single man, much less a family. However, rumors of the tsar's generosity spread all over the country and crowds flocked to the capital, intensifying the famine there. Boris surveyed grain stocks throughout his realm and ordered the royal granaries to sell to the people, but this source was soon exhausted. Much bread sold at fixed prices found its way into the hands of hoarders. In an attempt to arrest speculation the new tsar went so far as to execute some Moscow bakers who had given short weight, but none of these measures produced any real improvement.

Perhaps the steps the government took might have been successful if the famine had proved of short duration, but the repeated failure of the harvests nullified its efforts. Monasteries and boyars that had laid in large stocks of grain remained deaf to the appeals of the authorities. Patriarch Iov set an example for the rest when he refused to part with his surplus. Anticipating worse to come, wealthy peasants buried their grain in the ground. The government requisitioned grain wherever possible but was irresolute and inconsistent in its actions because Boris did not dare seriously to tangle with his richest subjects, and efforts to control the speculation rampant among traders similarly failed.

Godunov was well-disposed towards townspeople because he wished to preserve the most important source of financial revenue for the treasury, but the peasant millions were left to their fate. Even estates belonging to the court, which constituted the Godunov family's actual patrimony, would sell peasants available grain only if the latter would indenture themselves. Court bailiffs in the village of Kushalino told Moscow many needy peasants had come there and "stand in the streets with their wives and children and die of hunger and fever." On receiving this information the chancery promulgated a decree: "Have the poor kept warm and loan bread to those you can trust."[4] There was no free distribution of alms and bread in the countryside. Year in, year out the peasants had fed the country and their quitrent had filled the royal granaries, but under feudalism this was of little consequence. Starving peasants had to pay for bread they received by indenturing themselves. Ruined and transient peasants could not expect even loans and were doomed to a painful death.

Since it lacked sufficient reserves to feed the countryside the government tried another approach. For years the enserfed peasants had lived in hopes that the authorities might authorize departure years, but Boris' order to track down runaways had delivered a mortal blow to their desires. However, he displayed considerable flexibility when three years later he temporarily jettisoned his previous policies. On November 28, 1601 the country learned that peasants would be allowed to move on St. George's Day for a period of one year. The famine alone could not bring about such a major social change. The full impact of the first crop failure was not felt until autumn, 1601, for the people had not yet used up their stocks on hand. The three-year famine lay in the future and its severity could not then be fore-seen. Unafraid of famine, Godunov was terrified of the social up-heavals sober observers had long foretold. The peasants had been passive spectators of the change in dynasty and their views about electing the tsar had not been solicited. The people had trusted Tsar Fedor, no matter how insignificant he may have appeared. Govern-ment had conducted its affairs in his name and decrees emanated from the lawful sovereign. Boris had not been born to the purple. How could he aspire to occupy the seat of God on earth? The stoic peasant mind had not been able to resolve such a difficult question and with one bold move Boris tried to win the affection of the rural population. His rescript was uniquely designed to achieve his goal. In Fedor's name the peasants had lost their freedom and now Boris came forward as their champion by reestablishing the right of St. George's Day. His decree used simple language to explain to the peasants how merciful their great sovereign was for he had "granted exemption from taxation and confiscation to his whole kingdom and ordained that peasants be given the right to move."[5]

Grekov claimed Godunov's peasant policy conformed to the in-terests of the mass of serving-men but Koretskii has revised this view by showing that the reintroduction of St. George's Day ran counter to the petty gentry's concerns. The enactments of 1601-1602 tem-porarily restored the right of peasant movement only on land be-longing to provincial gentry, junior officers, and petty chancery people while categorically affirming the enserfment of peasants be-longing to the members of the boyar council, Moscow courtiers, secretaries, and clergy. This shows that Godunov had become a de-termined champion of the privileged nobility and the leading feudal ranks that had participated directly in his election. Likewise, St. George's Day was not reestablished in the area around Moscow or on crown lands, for Boris had no wish to stir up Moscow smallholders, who regularly came to the capital. Crown lands provided the treasury with substantial revenues and the authorities were determined to keep crown peasants where they were. Godunov avoided measures that might displease the nobility but displayed no hesitation in provoking the petty gentry, the largest complement in the ruling class. Platonov's view that Boris was the gentry tsar who linked his fate to the middle service estate is erroneous.

The authorities next did what they could to efface the disagreeable impression the temporary concessions granted the peasantry had produced on petty landlords. It was logical to assume the restoration of St. George's Day would cause peasants to flock to lands belonging to privileged landowners able to offer new arrivals loans and exemptions, but the government plugged this loophole by prohibiting rich landowners from soliciting peasants. Provincial gentry acquired the right to receive no more than one or two peasants from another estate at a time. Economic calculation underlay this decision.

Boris' epoch was the first in which Russia experienced universal famine after the peasants had been enserfed and this created unusual difficulties in small peasant production. For a century St. George's Day had served as an economic regulator. Whenever crops failed peasants were quick to leave landlords who refused to help them and go to proprietors willing to lend them seeds and equipment, but under serfdom peasants were trapped on impoverished service-tenure estates where they received no aid and from which they were legally forbidden to depart. Godunov's laws opened the jaws of the trap for the peasantry, but they also hindered enterprising gentry from attracting numbers of peasants who received no assistance on neighboring estates. Actuated mainly by financial considerations the government allowed peasants to move between middle and petty service-tenure estates, for unless peasants on ruined landholdings were permitted to move and receive aid they could not survive and keep paying the taxes that assured the treasury of income. Since petty landholders comprised the bulk of the feudal structure it follows that most of the peasant population had an opportunity to take advantage of Tsar Boris' edict. Restoration of St. George's Day might have helped small peasant production survive the years of crop failure, thereby dissipating the enserfed peasantry's discontent. Did this in fact occur? To enact a law was one thing; to realize it, another.

The peasants placed their own interpretation on the new tsar's overtures. They refused to pay taxes, imposts, fines or quitrent, and moved whenever they pleased without regard for the fact they were forbidden to settle in at least half the country. The peasants reacted so intensely that when the edict was reissued in 1602 it omitted clauses granting exemption from taxes and fines. Landlords resisted these concessions to the serfs, limited and temporary though they were, with all their power. Gentry opposition became so widespread that the authorities included measures in the 1602 edict designed to stop peasants from attacking and plundering landlords: "Lesser boyars are not to restrain peasants by force; they are not to levy fines on them, and anyone encouraging peasants to plunder and not dismissing such persons will incur our grave displeasure."[6] Mere threats failed to alarm the gentry when its revenues were jeopardized, for without peasants the minor landholder faced poverty and ruin, and a government that had instituted serfdom was not likely to apply serious sanctions against the gentry, its chief source of support. The efforts to improve conditions in the starving countryside had failed. Boris' subtle policy ended by satisfying no one. The dynasty retained the support of the higher feudatories but its popularity among the petty gentry was receding rapidly.

Boris had failed to win popular favor. Landlord coercion and the famine inflamed the peasantry. In 1603, for the first time in its history, Russia became an arena of mass revolt. Official sources tried to discredit the rising by calling the commons "bandits,"[7] but peasant war unquestionably had broken out in the country. Tsar Boris entrusted the struggle with the rebels to Associate Boyar Ivan Buturlin, who had served with distinction during the Livonian war. As chief of the Robbery Chancellery, Buturlin dispatched gentry units to attack "bandits" in Kolomna, Volokolamsk, Mozhaisk, Viazma, Medyn, Rzhev, Belaia, and other areas. The region affected by the rebellion surrounded Moscow on all sides and the "bandits" eventually approached close to the capital.

In May, 1603 Moscow undertook military preparations on an unprecedented scale. One might have thought the Tatars were again menacing the city. Boris divided Moscow into sectors and assigned their defense to five boyars and seven associate boyars. In autumn Associate Boyar Ivan Basmanov, charged with preserving order in the wooden Arbat sector, attacked the bandits, but the other commanders made no efforts to support him. The authorities were obviously more afraid of an urban rising than of the rebels. In a clash with government troops the latter displayed great tenacity and daring, but although Commander Basmanov was killed the rebels were defeated and Khlopko, their leader, was captured and hanged. Flames of revolt were sweeping over the country. The bandits seemed immune to capture and turned up everywhere. Moscow soon became convinced that military action alone was inadequate.

Adopting an ingenious stratagem to persuade insurgent slaves to lay down their weapons, on August 16, 1603 Tsar Boris issued an edict promising freedom to indentured slaves denied sustenance by their masters during the famine. The authorities urged slaves to come to Moscow in order to obtain an appropriate document from the Slave Chancellery. Their word was accepted even when their owners were not present. Slaves who had served as military attendants posed the greatest danger for they were accustomed to bearing arms, unlike laborers and peasants who had no military experience. It was they who had enabled the rebels to survive major encounters with government forces and it was to them the government directed its primary appeal.

The lower elements in society constituted the driving force behind the movement of 1603. The government could not cope with it until it rallied the entire petty provincial gentry, and when the danger lessened the gentry made Godunov compensate its members. Their pressure forced him to annul the concessions he had made to the peasantry: in 1603 he abrogated the law that had restored St. George's Day. Boris' reaffirmation of the previous policy of enserfment rendered a peasant war inevitable.

Chapter Twelve

GRIGORII OTREPEV

The story of the pretender who took the name of Dmitrii is one of the most dramatic episodes of this period.

Boris' election did not squelch boyar intrigue. The nobility first tried to substitute Khan Simeon, and later the pretender Dmitrii for Godunov. The boy, who had been almost forgotten, was mentioned the day after Fedor died. Lithuanian spies operating secretly in Smolensk learned many strange things about him. Some claimed Dmitrii was alive and had sent them a letter, while others asserted Boris had had Dmitrii killed but kept a double handy, calculating that failing to secure the throne himself he might put forward a false heir through

whom he might win the throne anyway. Godunov's enemies concocted fanciful tales. Deliberately defaming the new tsar they extolled his opponents, the Romanov boyars. They sowed rumors to
the effect that the eldest Romanov brother, having charged Boris
openly with murdering Ivan's two sons, had tried personally to punish
the malefactor.[1] It is impossible to believe such rumors; they are
absurd, but they show that those close to the Romanov family were
the ones responsible for activating Dmitrii's ghost.

After Boris' coronation stories about a pretender ceased to attract
attention, but when the tsar became seriously ill a contest for the
throne seemed unavoidable and Dmitrii's ghost appeared again. Three
years later the mysterious, elusive shadow became flesh and blood—a
man turned up in the Rzeczpospolita claiming he was the dead heir.
The Russian populace was told this Dmitrii was Grishka[2] Otrepev, a
monk who had run away from the Miracles monastery. It might be
assumed the authorities in Moscow had picked this name at random,
but this was not the case. The identity of the pretender, initially regarded as a petty thief and troublemaker, was established after careful investigation. The authorities could not prove Grishka and the
pretender were one and the same person beyond the shadow of a
doubt, but using testimony supplied by his mother, uncle, and other
relatives in Galicia they assembled detailed evidence concerning the
real Otrepev's career. Grigorii's uncle, Smirnoi-Otrepev, was a precise
witness and Boris sent him to Poland to expose his nephew.

A member of the petty gentry of Galich, Yurii Bogdanovich Otrepev, known as Grigorii in monastic life, was tonsured in a Russian
monastery and then fled to Lithuania. The royal chancellery concentrated intensely on these vital incidents in Otrepev's life but its
assertions were full of contradictions and the numerous discrepancies
in the official accounts require explanation.

The Russian authorities designed an initial version for consumption at the Polish court which ran literally thus: "Yushka Otrepev, as
he was known in the world, refused to obey his father out of wickedness, fell into heresy, was a robber and thief who gambled, caroused,
and often ran away from his father until after a life of crime he was
tonsured."[3] The author of this edifying tale about a corrupt son of
the gentry apparently was Smirnoi-Otrepev, after he returned from
Poland where he had failed to meet with his nephew.

The tsar's diplomats spoke of Otrepev not merely in Cracow but
in Vienna as well. Boris sent a personal message to the emperor, the
original of which, still unpublished, is preserved in the Vienna archives

and I have managed to study it. Concerning the fugitive monk Boris wrote: "Yushka Otrepev was a slave to our courtier, Mikhail Romanov, and while in his service began stealing, for which Mikhail expelled him from his court. Then the vagabond started stealing more than ever and for this they wished to hang him, but he avoided the punishment of death, was tonsured in remote monasteries, and called the monk Grigorii."[4] In faraway Vienna Muscovite diplomats were more forthcoming than in Cracow. Here they first revealed the identity of the pretender's patron, but although they linked the names of Otrepev and Romanov they implied the whole influential boyar party had encouraged the adventurer. They concealed from the Poles the fact that Otrepev had served the house of Romanov and tried to convince the Austrians the Romanov family had not been a party to the intrigue and its members had voluntarily gotten rid of the pretender. Comparison of the two official versions of Grishka's tonsure are conducive to the assumption that the royal chancellery falsified this episode in his life. The reason for it is clear. The Muscovite authorities wanted to show that Otrepev was an ordinary criminal, not a political figure who had influential backing.

These explanations were made abroad while the name of the pretender was forbidden to be mentioned in Russia. Reference to a Dmitrii who had miraculously survived was rigidly suppressed, but when the False Dmitrii finally entered the country it was no longer possible to maintain silence. He proved a far more formidable enemy than Moscow had assumed, for although he was defeated in battle nothing could exorcize his presence.

The efforts to show that Otrepev was a young scoundrel whom drink and brigandage had forced to seek refuge in a monastery were no longer convincing and diplomats had to stop telling such stories. The church next took up the task of exposing him. The patriarch told the people Otrepev "had lived at the Romanov court, where he turned to thievery; to save himself from execution he became a monk and spent time in numerous monasteries." He then worked at the patriarchal court and fled to Lithuania.[5] To comprehend how contemporaries understood the patriarch's revelations it should be remembered that in those days the charge of robbery most frequently meant defiance of authority, treason, and other political crimes. Diplomatic documents listed drunkenness and thievery as the reasons for Grishka's becoming a monk, and the patriarch's proclamation implied that he had committed these crimes while he was in the service of the Romanov family.

After the fall of the Godunov dynasty and the death of the First False Dmitrii, Tsar Vasilii Shuiskii, ringleader of the conspiracy that eliminated the pretender, launched a new investigation into the Otrepev affair and made available a more detailed history of Grishka than Boris had done. In particular, he informed the Poles that Yushka Otrepev had been a slave in service to the Romanov brothers, the sons of Nikita, and had served Prince Boris Cherkasskii, but after committing acts of theft had become a monk.[6] These new official revelations proved that Otrepev had been associated with at least the Romanov and Cherkasskii families, both high noble boyar houses.

Political consideration motivated such frankness. On coming to power Shuiskii had tried to win support from surviving members of the Romanov family by appointing the monk, Fedor Romanov, patriarch and making his brother Ivan a boyar. His crafty approach failed to produce the desired result, for as soon as they had a chance the members of the Romanov family joined a conspiracy against Shuiskii. The new tsar no longer had any reason to spare his rivals. He abandoned the fiction that Otrepev had been expelled from the Romanov court and revealed further details about his early life. Shuiskii's version is more reliable than Godunov's, for after the latter's fall the fact that the boyar opposition had abetted the pretender's intrigue was no longer significant. Furthermore, Shuiskii was addressing the Polish court, which was well informed about its former protégé. The tsar, insecure on the throne, had to adhere to facts, for the Polish side was in a position to refute fabrications concerning Otrepev.

That Otrepev served boyars in the house of Romanov may apparently be accepted as historical fact. What part did this play in the adventurer's life? Contemporaries had nothing to say about it, but the author of the *Tale of the Defrocked One,* a chronicler who lived under the first Romanov tsars, threw caution to the winds and lifted a corner of the curtain. He wrote: "Grishka Otrepev was afraid of Tsar Boris, who had instituted persecution of the great boyars, and hid . . . . The prince sent Fedor Nikitich Romanov and his brothers into confinement, just as he sent Boris Kelbulatovich . . . into confinement. Now this Grishka Otrepev often visited the luxurious home of Prince Boris Kelbulatovich and was honored by Prince Boris Kelbulatovich, and for this reason Tsar Boris came to suspect him, but this cunning man soon escaped from the tsar, hid in a monastery, and was tonsured."[7] Devoted to the Romanov interest, the author of the *Tale* seemed to be saying "Enough. Otrepev never served either Mikhail Romanov or Boris Cherkasskii; he used merely to drop in at

Panning Salt

the Cherkasskii court." Well informed about the Cherkasskii family, the chronicler knew its members had been disgraced along with the Romanov family and Prince Boris' wife and son, Ivan, had gone into exile with him. This makes the statement that the Cherkasskii family esteemed Otrepev more interesting; it meant that Yurii Bogdanovich was not simply one of the mass of courtiers but had achieved distinction in Prince Cherkasskii's service.

For a long time scant attention has been paid to the *Tale of the Defrocked One,* which has not been considered a valid source because of the amount of unreliable detail present in it, and it has been overlooked that the fictitious stories the *Tale* contains invariably refer to the time Otrepev spent in Lithuania. The author knew far more about Grishka's adventures in Muscovy, but the unique information that can be derived from this provocative source should not, of course, be utilized unless it has been thoroughly verified, an essential task that must be undertaken.

The Moscow period in Otrepev's life is barren of incident. After service at various boyar courts he spent time as a monk and then disappeared to Lithuania. Most puzzling is the time during which he sojourned in provincial monasteries. Contemporaries, having no direct knowledge of his wanderings, invariably contradicted one another; they had difficulty enumerating even the places where he stayed. One chronicler claimed Grishka spent three years in a small monastery near Galich and two quiet years at the Miracles monastery. The information this chronicler possessed was insubstantial; he somehow confused the monastery of St. John the Baptist in Zheleznyi Borek in Galicia with the monastery of the Life-Giving Trinity in the Kostroma district, and his account of Otrepev's visit to Queen Mariia Nagaia in a nunnery located on the Vyksa river is pure invention.

The author of a work known as *A Different Tale* described Otrepev's sojourn in various monasteries otherwise. He claimed Grishka first inhabited the Spaso-Evfimiev monastery in Suzdal, transferred to the Miracles monastery, and ended up in the monastery of St. John the Baptist in Zheleznyi Borek. Composed under the Romanov tsars, *A Different Tale* offers its readers a romantic legend: at fourteen Yushka was moved to become a monk after he had an inspiring conversation with an abbot from Viatka he met by chance in Moscow. This story contains too many political overtones to merit credence; it was rather his service at the court of disgraced boyars, not an inspiring conversation, that caused Yushka to enter a monastery, but under the Romanov tsars it was dangerous to recall a link between the originator of the dynasty and an abandoned heretic.

To determine the truth it is best to use materials composed at an earlier date. In Shuiskii's time the authorities established that Grishka had definitely spent some time in two provincial monasteries in Suzdal and Galich and then served a year as a deacon at the Miracles monastery. This detail merits special attention. The royal chancellery, making a timely investigation into the Miracles monastery phase of Otrepev's life, followed fresh leads. The abbot of the Miracles monastery was called upon to explain why he had admitted Grishka. The account of Otrepev's life compiled in Shuiskii's time makes no mention of how long the monk sojourned in provincial monasteries, but Prince Shakhovskoi, one of Grishka's best-informed contemporaries, comes to the rescue. He categorically affirmed that Grigorii had been a monk only a short while before he settled in the monastery in Moscow: "Soon after his tonsure this monk came to the royal city of Moscow, where he entered the pure cloister of the Archangel Michael."[8] If Shakhovskoi is to be believed, Otrepev did not stay at but merely visited provincial monasteries, and forgetting this later writers unwittingly exaggerated the period of time he spent as a monk.

A simple arithmetical calculation may prove of assistance. Grigorii went abroad in February, 1602 after spending approximately a year at the Miracles monastery. This means he entered the Kremlin cloister early in 1601 and, if it is assumed Yushka donned the cowl shortly before that, he became a monk in 1600. A sequence of proofs is emerging; it was precisely in 1600 that Boris degraded the Romanov and Cherkasskii boyars, and this surely provides a basis for the view that Otrepev's tonsure was motivated largely by the fall of the Romanov faction. Another striking coincidence is that again in 1600 all Russia heard the rumor that Dmitrii had survived miraculously, a story that very likely suggested to Otrepev the role he might assume.

The Otrepev family apparently had longstanding connections with Uglich, the abode of the dead heir. Grigorii's ancestors had come to Russia from Lithuania; one settled in Galich, others in Uglich. In 1577 Smirnoi-Otrepev and his younger brother Bogdan, new arrivals without service experience, received a service-tenure estate in Kolomna, when Bogdan was barely fifteen years old. A few years later a son, Yurii, was born to Bogdan at approximately the same time as Tsar Ivan's son Dmitrii was born. Yushka came of age at the end of Fedor's reign. Bogdan Otrepev rose to the rank of squadron commander in the fusiliers and died young. Probably endowed with the same turbulent nature his son possessed, he lived in the German Suburb of

Moscow, where foreigners freely trafficked in wine and drunken brawls were of frequent occurrence. A Lithuanian killed Bogdan in one such encounter.

Yushka was only a child when his father died and his mother brought him up. She made him learn to read holy writ and when opportunities for education at home were exhausted sent him for further study to Moscow, the home of his brother-in-law, Semeika Efimev, who was destined to play a prominent role in Yushka's life. As soon as he entered religious life Grishka started transcribing books at the patriarchal court. He could never have obtained such a position unless he wrote clearly. He may have learned to write in Secretary Efimev's home, for Muscovite chanceries esteemed calligraphy and those like Efimev who worked in them knew how to write a fine hand.

Early accounts portrayed young Otrepev as a corrupt scoundrel, but by Shuiskii's time such ideas had been abandoned and under the Romanov tsars authors freely expressed amazement at the young man's exceptional capacities although voicing pious suspicion that he may have had converse with unclean spirits. Otrepev learned quickly and soon became well educated. Poverty and the loss of his father seemed to have denied the able student a distinguished career, but Yurii finally took service with Mikhail Romanov. Many considered the Romanov family heir to the throne and service at its court might presage a splendid future. The Otrepev family's ancestral home was located on the Monza river, a tributary of the Kostroma, where the village of Domnino, a handsome patrimonial estate belonging to the Romanov family, was situated. The proximity of the two holdings may have influenced Otrepev to apply to the court the Romanov boyars maintained in Moscow.

Shuiskii's pronouncements termed Yurii Otrepev a boyar slave but these hostile statements cannot be taken seriously. Yushka served Mikhail Romanov of his own volition, for otherwise he could not have transferred to the service of the Cherkasskii house. The members of the Otrepev family served as officers in fusilier detachments. In boyar courts gentry holding their rank were attendants and stablers. The fact that Yushka was honored by the Cherkasskii family meant that his career was off to an auspicious start, but the disgrace that overwhelmed the Romanov forces in November, 1600 nearly ruined him. The Romanov palace was the site of a pitched battle when the family's armed retainers desperately resisted the tsar's fusiliers. In such situations Tsar Ivan had exterminated boyar households but

Boris did not choose to follow his example; he tortured prominent servitors (many of whom died from it) and forbade anyone to accept into service persons from boyar suites he had dissolved. Principal figures and their close associates were harshly dealt with; Associate Boyar Mikhail Romanov and Boyar Boris Cherkasskii died in exile.

Yushka Otrepev obviously found himself in a difficult situation. The patriarch declared only tonsure saved him from certain execution but Boris was even more explicit: "The gallows awaits the boyar servitor!" No pious conversation but fear of death impelled Otrepev to enter a monastery. The courtier, twenty years old and full of hope, energy and strength, had to forsake the world and even forget his own name, becoming henceforth the humble monk Grigorii. It is clear that in his wanderings the new monk spent time at the monastery at Zheleznyi Borek in Galicia, where some accounts say he was tonsured, and at the Spaso-Evfimiev monastery in Suzdal. A glance at the map shows that both these places lie northeast of Moscow. This servant of disgraced boyars would naturally seek refuge in his homeland.

Tradition holds that a spiritual elder was assigned to instruct Grishka in the Spaso-Evfimiev monastery but when life as a novice grew confining Otrepev left the Suzdal cloister, although he apparently stayed there longer than he did in any other monastery he visited. The transition from life in boyar palaces to vegetating in monasteries was very unpleasant and Grigorii could not help feeling depressed. Moscow and its distractions beckoned to him and soon he quitted the provincial backwater. He ventured again to show his face in the capital mainly because the tsar had banished the Romanov family, terminated the investigation, and the disgraced who were still alive had soon been forgiven. Furthermore, as contemporaries pointed out, in Old Russia becoming a monk frequently saved criminals from punishment.

How could a disgraced monk enter the Miracles monastery, the most aristocratic in the Kremlin? Shuiskii's secretaries answered this question satisfactorily, after finding witnesses who described how this provincial individual made his way into the Kremlin. Grigorii had patrons: "The God-born protopope Evfimii intervened on his behalf with Abbot Pafnutii of the Miracles monastery ('now metropolitan of Krutitsa,' the secretaries added parenthetically), ordering him to be admitted to the monastery and to live in a cell with Evfimii's uncle Zamiatin, and Abbot Pafnutii, moved because he was a poor orphan, took him into the Miracles monastery and made him a novice."[9] Otrepev did not long remain under the tutelage of Evfimii's uncle, for the abbot soon noticed him and brought him to his own cell where, as Otrepev himself said, he was occupied with literary tasks, telling monks of his acquaintance: "When I lived in Abbot Pafnutii's cell in the Miracles monastery I composed paeans in honor of the Moscow miracle-workers Peter, Aleksei and Iona."[10] Otrepev's work was valued and he began his swift, almost meteoric ascent.

Although Grigorii was young and had spent only about a year in the monastery, Pafnutii promoted him to deacon. The post of assistant to the powerful abbot of the Miracles monastery might have satisfied anyone other than Otrepev, but he left Pafnutii to join the patriarchal court. Eventually the patriarch would use the extenuating argument that he had invited Grishka merely to copy books, but at the patriarchal court Otrepev both transcribed books and composed canons to the saints. The patriarch observed that bishops, abbots, and the entire spiritual assembly were acquainted with the monk Grigorii. This was probably true, because the patriarch always brought a host of assistants to the assembly and the boyar council. Otrepev was among their number and said to his friends: "The patriarch discerned my capacity and began to bring me with him to the royal council. I acquired great renown." His claim to "great renown" should not be considered mere boasting.

After the severe reverses he had suffered in the service of the Romanov family it was amazing how quickly Otrepev adapted to his new mode of life. Although he had never planned to be a monk he showed signs of real distinction in his new career. The ambitious youth secured preferment because of his unusually enterprising nature, not as an ascetic. In months he mastered what it took others a lifetime to comprehend. Church leaders at once appreciated his vigorous intellect and literary talents, but the young man possessed additional qualities that attracted and bound men to him. He had been a lackey to Evfimii's uncle, Zamiatin, assistant to the abbot of the Miracles monastery, and an attendant to the patriarch; hence, he must have been endowed with exceptional capacities because he carved out so successful a career in less than a year. Otrepev was a man in a hurry; undoubtedly he sensed he was not fated to live long . . . .

Tsar Boris had the ambassadorial chancellery circulate a story to the effect that Otrepev had fled from the patriarchal chancellery after he was exposed as a heretic, flouting his parents' authority and defying God Himself: "He dabbled in black magic, summoned unclean

Brewing Beer

spirits, and disavowed God." As punishment the patriarch and the whole ecumenical assembly, "according to the laws of the holy fathers and an assembly decree, sentenced Otrepev to exile and confinement for life in Beloozero." The Muscovite authorities sent a comparable version to the Polish court, in which they sought to prove that a court had condemned Otrepev. This would provide them with an excuse to demand the Poles surrender a fugitive criminal. In Shuiskii's time the ambassadorial chancellery compressed Otrepev's condemnation into a single sentence: the monk Grigorii had lapsed into heresy and the assembly had tried (!) to confine him for life in exile. No mention was made of an assembly decree sentencing Otrepev.

The version circulated abroad differed from the one destined for domestic consumption. After the fall of the False Dmitrii, Shuiskii's secretaries compiled a selection of documents containing a brief commentary on the pretender's personality. Under the heading of his service career it was stated that in 1602, after fleeing from the Miracles monastery to Lithuania, "in Kiev and its environs the deacon, monk Grigorii . . . took to black magic, abandoned his angelic image, blasphemed, and with his hostile actions fell entirely away from God."[11] This indicates that Otrepev did not become a heretic until he fled abroad and means that prior to his flight the patriarch had no grounds for condemning Otrepev to death. When the Muscovite bishops informed the Poles that they had exposed Monk Grigorii and condemned him to death they were lying. In reality, they did not oppose Otrepev until the False Dmitrii had appeared in Lithuania.

The Muscovite authorities had little difficulty in discovering what Grigorii Otrepev had been doing in Russia, but they encountered enormous problems ascertaining the nature of his activities abroad until Godunov's police managed to locate two itinerant monks, who had been with Grishka when he left Russia and had known him in Lithuania. Unfortunately these mendicants, who mysteriously appeared before the authorities, inspired trust in no one, not even the government, which unceremoniously termed them bandits. No reliable witnesses were forthcoming in Moscow until two years later, when Boris was dead and a rising had overthrown and slain the First False Dmitrii. Vasilii Shuiskii, leader of the conspirators, needed evidence to prove incontrovertibly the Tsar Dmitrii he had ousted was a pretender. It was most opportune that at that very moment the monk Varlaam appeared in Moscow and addressed a celebrated *Communication* to the government.

Varlaam's composition has been considered a devious forgery designed to satisfy those then in power and even such a profound scholar as Platonov, who was cautious in his conclusions, called the *Communication* a strange tale, not the testimony of a reliable witness. However, attitudes towards the *Communication* have altered with the passage of time. Recently discovered archival texts differ from the original chronicle version in that they do not contain the citations from charters issued by the First False Dmitrii, the cause of the original mistrust. Subsequent suspicion that the work was a forgery disappeared when the original records of the royal archive in the early seventeenth century were found to contain direct reference to an investigation of Elder Varlaam Yatskii. Otrepev was accompanied by two monks, Varlaam and Misail, when he fled abroad and Boris' manifestos had made the name of Otrepev's confederate, called Thief Varlaam, well known. Varlaam tried to return to Russia a few months after the First False Dmitrii's coronation but the latter's commanders detained him at the border and would not allow him to proceed to Moscow.

The situation changed when False Dmitrii died. The Muscovite clergy had condemned both Otrepev and his confederate *in absente;* thus, when he was summoned to a hearing Varlaam had every reason to expect he would be imprisoned. Harboring little hope for a successful outcome of his trial, the fugitive monk ended his petition with a surprising request: "Merciful Tsar, Sovereign, Grand Prince Vasilii Ivanovich, spare me, your pilgrim, and send me to Zosima and Savateia at Solovki."[12] This monastery, situated on barren islands in the Arctic Ocean, had long been a place of exile for particularly dangerous political criminals. Varlaam asked to be sent there because the pretender's murder had so unnerved him that he considered banishment to the remote north the safest course for him to follow.

Varlaam's composition displays one striking feature. If the new authorities had bribed the fugitive monk to write a spurious *Communication* at their dictation he would have spared no eloquence to vilify the pretender, but the astonishingly artless account in the *Communication* seeks not so much to assail Otrepev as to vindicate Varlaam. He feared punishment for having abetted Grigorii but his efforts to show he had been a foe of the defrocked monk are amazingly naive.

Varlaam manifested thorough knowledge of the pretender's first moves in Lithuania. No other Russian knew that in Sambor Otrepev arranged for the death of a Muscovite courtier who was trying to expose him, an event proved by an incontestable document, a letter written by Jerzy Mniszech from Sambor immediately after Godunov's agent was executed. When the pretender caused this first Muscovite to lose his life Varlaam was languishing in prison in Sambor, calling the executed courtier a comrade and asking the Muscovite authorities to question Jerzy Mniszech so as to satisfy themselves he was telling the truth. While Varlaam was being interrogated Jerzy Mniszech and False Dmitrii's widow were under investigation in Moscow and might possibly be examined.

Historians have expressed surprise that Varlaam could remember the exact date of August 15, on which the pretender left Sambor for his march on Moscow, and for this reason he has been suspected of a hoax and of using later documents to compose his *Communication,* but Varlaam's preciseness is easily explained. The elder could not forget the day he was released from prison in Sambor, which was the day the pretender left that town. Varlaam believed it was the gracious intercession of Marina Mniszech that freed him from prison after five months. He clearly did not understand the real reasons for his release although they are fairly simple. For four months False Dmitrii had been enjoying success but then his army was defeated; he himself barely escaped capture, and Jerzy Mniszech already had left the camp of the pretender, whose adventurous scheme now seemed doomed to failure. Under the circumstances the leaders in Sambor were no longer concerned with False Dmitrii's safety and freed Varlaam from prison.

Elder Varlaam proved to be of real value to the courts in Moscow investigating Grishka Otrepev's adventurous career. As he strove to exculpate himself of the charge of having cooperated with Otrepev, Varlaam set out the facts pertaining to the departure of the three itinerant monks for Lithuania as best he could, and his work is filled with precise dates. Are they reliable? To answer this question it should be remembered that Varlaam was describing events that had occurred two to five years earlier, clearly not a long period of time, and furthermore he was familiar with church holidays. He recalled leaving Moscow the week after Easter, holding service in Novgorod-Seversk on Annunciation Day, and crossing the frontier three weeks after Easter, etc.

Varlaam purposely omitted details about what happened before he went to Lithuania and made it seem as though he had met Otrepev by chance only the day before they left Moscow: once he was going along the Varvarka (the most populous trading street, which now passes by the modern Hotel Rossiia) when he was suddenly overtaken by a young monk called Grigorii Otrepev, who suggested they should

go to Chernigov and ultimately visit Christ's tomb. Varlaam agreed
and the next day the monks set out from Moscow. Scholars have
doubted Varlaam would have undertaken such a long arduous journey
on such short notice as the result of a chance encounter with an unknown man and of course the most dubious aspect of Varlaam's
account is his contention that he had not previously been acquainted
with Otrepev, but there is nothing surprising about their sudden departure. It was the end of winter in 1602 when the famine was raging
in Moscow. Varlaam took pains to emphasize that he had accepted
Otrepev's offer in order to save his soul, but it was actually their
mortal bodies, not their immortal souls, that made the monks undertake their hasty journey. Misail, Otrepev's friend from the Miracles
monastery, had joined Girgorii previously.

No one in Moscow paid attention to the monks as they departed.
At first they chatted quietly on the main trading street; the next day
they met in Icon Row, crossed the Moscow river, and hired a con-
veyance to take them to Bolkhov. No one bothered the itinerant
monks even in border towns. Otrepev openly performed service in a
church. For three weeks the friends collected money to build a remote cloister but appropriated the proceeds for their own use. The
legendary *Tale of Otrepev* vividly describes a scene in a tavern, which
Pushkin's tragedy has made widely known. The three runaways were
stopping in a village on the frontier when they chanced to learn that
barricades had been erected across the road. Otrepev became deathly
afraid and muttered to his companions: "This barrier is because of
us. I deceived Patriarch Iov and betook myself to flight with you."
This story is fictitious; nobody noticed Otrepev's and his friends'
departure from Moscow and the authorities had no reason to take
measures to apprehend them. The renegades crossed the frontier
without incident; first they spent three weeks in the Pechora monastery of Kiev, and then they moved to the estate belonging to Prince
Konstantin Ostrozhskii in Ostrog.

Varlaam's testimony that the fugitives spent time in Ostrog during
the summer of 1602 is supported by incontrovertible evidence. In
the repository of the Zagovorskii monastery in Volynia, A. Dobro-
tvorskii found a book printed in Ostrog in 1594 bearing the inscription: "The year from the Creation of the World 7110 (1602—R.S.),
in the month of August, on the fourteenth day, this book of the
mighty Vasilii was given to us, Grigorii, and his brethren Varlaam and
Misail, by Konstantin Konstantinovich, called Vasilii in holy baptism,
by God's grace Prince of Ostrog and Commander of Kiev."[13] This

shows that while spending the summer in Ostrog Otrepev had managed to attract the magnate's favor and received a splendid gift from him.

On leaving Ostrog the three monks successfully made their way to the Dermanskii monastery, which belonged to Ostrozhskii, but Otre-pev had not left the patriarch's court and the Miracles monastery in the Kremlin in order to bury himself in a small remote monastery in Lithuania. Varlaam stated that Grigorii left Ostrozhskii's domain, doffed his monastic habit, and at last proclaimed himself heir to the Muscovite throne. An unknown hand has supplemented the dedica-tory inscription in the book bestowed by the "mighty Vasilii," in-serting "heir to the Muscovite throne" over the word "Grigorii." The author of the addition might have been one of the book's three pos-sessors or a sympathizer who believed Girgorii's claim. The addendum to the dedicatory inscription is only remarkable because it supports Varlaam's allegation.

To authenticate Varlaam's *Communication,* Paul Pierling, S.J., was the first to draw attention to an odd source, the pretender's *Confes-sion.* When Adam Wisznewecki informed the Polish king that an heir to the Muscovite throne had appeared, the latter requested a detailed explanation and Prince Adam transcribed the pretender's own version of how he was miraculously saved. This interview, which incidentally has never been translated from Latin to Russian, produces a strange impression. The pretender gives many details about secret happenings at the Muscovite court but takes refuge in clumsy fantasy when he tells of the amazing circumstances under which he was saved: a tutor who had learned of the plan to murder him put another child of the same age in his place and this unfortunate was killed in Dmitrii's bed. The queen mother ran into the bedchamber and beheld the slain lad, but since his face had turned blue she failed to notice the substitution.

At this crucial moment in his career the pretender ought to have advanced every argument he could but he was unable to offer any genuine proof of his royal origin. He avoided stating facts and naming names that could be checked and refuted, and admitted his miracu-lous preservation was still unknown to anyone, including his mother who was then confined in a Russian nunnery. Study of the pretender's story discloses the remarkable fact that he appeared in Lithuania without a well-contrived, convincing provenance. His *Confession* reads like an awkward improvisation that involuntarily proves its author was a pretender, although not everything he said in it was false.

The newly proclaimed heir lived openly in Lithuania and anything he said could be checked; thus, if he had tried to conceal generally known facts he would immediately have been exposed as a fraud. Since everyone knew he was a monk when he arrived in Lithuania, he had to explain why he was tonsured. His story ran: before dying the tutor had entrusted the boy he had saved to the care of a gentry family. Its head, a "faithful friend," let the youth live in his home but before his death advised him to avoid danger by entering a cloister and adopting the monastic life. Yushka took his advice and visited numerous Russian monasteries until a monk discerned that he was the heir to the throne. After this Dmitrii decided to flee to Poland . . . . The pretender's version uncannily resembles Grigorii Otrepev's history during the Muscovite period of his life; it should be recalled that Grishka grew up in a gentry family and traversed Muscovy in a monk's habit.

Describing his movements in Lithuania, the pretender mentioned he had stayed with Ostrozhskii, then with Gavriel Khoiskii in Goshcha, and finally went to Wisznewecki in Brachin, where the latter took down the pretender's story in 1603. It is noteworthy that Varlaam, Grigorii's traveling companion, enumerates the same places and dates: Grishka turned up at Wisznewecki's estate in Brachin after he had been in Ostrog and Goshcha. Pierling, the first to note this striking coincidence, considered it unassailable proof that Otrepev and the First False Dmitrii were one and the same person, and in fact the accounts of the pretender and Varlaam are so close in giving times and places as to exclude chance correspondence, and a concert between them is also ruled out for Varlaam could not have known of the secret report Wisznewecki sent to the king nor could the pretender foresee what Varlaam would write after his death.

Besides the *Confession,* material he wrote himself provides important data for assessing the pretender's personality. Two scholars, J.A. Baudouin de Courtenay and S.L. Ptashitskii, made a paleographical analysis of a letter the pretender wrote to the pope and established a paradoxical fact. Dmitrii possessed a cultivated literary style but made serious grammatical errors, leading inevitably to the conclusion that he was simply copying a text the Jesuits had composed for him. Graphological analysis of the letter has demonstrated that the False Dmitrii was a Great Russian who knew Polish poorly while writing Russian freely. His handwriting was remarkably refined and displayed characteristics associated with the style of writing favored in Moscow chanceries. This is a further factor conducive to equating the False Dmitrii with Otrepev. The fact that Grigorii wrote a fine hand was the reason the patriarch personally had chosen him for his chancellery to copy books. In Russia literary skills were not uncommon, but calligraphy was rare among literate people. To write an elegant script was then incomparably more important in identifying an individual than it is today. Otrepev had chafed under the confining life of a monk he had been forced to adopt and the pretender continued to harbor hostile feelings derived from his former involuntary status. In conversations with Jesuits he was never able to restrain his anger and irritation whenever the talk touched upon monastic life.

Analysis of the biographical information available concerning Otrepev and the self-proclaimed heir to the throne shows that many significant details in them correspond. Otrepev disappeared while proceeding from Lithuania to Ostrog, Goshcha and Brachin, and False Dmitrii first appeared along the same route at the same time. The itinerant monk was transformed into the heir during this part of his journey and a number of persons witnessed the metamorphosis. Naively claiming he had taken leave of Grishka before the latter was proclaimed heir, Varlaam stated Otrepev studied with Protestants in Goshcha, where he spent the winter with Prince Yanush Ostrozhskii. The prince confirmed this in a personal letter of 1604, saying he had known Dmitrii for some years, the latter had spent considerable time in his father's monastery in Derman, and (clearly in Goshcha) then had gone over to the Anabaptists. The prince's letter shows that Varlaam had not told the truth; Prince Yanush knew Otrepev only as the heir Dmitrii while he was in Goshcha and even earlier in Derman.

Apparently when still in the Pechora monastery in Kiev Otrepev tried to pass himself off as Dmitrii. The registers of the Military Records Bureau contain a curious notation that when Otrepev became seriously ill he revealed he was the heir to the Pechora abbot: "And I got about as a probationer; I am not yet a monk; I am in flight, hiding from Tsar Boris . . . ." The Pechora abbot, in Varlaam's words, showed Otrepev and his associates the door: "Four of you came; four of you go!"

Otrepev seems often to have performed this same clumsy maneuver and the Pechora monastery was not the only place in which he pretended to be ill: Russian chronicles note that Grigorii was also sick at Wisznewecki's estate. In his *Confession* he revealed his royal origins to a priest, but Wisznewecki's report to the king makes no mention of this episode. No matter what he did the adventurer's efforts to curry support among the Orthodox clergy in Lithuania met with nothing but failure; he had been ignominiously dismissed from the Pechora monastery in Kiev, and it was no better in Ostrog or

Goshcha. Not fond of recalling this period, in his *Confession* to
Wisznewecki the pretender vaguely noted in passing that when he
sought refuge with Ostrozhskii and Khoiskii he spent his time with
them "in silence."

The Jesuits described the affair differently. They claimed that
when the pretender asked Ostrozhskii for help the latter supposedly
ordered his guards to throw him out. Doffing his monastic garb the
pretender was destitute and had to work in Lord Khoiskii's kitchen.
This was the lowest ebb in Otrepev's fortunes. Grigorii was a kitchen
helper and had lost all his former protectors at once, but he did not
despair. Fate's heavy blows might ruin anyone but Otrepev, for he
soon found powerful new patrons among the Polish and Lithuanian
magnates. The first was Adam Wisznewecki, who provided Otrepev
with proper attire and had him conveyed in a carriage attended by
his own bodyguards.

The king and his chief officers, including Chancellor Lew Sapieha,
became interested in Wisznewecki's intrigue. The chancellor had in
his service a slave named Petrushka, a fugitive from Muscovy of
Livonian origin, who had been brought as a prisoner to Moscow when
he was only a year old. Secretly fostering the intrigue Sapieha announced that his servant, who was now graced with the name of
Yurii Petrovskii, had been well acquainted with the heir Dmitrii in
Uglich, but when he met the pretender Petrushka did not know what
to say until to save the situation Otrepev declared he recognized his
former servitor and questioned him with aplomb. The slave then proceeded to recognize the heir by characteristic tokens: he had a wart
near his nose and his arms were unequal in length. Such features of
Otrepev as these had obviously been described to the slave earlier by
those setting the stage.

Sapieha had rendered the pretender a priceless service and the
way now lay open for him to acquire the patronage of Jerzy Mniszech;
one of the latter's slaves also acknowledged Otrepev as the heir Dmitrii. Such were the principal figures in Lithuania who declared that
Otrepev was of royal origin. They were joined by the Khripunov
brothers, renegade members of the gentry who had fled from Moscow to Lithuania in the first half of 1603. Varlaam had named the
entire group of individuals who recognized the heir abroad, only forgetting the adventurer's first two confederates, Misail and himself . . . .
It is hard to imagine that the pretender's naive tales and the words of
the witnesses around him could have convinced anyone; Wisznewecki
and Mniszech had no doubt they were dealing with a clumsy impostor,

and the change in the adventurer's fortunes did not occur until a real force rose to support him.

Many indications show that from the outset Otrepev maintained an interest in the Zaporozhian cossacks. Stepan, a man from Yaroslavl who kept an icon shop in Kiev, deposed that while still a monk Grishka used to frequent his place of business in the company of cossacks, and an Elder Benedikt saw Otrepev, after he had renounced monastic life, with a unit of the Dnieper cossacks. Grishka was eating meat with them (clearly at a time of fasting, which is what elicited the elder's condemnation) and proclaiming himself the heir Dmitrii.

To visit the Zaporozhians was why Otrepev secretly left Goshcha. Varlaam wrote that after spending the winter there Grigorii disappeared from the place in early spring. It is striking that the defrocked monk negotiated with Protestants both in Goshcha and among the Zaporozhians, at whose headquarters he was honorably enrolled in the company commanded by Officer Gerasim Evangelik. The cossacks were in turmoil. The turbulent Zaporozhian freebooters were preparing to attack the tsar of Moscow. The Military Service Register for 1602-1603, recently discovered, shows that in the first half of 1603 Godunov sent gentry to Belaia on the frontier to calm them and the local chronicler asserts this was precisely the time when barriers were erected on the Lithuanian frontier in two border areas.

Reports concerning a cossack attack started circulating at the time the self-proclaimed heir was said to have appeared at their headquarters, where the revolutionary army that subsequently marched with the pretender on Moscow began to form in 1603. The cossacks enthusiastically stockpiled weapons and recruited followers. Disturbed by the extent of the military preparations the Zaporozhians were making, the Polish king issued a special rescript on December 12, 1603 forbidding the sale of weapons to the cossacks, but they simply ignored his fulminations.

Couriers from the Don approached the newly appeared heir. The Don army was ready to march against Moscow. The country of serfs was reaping the fruits of its policy of constraining the free cossacks. The pretender sent his standard, a red banner with a black eagle, to the Don, and his emissaries devised a treaty of alliance with the cossack army. With the borderlands in ferment numerous rebel units penetrated deep into Russia and the Godunov dynasty seemed about to fall. Otrepev sensed that the developing situation portended splendid opportunities for him, because cossacks, runaway slaves, and enserfed peasants hoped the heir Dmitrii would help them throw off the hated regime of serfdom Godunov had fastened on the country. Otrepev had a chance to lead a broad popular revolt.

A few historians have contended it was an unknown cossack who pretended to be Dmitrii, but if that had been the case what would have prevented such a person from fleeing into the steppe after the setbacks the cossack forces experienced at Kiev and Ostrog? The facts do not support this hypothesis. The actual False Dmitrii-Otrepev, of gentry origin and background, trusted neither the turbulent free cossacks nor the humble peasants who came to his camp. The pretender had managed to become a cossack chieftain and leader of a popular movement but he preferred to come to terms with Russia's enemies.

Chapter Thirteen

DISASTER

Three years of famine and devastation had made the people apathetic and signs of fatigue multiplied everywhere. The fighting capacity of the gentry levy declined and Russia experienced a number of military defeats. Tsar Boris tried to strengthen Russia's position in the northern Caucasus, where he sent Ivan Buturlin, one of his best commanders, but after a few initial successes Circassians and Turks destroyed the Russian force of 7,000 men.

A truce concluded with Poland in 1600 did not bring security to the western frontier. King Sigismund III, planning to undertake a great eastward expansion, vigorously supported False Dmitrii and made a secret covenant with him. In exchange for vague promises the pretender agreed to hand the fertile Chernigov-Seversk region over to Poland and promised to surrender Novgorod and Pskov to the Mniszech family, his immediate patron. False Dmitrii was carelessly carving up Russia to satisfy his creditors, but his deceitful actions failed to produce the benefits he hoped for. Discerning politicians in the Rzeczpospolita, including Zamojski, strongly opposed war with Russia, and the king failed to live up to his undertakings; no Polish army participated in False Dmitrii's campaign. Otrepev assembled under his banner some 2,000 mercenaries, consisting of a diverse rabble and bandits anxious for plunder. This force was too small to intervene effectively in Russia, but the invasion was supported by the Don cossack army.

Although the tsar's commanders, who had large numbers at their
disposal to oppose the pretender, acted sluggishly and indecisively
the interventionists soon came to realize they had badly miscalcu-
lated. Defeated at Novgorod-Seversk most of the mercenaries abandoned the pretender's camp and left the country. Jerzy Mniszech, the
pretender's destined father-in-law and commander-in-chief, followed
them. The invasion had failed, but the armed support the Poles provided enabled False Dmitrii to remain in Russia during the first critical months until a wave of popular revolt engulfed the whole southern
frontier.

When Boris first learned a pretender had appeared in Poland,
making no effort to conceal his feelings, he told the boyars openly
that they were responsible and had contrived this in order to over-
throw him. It thus seems incomprehensible that he would later entrust these same boyars with an army and dispatch them to do battle
with the pretender, but reasons for his action may be found. The
famine had intensified social conflicts and massive rebellion and a
cossack revolt along the frontier from the Don to the Yaik rivers
posed deadly danger for the feudal state. These popular movements
threatened to crush the incipient serf regime, which had come into
existence but was not yet consolidated. Under the circumstances the
feudal groups in power had little choice but to rally round the dynasty
in order to protect their own interests. The mass of the gentry reacted
cautiously to the self-proclaimed cossack ruler and only a few low-
ranking officers went over to him. More often mutinous cossacks and
townspeople would surrender fortresses to the pretender and hand
their commanders over to him.

Otrepev, now riding the crest of a popular movement, tried to act
like a cossack hetman and national champion, but the former boyar
servitor and defrocked monk had no real understanding of the genuine
concerns of the people. The universal revolt against Godunov was
rooted in an instinctive protest by the oppressed people, but they
were incapable of finding leaders and formulating goals. This was
exactly why the adventurer, who had appeared at such an opportune
time, was able to utilize the movement for his personal advantage.

Deserted by most of his mercenaries, Otrepev hastily organized an
army composed of the cossacks, fusiliers, and townspeople who were
constantly flocking to him and a witness, Jacques Margeret, said the
pretender had armed and enrolled peasants. This army was completely
defeated by the tsar's forces in a battle near Dobrynichi on January
21, 1605. If the commanders had initiated a vigorous pursuit they
might have been able to arrest the pretender or expel him from the

тъсмр̃ти .

влаженсакъземлⷩтон . ноужⷶ
томвлⷶⷶⷶⷶтестоⷶⷶⷶⷶⷶⷶⷶⷶⷶⷶⷶⷶⷶⷶⷶ
ⷶⷶⷶⷶⷶⷶⷶⷶⷶⷶ ⷶⷶⷶⷶⷶⷶⷶⷶⷶⷶⷶⷶⷶ . ⷶⷶⷶⷶⷶⷶⷶⷶⷶⷶⷶ
ⷶⷶⷶⷶⷶⷶⷶⷶⷶⷶⷶⷶⷶⷶⷶⷶⷶⷶⷶⷶ . ⷶⷶⷶⷶⷶⷶⷶ

Harvest

country, but they procrastinated and failed to move. The boyars were not betraying Boris. They had to operate among a hostile populace in revolt against the institution of serfdom; therefore, False Dmitrii's authority soon again was acknowledged in many southern fortresses, and cossack detachments threatened the royal army's communications. The protracted campaign had exhausted the army; members of gentry units took matters into their own hands and scattered to their homes. It took the commanders nearly six months to take Kromy, the headquarters of Hetman Korela and the Don cossacks; in Platonov's picturesque phrase the fate of the dynasty was decided at the burning walls of the fortress.

Discerning the growing disaffection among his subjects the tsar was anxious to discover their secret thoughts, and this led the authorities to urge slaves and indentured persons to inform against their masters in an effort to penetrate the feudatories' private domain. At the end of his reign Ivan the Terrible had promulgated a special rescript forbidding slaves to inform on their lords, but Boris now elevated slaves who had turned informer to gentry status and assigned them service-tenure estates, and in the square in front of the petitions chancellery the authorities publicly offered rewards for information. After Boris died False Dmitrii issued a specific law confiscating the estates belonging to these new gentry members who formerly had been slaves, most of whom had appeared in Godunov's time. Contemporaries claimed the denunciations made by slaves were a source of great disturbance in the realm.

However, the main cause of the turbulence remained the policy of enserfment the government was following, and Boris had to pay for it. He was surrounded by disarray and treachery. Agitation in favor of False Dmitrii was spreading everywhere like a plague and Boris' weakness made him cruel. After the affair of Khlopko, the rebel leader, in 1603 torture and execution became daily occurrences and rebellious slaves, townspeople and peasants could expect no mercy. Marshalling all its resources to save itself from popular wrath, the serf government lashed out savagely at the lower orders, not the gentry. The authorities fully understood the danger as mobs of humble peasants turned rebel and made their way to the pretender's camp. As a punishment for what was termed brigandage the Komaritskii district endured measures of exceptional brutality. Men were hanged by their feet, singed and shot at with arrows; women and children were drowned, and the survivors were sold as slaves. Semen Godunov, who had succeeded Dmitrii Ivanovich Godunov, was now head of the

Agriculture

secret police and he had so perfected his system of investigation that
foreigners were not exaggerating unduly when they said several spies
had been assigned to each Muscovite.

Formerly active and energetic, at the end of his life Boris grew
increasingly remote from affairs. He rarely left the palace and ceased
to receive petitions or hear complaints. The circle of men who had
supported him all his life with advice and assistance was swiftly growing smaller. The tsar had become seriously ill and his physical and
mental condition was rapidly deteriorating. A superstitious man, Boris
long had dabbled in black arts and his inclination was transformed
into a passion when luck at last deserted him. Finding no support
among his closest associates the tsar turned to diviners. A Polish dip-
lomat in Moscow wrote that Boris was devoted to prophecy and
would do nothing without first consulting soothsayers; he listened to
their advice, relied on their skills, and obeyed them. In despair after
the string of misfortunes he had sustained the tsar lost confidence in
himself and, it seems, his judgment as well. Foreseeing his end was
near Boris pondered painfully whether he might anticipate salvation
in a future life and consulted theologians and Elder Elena, a holy
fool celebrated in Moscow, to resolve his doubts. Forty years after
he died Daritsa, a witch, officially testified that fortune-telling had
been practiced at Boris' court. Terrified of the pretender, Boris sent
several covert assassins to his camp and later had Dmitrii's mother
brought to Moscow in hopes of learning from her whether the heir
was indeed alive or had perished long ago. On April 13, 1605 in the
Kremlin palace Boris died suddenly. It was rumored that overcome
with fear he had taken poison, but this was merely idle talk. Jacques
Margeret, who was with the tsar in the palace, deposed that he had
died of an apoplectic stroke.[1]

Shortly before his death Boris had decided to entrust command
of the armies to his favorite commander, Petr Basmanov, who had
distinguished himself in the first campaign against the pretender. This
young officer, who was not of noble origin, was supposed to save the
dynasty but later events showed that Boris had made a monumental
miscalculation. A son of Ivan's notorious favorite in the oprichnina
[Aleksei Basmanov—ed.] Petr had been intent on his own career and
did not properly understand what this honor entailed. Forced to
reckon with the institution of precedence Boris formally named as
army chief Boyar Prince Mikhail Katyrev-Rostovskii, who owed his
entire career to the new tsar, and designated Petr Basmanov his
adjutant. After a meteoric rise in the oprichnina the Basmanov family

had long ago virtually died out and Petr faced formidable opposition to any bid he might make to restore the dignity its members had once enjoyed. When he arrived at headquarters Boris was already dead, and Basmanov sharply protested because Boyar Andrei Teliatevskii had been assigned to him. He considered this an affront to his precedence rank.

Loss of family honor affected the untried commander-in-chief much more than the precarious military position. In the presence of the boyars Petr declared that Semen Godunov had made him a slave to Teliatevskii, the former's father-in-law, but he preferred death to such disgrace. Unable to control his feelings, on entering headquarters the young commander "wept for an hour lying on a table."[2] The precedence quarrel with the father-in-law of the all-powerful Semen Godunov sent Basmanov into the ranks of the opposition that had long been forming in the field army. The greatest discontent was voiced by gentry from Riazan and Seversk, most of whose members had forsworn their oath to Fedor Godunov. Members of the prominent gentry family of Liapunov in Riazan were active among the disaffected conspirators. In Godunov's time they had often been punished for taking part in disorders in Moscow and illegally selling weapons to the Don cossacks. Now they initiated secret negotiations with the cossacks they were besieging in Kromy.

As soon as the conspirators created a disturbance, Commanders Basmanov and the Golitsyn brothers joined them. At a signal the Don cossacks made a sortie from Kromy and attacked the royal camp while the conspirators simultaneously burst into the command post in the middle of the camp and seized Commander Ivan Godunov. The ensuing panic made it impossible for the loyal commanders, Prince Mikhail Katyrev-Rostovskii and Teliatevskii, to organize resistance and they fled. Most of the gentry levy did not support the conspirators but the men of Novgorod and Pskov, who made up the largest contingent in the army, showed little enthusiasm to fight for the Godunov cause. For three days remnants of their units, heading north, passed through Moscow. Fedor Godunov's government could not carry out a new mobilization and its military support crumbled away.

Although Moscow had displayed no reluctance to take an oath to Fedor Godunov, because the treasury had distributed vast sums ostensibly to pray for Boris' soul but actually to ensure calm, disturbances were increasing daily. The nobility at once profited from the interregnum to get rid of the dynasty under which it chafed. Recalled from the front Fedor Mstislavskii behaved so equivocally that Semen Godunov ordered him secretly executed, but the attempt failed. Deprived of the support of the gentry levy the Godunov family lost control of the capital. The boyar council and the people secured a decree of general amnesty and many persons Boris had disgraced and banished returned to Moscow, the most formidable of whom was Bogdan Belskii.

False Dmitrii, slowly proceeding the while toward Moscow, sent couriers ahead with letters addressed to the populace. When rumors spread that the true tsar was on his way, Moscow was in ferment; some prepared to fight and others made ready to welcome Ivan's son. In terror Fedor Godunov, his mother, and their loyal boyars shut themselves up in the Kremlin and strengthened the guard. These military measures were designed to cow the inhabitants, for the rulers as witnesses observed were more afraid of their own people than the enemy or Dmitrii's partisans.[3] On June 1 Gavrila Pushkin and Naum Pleshcheev, False Dmitrii's legates, reached Red Village, a prosperous trading suburb of Moscow, and their arrival was the signal for the revolt that had long been brewing. The residents of Red Village marched on Moscow, where the populace joined them. The crowd swept aside the guards, poured into Kitaigorod, and crammed Red Square. The Godunov faction sent fusiliers against the mob but they were powerless to deal with it. From the Place of Execution, Gavrila Pushkin read a conciliatory proclamation from the pretender which promised many favors to the people of Moscow, "from boyars to commons."[4]

The members of the Godunov family might have remained under siege in the Kremlin, as Boris had done more than once, but their opponents made sure the gate leading into the fortress was kept open. Boyars mingled openly and covertly with the people, agitating against Fedor Borisovich. Dmitrii's former guardian, Bogdan Belskii, took advantage of the situation to settle old scores. He swore to the people he had saved Ivan's son and with his words the mob threw off all restraint. Bursting into the Kremlin the people began razing Godunov's palaces. The revolt also enabled the lower orders to vent their spleen: townspeople destroyed the residences of many persons of substance and traders who had profited from the famine. After thus entering the Kremlin, Belskii tried to rule in Dmitrii's name but the pretender considered him too menacing a figure. The deposed queen was Belskii's sister and Otrepev could not trust him to execute members of Boris' family. Belskii had to make way for Boyar Vasilii Golitsyn, whom the pretender dispatched to the capital.

False Dmitrii procrastinated, delaying his entry into Moscow until he had removed every obstacle from his path. His representatives arrested Patriarch Iov and sent him in disgrace to a monastery. Although the Moscow rising had shown how inconsequential Boris' appointee was and had deprived him of all authority, Iov was removed not only because of his devotion to the Godunov cause but because Otrepev had another reason for concern. As a deacon he had served the patriarch, who knew him well. After Iov was dismissed Prince Vasilii Golitsyn entered the Godunov family residence with fusiliers and smothered Boris' son and heir Fedor, and his mother. Nor did the boyars leave Boris undisturbed: they disinterred his corpse from the cathedral of the Archangel and buried it with the remains of his wife and son in a remote cemetery outside the city.

During Boris Godunov's reign Russia experienced marked changes. Ivan's *de facto* successor expanded and confirmed privileges for the gentry. The institution of serfdom was established. The laws abrogating the rights of St. George's Day won Boris the support of feudal landlords, but the lower orders rose against him. The fall of the Godunov dynasty was the prelude to a massive peasant war that would shake the feudal state to its very foundations.

NOTES

EDITOR'S INTRODUCTION

1. V.I. Koretskii, *Formirovanie krepostnogo prava i pervaia krest'ianskaia voina v Rossii* (Moscow, 1975) has stated flatly (p. 79) that the nonjuridical school of thought on this central issue has become a thing of the past. For the literature on this complex topic see Richard Hellie (also a member of the juridical school), *Enserfment and Military Change in Muscovy* (Chicago, 1971), pp. 1-18.

2. D.S. Likhachev, *Chelovek v literature Drevnei Rusi* (Moscow, 1970, pp. 12-15) has observed that not until Ivan the Terrible and Boris Godunov appear on the scene is it possible to distinguish the individual personality of one ruler of Russia from another in the sources.

3. The impression conveyed by *Vremennik Ivana Timofeeva*, which Professor Skrynnikov frequently cites, and the *Povest'ot prezhnykh let o nachale tsarstvuiushchego grada Moskvy*, attributed to Prince I.M. Katyrev-Rostovskii.

4. Gerard Grevenbruch, *Tragoedia Moscovitica, sive de vita et morte Demetrii, qui nuper apud Ruthenos imperium tenuit, narratio*, Cologne, 1608.

5. *Io. Inno. Petricii Historia Moscovitica*, Cracow, 1641.

6. Anon., "Narratio succincta de adversa et prospera fortuna Demetrii moderni Moschoviae ducis," in B. von Wickmann, ed., *Sammlung bisher noch ungedruckter kleiner Schriften zur ältern Geschichte und Kenntniss des russischen Reichs* (Berlin, 1820), pp. 401-422. This work was known since its appearance in 1661.

7. M.M. Shcherbatov, *Istoriia rossiiskaia* (Spb., 1790), pp. 290-301.

8. In his work, the modern *locus classicus* on the establishment of the patriarchate in Russia, A.Ya. Shpakov, *Gosudarstvo i tserkov' v ikh vzaimnykh otnosheniiakh v Moskovskom gosudarstve* (Odessa, 1912, pp. 56-60), tenders this horrendous bill of particulars. Shpakov was one of the first revisionist historians of Boris' administration, whose ideas Platonov subsequently amplified.

9. N.M. Karamzin, *Istoriia gosudarstva rossiiskogo*, Vols. 9 and 10, (Spb., 1852), (Vol. 10), pp. 120-132.

10. A.S. Pushkin, *Boris Godunov*. See Note 1, Chapter 1.

11. I.I. Polosin, "Uglicheskoe sledstvennoe delo," in the collection of his essays *Sotsial'no-politicheskaia istoriia Rossii XVI-nachala XVII v.* (Moscow, 1963), pp. 218-245.

12. S.M. Soloviev, *Istoriia Rossii s drevneishikh vremen*. Book 4, Vols. 7-8 (Moscow, 1960), pp. 313-425.

13. V.O. Kliuchevskii, *A History of Russia*. Trans. by C.J. Hogarth. Vol. III (New York, 1960), pp. 17-31.

14. E.A. Belov, "O smerti tsarevicha Dimitriia," *Zhurnal Ministerstva narodnogo prosveshcheniia*, 168 (1873), pp. 1-44, 279-320.

15. N.I. Kostomarov, "O sledstvennom dele po povodu ubieniia tsarevicha Dimitriia," *Sobranie sochinenii*, 5 (1904), pp. 451-465.

16. A sign that Platonov was interested in the Uglich commission report may be found in the fact that he encouraged his associate A.I. Tiumenev to publish "Peresmotr izvestii o smerti tsarevicha Dimitriia" (*Zhurnal Ministerstva narodnogo prosveshcheniia*, 15-n.s. (1908), pp. 93-135, 323-359) which supported and substantially improved upon Belov's position. Platonov's own biography of Boris appeared in Prague in 1921. It is available as *Boris Godunov, Tsar of Russia*, trans. by L. Rex Pyles, with an introductory essay, *S.F. Platonov: Eminence and Obscurity*, by John T. Alexander (Gulf Breeze, Fla., Academic International Press, 1972). Platonov succinctly restated his views about Boris in *The Time of Troubles* (Trans. by John T. Alexander, Lawrence, Kan., 1970, pp. 51-78). A bibliographical essay the translator appended to this work contains a useful comprehensive source list, mostly in English, with an appraisal of the studies cited in it. See Chapter 5, Note 11.

17. S.F. Platonov, *Ivan the Terrible*. Trans. by Joseph L. Wieczynski. With *In Search of Ivan the Terrible*, by Richard Hellie (Gulf Breeze, Fla., Academic International Press, 1974).

18. Le P. Pierling, S.J., *La Russie et le Saint-Siège*, Vol. III (Paris, 1901), pp. 12-50.

19. K. Waliszewski, *La crise revolutionnaire 1584-1614* (2nd ed., Paris, 1906), pp. 39-59.

20. Stephen Graham, *Boris Godunov*, New Haven, 1933. The book has an intriguingly elliptical preface by George Vernadsky.

21. A.M. Nikolaieff, "Boris Godunov and the Ouglich Tragedy," *Russian Review*, 9 4 (1950), pp. 275-285.

22. George Vernadsky, "The Death of the Tsarevich Dimitry, a Reconsideration of the Case," *Oxford Slavonic Papers*, 5 (1954), pp. 1-19.

23. George Vernadsky, *The Tsardom of Muscovy 1547-1682*, Part 1 (New Haven, 1969), pp. 184-229.

24. Constantin de Grunwald, *La vraie histoire de Boris Godunov*, Paris, 1961.

25. Ian Grey, *Boris Godunov, the Tragic Tsar*, London, 1973.

26. Philip L. Barbour, *Dimitry Called the Pretender, Tsar and Great Prince of All Russia, 1605-1606*, Boston, 1966.

AUTHOR'S INTRODUCTION

1. V.O. Kliuchevskii, *Sochineniia*, Vol. III (Moscow, 1957), p. 24.

CHAPTER 1

1. An English translation of A.S. Pushkin's play, *Boris Godunov*, by Alfred Hayes is found in Avraham Yarmolinsky, ed., *The Poems, Prose and Plays of Alexander Pushkin* (2nd ed., New York, 1964, pp. 333-411. See p. 337) (ed.).

2. Ivan I (1304-1341), nicknamed Kalita (Moneybags), a grandson of Alexander Nevskii, was considered the founder of the dynasty that ruled Moscovy down to Fedor's death. He became grand prince of Vladimir and Moscow in 1325, when the Tatars controlled Russia and severely punished attempts to

resist their authority. Ivan Kalita carefully avoided provoking the Tatars and actually cooperated with them on occasion, so that his principality remained relatively free of Tatar raids. Kalita even used Tatar detachments to subjugate adjacent Russian princes. This was the beginning of the process known as "the gathering of the Russian lands" under Moscow's aegis, which Kalita's successors continued, employing a variety of means, until the process was relatively complete after Vasilii III acquired suzerainty over Pskov in 1510 (ed.).

3. The Mongol-Tatar forces that devastated and conquered Russia under their leader Batu-khan in the mid-thirteenth century were known as the Golden Horde. Their capital was Sarai, on the lower Volga, where Russian princes had to go in order to obtain a *yarlyk,* or patent of authority, from the khans. In time the Horde fragmented and its components engaged in civil war; under Moscow's leadership Russia defeated them and finally renounced the Golden Horde's suzerainty. Ivan IV conquered the Tatar enclaves of Kazan and Astrakhan in the 1550s, but the Tatars in the Crimea remained a constant threat to Moscow during Boris Godunov's time and until considerably later (ed.).

4. S.B. Veselovskii, *Issledovaniia po istorii klassa sluzhilykh zemlevladel'-tsev* (Moscow, 1969), pp. 162-168.

5. Besides crown and church, members of the hereditary nobility possessed much of the land (and the peasants who worked it) in the grand duchy of Muscovy. Their estates, which might be scattered in a patchwork throughout the realm, were known as *votchiny.* To meet increasing demands for military service, and in time to strengthen the position of the grand prince the practice arose for the crown to assign land to other elements of society in return for military service. Such lands were held on service-tenure (pomestia) and their number steadily increased, especially during Ivan IV's time. The status of the peasants, whose labor was essential to work these lands, was in flux, and Professor Skrynnikov shows how Boris Godunov finally decided the issue in favor of landowners and landholders, thereby greatly contributing to the establishment of serfdom in Russia (ed.).

6. In 1570 Tsar Ivan suddenly led the oprichnina army in an attack on Novgorod, an action accompanied by arbitrary violence, terror, and loss of life, which was one of the most brutal and capricious incidents of the oprichnina years. Professor Skrynnikov, in his article "Oprichnyi razgrom Novgoroda," in N.E. Nosov, *et al.,* eds., *Krest'ianstvo i klassovaia bor'ba v feodal'noi Rossii* (Leningrad, 1967, pp. 157-171), has argued plausibly that the Lithuanian secret service took advantage of the continuing existence of separatist tendencies in Novgorod to stage an ingenious provocation that caused Ivan to suspect the city's loyalty and aroused him to use troops against his own people that might have been directed against Poland at this point in the Livonian war (ed.).

7. Aleksei Fedorovich Adashev, a wealthy member of the gentry from the Kolomna region, attracted Ivan's attention in the early 1550s, when the tsar was in a reforming mood. Enjoying a reputation for piety and incorruptibility, Adashev first worked in the petitions chancery and later moved to the treasury, an important office, where he was responsible for a variety of reforms in the

areas of landholding, finance, and military service which to some degree advanced the gentry at the expense of the nobility. Adashev joined forces with the priest Silvester, who had acquired an ascendancy over the young tsar; the two men were the chief figures at court until 1560, when Ivan began to chafe under their tutelage and believe they were circumscribing his autocratic power. Their fall was swift and dramatic. Ivan banished Silvester to a remote monastery, and Adashev, who had opposed the Livonian war because he favored a strong line against the Crimean Tatars, was assigned a subordinate command in Livonia, where he died in 1561. Ivan subsequently conducted reprisals against his family (ed.).

8. R.G. Skrynnikov, *Rossiia posle oprichniny* (Leningrad, 1975), p. 11.

9. *Istoricheskii arkhiv*, 4 (1949), pp. 30-37. See G. Kotoshikhin, *O Rossii v tsarstvovanie Alekseia Mikhailovicha* (Spb., 1906), p. 24.

10. This is Ivan Ivanovich, the tsar's elder son and heir, born in 1554. Aleksandrovskaia Sloboda, a village sixty miles from Moscow located in thick woods, was a place in which Ivan felt secure from the boyar conspiracies he believed were forming against him. Spending increasing amounts of time there, he turned the village into an armed camp and a headquarters from which he conducted government affairs. It contained torture chambers where suspects might be interrogated, and the equivalent of a monastery where Ivan and other leaders of the oprichnina could play monk in their spare time (ed.).

11. *Vremennik Ivana Timofeeva* (hereafter VIT) (Moscow, 1951), p. 56.

12. *Chteniia v Imperatorskom obshchestve istorii i drevnostei rossiiskikh pri Moskovskom universitete* (hereafter ChIOIDR), 3 (1911), p. 28.

13. ChIOIDR, 1 (1897), pp. 6-7.

14. The concept of dishonor was highly developed since it was related to the vital question of precedence, which determined a man's position in society. It could be, and frequently was, an actionable matter to be decided by the courts, especially if the litigants were prominent individuals (ed.).

15. *Tsentral'nyi gosudarstvennyi arkhiv drevnikh aktov* (hereafter TsGADA) [the main repository of material on early Russian history, located in Moscow], Fond 181, No. 141, leaf 91.

16. The Englishman, Sir Jerome Horsey, is an essential primary source for this period. He recorded impressions of the almost twenty years (1573-1591) he spent in Russia, where he formed connections in high places and was in a position to provide information of value. However, his commercial activity was not always above reproach; his narrative tends to be self-serving and must be approached with caution. Professor Skrynnikov cites a Russian translation of Horsey found in ChIOIDR, 2 (1907); a good annotated edition is Lloyd E. Berry and Robert O. Crummey, eds., *Rude and Barbarous Kingdom. Russia in the Accounts of Sixteenth-Century English Voyagers* (Madison, 1968), pp. 249-369 (ed.).

17. *Haus-, Hof- und Staatsarchiv*, Russland I, Fascicule 3 (hereafter HHS), Folios 62-64, Vienna.

18. This is the first reference to Dmitrii of Uglich who figures so prominently in this narrative (ed.).

CHAPTER 2

1. *Scriptores rerum polonicarum* (hereafter SRP), Vol. 8 (Cracow, 1885), p. 174.

2. *Materialy po istorii SSSR XV-XVII vv.* (hereafter MIS), 2 (1955), p. 87.

3. The Cap of Monomakh was named in honor of Vladimir Vsevolodovich Monomakh, grand prince of Kiev 1113-1125, who earned an enviable reputation as a warrior in Russia's interest. It was used to crown subsequent sovereigns, as can be seen in the present instance, although its design was most likely modeled on headgear worn by Tatar princes (ed.).

4. Giles Fletcher (1546-1611), an English scholar, jurist and politician, was sent by Queen Elizabeth to renegotiate the status of the Muscovy Company. His mission was unsuccessful and he found himself with time on his hands, which he employed in culling firsthand information about Russia. He too ranks as a primary historical source, in some ways more important than Horsey for he was a more sober and responsible observer. Professor Skrynnikov cites Fletcher in a Russian translation, *O gosudarstve russkom* (Spb., 1906). There are three good modern editions: Lloyd E. Berry, ed., *The English Works of Giles Fletcher, the Elder* (Madison, 1963); Albert J. Shmidt, ed., *Of the Russe Commonwealth* (Ithaca, 1966), and a facsimile edition by Richard Pipes and John V.A. Fine, Jr., eds., *Of the Russe Commonwealth, 1591* (Cambridge, Mass., 1966). Berry and Crummey, *Rude and Barbarous Kingdom . . .* (pp.87-246) have supplied the text with a good introduction and careful notes (ed.).

5. Fletcher, pp. 152-153.

6. Antonio Possevino was sent to mediate the Livonian war and deserves credit for ending the conflict at the Truce of Zapol'skii Yam in 1582. He was a discerning and discriminating observer of Muscovy, where he came in contact with highly placed people, including the tsar with whom he held three disputations on religion in the hope of persuading Ivan to submit the Orthodox to the Pope. His observations about Russia are available in Hugh F. Graham, ed. and trans., *The Moscovia of Antonio Possevino, S.J.* (Pittsburgh, 1977), (ed.).

7. VIT, p. 178.

8. *Skazaniia Avraamiia Palitsyna* (hereafter SAP) (Moscow, 1955), p. 104.

9. *Dopolnenie k aktam istoricheskim,* Vol. II (Spb., 1846), p. 194.

10. Gedimin was grand prince of Lithuania from 1316 to 1341. Spurred by the need to resist the Knights of the Cross he organized the country into a powerful military and political confederation which came to include territory that had been part of the Kievan state. Russian language and customs became influential there. In time descendants of the house of Gedimin were accorded the same honor and rank in Muscovy as descendants of the house of Rurik. After Lithuania affiliated with Poland and its leaders became hostile to Russia, Muscovite grand princes were delighted to welcome Lithuanian nobles who defected. Prince Mstislavskii was a scion of one such family (ed.).

11. N.G. Ustrialov, ed., *Skazaniia inostrantsev o Dmitrii Samozvantse,* Vol. III (Spb., 1832), p. 256.

12. ChIOIDR, 2 (1907), pp. 52-53.

13. *Historica Russiae monumenta,* Vol. II (Spb., 1841), pp. 2-3.
14. TsGADA, Fond Solovetskogo monastyria No. 211, opus 1, No. 3, leaves 8-8 ob.
15. SRP, Vol. 18, p. 422.
16. TsGADA, Fond 79 (Snosheniia Rossii s Pol'shei), Book 16, leaf 141.
17. *Ibid.,* Book 17, leaf 143.
18. A.N. Popov, *Izbornik slavianskikh i russkikh sochinenii i statei, vnesennykh v Khronografy* (Moscow, 1869), p. 187.
19. SRP, Vol. 18, p. 424.
20. TsGADA, Fond 79, Book 15, leaf 629 ob.
21. HHS, Folio 63. Photocopy of a document in the Vienna archives.
22. *Archiwum główne akt dawnych w Warszawie. Archiwum Radziwiłłów,* Vol. V, N 11223. I am very grateful to B.N. Floria for bringing to my attention texts of letters by S. Pac, L. Sapieha, and A. Barakovskii.
23. TsGADA, Fond 79, Book 18, leaf 123 ob.
24. HHS, Folio 63.

CHAPTER 3

1. The Russian equivalent of "queen" is *tsaritsa.* The city named in Irina's honor is now Volgograd, formerly Stalingrad (ed.).
2. Richard Chancellor's arrival in Moscow in 1553 led to rapid growth of trade between the two countries, to their mutual advantage. Russia needed England's manufacturing expertise, while England valued raw materials imported from Russia. The Muscovy Company, composed of English traders working in Russia, was established. Tsar Ivan, who in general looked with favor upon England, granted the company exemption from taxes. The areas where the English operated were included in the oprichnina, thereby indicating that economic factors were important in creating Ivan's personal appanage. Desire for expanding trade with the West was one of the root causes of the Livonian war (ed.).
3. Fletcher, p. 123.
4. *Gosudarstvennaia Publichnaia Biblioteka im. M.E. Saltykova-Shchedrina* (hereafter GPB), sobranie Ermitazhnoe, d. 390, leaf 733.
5. *Biblioteka polskiej akademii nauk w Korniku,* N 1539/13.
6. *Biblioteka polskiej akademii nauk w Krakowie,* Rkp. Jag. bibl., N 1136. B.N. Floria was the first to discover these reports in the Polish archive.
7. Yu. Tolstoi, *Pervye 40 let snoshenii mezhdu Rossiei i Angliei* (hereafter PMR) (Spb., 1875), p. 286.
8. HHS, Folio 63.
9. ChIOIDR, 2 (1907), p. 61.
10. GPB, sobranie Kirillo-Belozerskogo monastyria, No. 78/1317, leaves 69-69 ob.
11. A.P. Barsukov, *Rod Sheremetevykh,* Vol. II (Spb., 1882), pp. 8-9.
12. HHS, Kart. 4, Folio 97.
13. Prince Vladimir Andreevich, Ivan's cousin, was forced to commit suicide in 1569 because the tsar feared the boyars would coalesce around him. He also

slew members of Vladimir's family but spared a daughter, Mariia. He later quixotically married her off to Duke Magnus of Denmark, the man Ivan once intended to make heir to the Russian throne and did establish as the puppet king of the parts of Livonia under Russian control. Magnus achieved no success, but the tenuous connection Mariia Staritskaia had with the royal house worried Godunov. He employed Horsey, his agent, to entice Mariia back to Russia with a promise she would not be harassed, but then proceeded to immure her in a nunnery (ed.).

14. Fletcher, p. 127.
15. TsGADA, Fond 79, Book 22, leaf 29.

CHAPTER 4

1. *Russkaia istoricheskaia biblioteka* (hereafter RIB), 13 (1909), p. 928.
2. A.Ya. Shpakov, *Gosudarstvo i tserkov v ikh vzaimnykh otnosheniiakh v Moskovskom gosudarstve* (hereafter GMG) (Odessa, 1912), p. 140.
3. *Vestnik Evropy,* 19 (1820), pp. 22-23.
4. GMG, p. 109.
5. *Vestnik Evropy,* 19 (1820), p. 74.
6. F. Ternovskii, *Izuchenie vizantiiskoi istorii i ee tendentsioznoe prilozhenie k Drevnei Rusi,* Kiev, 1875.
7. E.F. Shmurlo, *Rossiia i Italiia,* Vol. II, Part I (Spb., 1908), p. 167.
8. Ternovskii, *op. cit.,* p. 72.
9. GMG, pp. 117-118.
10. Ternovskii, *op. cit.,* p. 72.
11. GMG, p. 120.
12. *Ibid.,* p. 156.
13. The Apollinarian heresy, as the term is used here, was a broad rubric under which were comprehended various Christological views associated with Monophysitism (ed.).
14. *Sobranie gosudarstvennykh gramot i dogovorov* (hereafter SGGD), Part II (Moscow, 1819), p. 93.

CHAPTER 5

1. *Pskovskie letopisi,* Vol. II (Moscow, 1955), p. 264.
2. Rugodiv was the original name of Narva, the port town on the Baltic Russia had expended so much unsuccessful effort to control (ed.).
3. *Razriadnaia kniga 1475-1598 gg.* (Moscow, 1966), p. 427.
4. *Ibid.,* p. 443.
5. GPB, sobranie Ermitazhnoe, d. 390, leaf 768.
6. MIS, p. 93.
7. The year after they sacked Moscow the Tatars appeared in large force, bent on subjugating Muscovy. A combined oprichnina and zemshchina army encountered them at the village of Molody south of Moscow and decisively defeated them. This event influenced Tsar Ivan to decide to abolish the oprichnina (ed.).

8. The Battle of Kulikovo Field in 1380 had great significance. Led by Moscow, whose grand prince was Dmitrii Donskoi, a combined Russian force inflicted a defeat on the Tatars. It did not matter that the following year the Tatars sacked and burned Moscow and formal submission to their yoke was maintained for another century; the enormous psychological impact of the victory at Kulikovo confirmed Moscow's preeminence in Russia (ed.).

9. RIB, p. 1283.

10. B.N. Floria, *Russko-Pol'skie otnosheniia i baltiiskii vopros v kontse XVI-nachale XVII v.* (Moscow, 1973), pp. 61-62.

11. S.F. Platonov, *Boris Godunov* (Prague, 1921), p. 54. (This study is available as S.F. Platonov, *Boris Godunov. Tsar of Russia.* Ed. and trans. by L. Rex Pyles, Gulf Breeze, Florida: Academic International Press, 1974 (ed.).

12. The term "Wild Field" was used to designate the steppeland contested between Russia and the Crimean Tatars. The latter's ceaseless raids forced Russia to construct a series of fortresses to protect the interior from them. Over a long period of time natural disasters and repression at the center had led doughtier peasants and other individuals to move to the periphery, an action of which the government informally approved for it helped in the defense against the Tatars. This was the origin of the cossacks, and the life they were obliged to lead fostered the development of a fiercely independent spirit among them. However, as later chapters in this book demonstrate, when serfdom became a burning issue the government attempted to restrict peasant movement into the Wild Field, with unfortunate consequences for the entire country (ed.).

13. The cossacks undertook their expedition beyond the Urals at a highly inauspicious time. Defeated by the Rzeczpospolita, Russia's armies were still fighting the Swedes in the Baltic area, as well as groups revolting in the Volga region and the Kazan district. As soon as Ivan IV learned of Ermak's advance he sent the Stroganov family a threatening directive to recall the "headmen-thieves" immediately and not allow them to provoke the Siberian khan in the future. Ermak's success did encourage the Muscovite authorities to dispatch 500 fusiliers to Siberia, but these forces were not enough to assure victory. Surprised in ambush Ermak perished with hundreds of cossacks, and hunger and sickness inflicted heavy losses on the fusilier detachment. The survivors had to return to Russia.

CHAPTER 6

1. Cf. *Boris Godunov,* p. 370. This translation is by the editor.

2. SGGD, Part II, pp. 300, 311. Why was the official version so quickly altered? Political calculations motivated the change. The people had dealt with the False Dmitrii but disturbances in Moscow had not subsided. The capital was awash in rumors detrimental to the new tsar, Vasilii Shuiskii. Everyone was claiming that miracles were occurring by the corpse of Royal Tsar Dmitrii. Flames leapt from the ground near his body, which had been thrown into a pit and covered with earth but suddenly turned up in a different cemetery. In an

effort to stop these damaging rumors Vasilii disinterred the pretender's corpse, cremated it, and scattered the ashes to the winds. None of this proving efficacious, Tsar Vasilii decided to invoke the miraculous aid of the true Dmitrii in order to scotch the miracles of the False Dmitrii. On his orders the corpse of the Uglich heir was exhumed, brought to Moscow, and placed on exhibition. Early in June, 1606 the church began spreading rumors concerning miracles the body of the pious heir reputedly had performed, but no matter how much it desired to accommodate the tsar the church could not canonize Dmitrii, because he had committed suicide. Church law regarded suicide, even if involuntary, as a mortal sin. While still a contender for the throne Shuiskii had advanced one version of Dmitrii's suicide; when he became tsar he had to dissociate himself from that version.

3. *Ibid.*, pp. 311-312.

4. RIB, p. 767.

5. V.K. Klein, ed., *Uglicheskoe sledstvennoe delo o smerti tsarevicha Dmitriia, 15 Maia 1591 g.* (hereafter USD), Part II (Moscow, 1913), pp. 3, 7, 16, 40, 48.

6. Rumor eventually charged that the "accursed beldame" Vasilisa was in secret contact with Godunov and the assassins he had dispatched, but it was not Boris who had sent Volokhova to Uglich. For many years as one of Ivan IV's chamberlains she had been in charge of the wardrobe in the royal bedroom and enjoyed the suspicious tsar's full confidence. When Ivan died Vasilisa took service with his widow. In Uglich she married her daughter to Nikita Kachalov, nephew of Secretary Mikhail Bitiagovskii. The queen detested him, and so Mariia never forgave her, especially as the two had formerly been close. The Volokhov family's fate was tightly entwined with that of the Bitiagovskii family and Kachalov. The queen's version of the heir's murder implicated only this family group.

7. USD, p. 40.

8. USD, pp. 17, 37.

9. USD, pp. 10, 45-46, 49-50.

10. USD, pp. 48.

11. USD, p. 20.

12. USD, p. 49.

13. USD, p. 13.

14. USD, p. 28.

15. USD, p. 14.

16. USD, p. 26.

17. The court appearance of the peasant Denis, charged with removing nuts from the bolts that held railroad tracks together to use as sinkers, is a humorous example of mutual incomprehensibility. Professor Skrynnikov refers to A.P. Chekhov, "Zloumyshlennik," *Sochineniia*, Vol. IV (Moscow, 1976), pp. 84-87. An English translation: Robert Payne, ed., *The Image of Chekhov (Forty Stories by Anton Chekhov in the Order in Which They were Written)* (New York, 1969), pp. 78-83 (ed.).

18. USD, pp. 11, 15, 40, 46.

19. USD, p. 47. On May 22 Metropolitan Gelvasii conducted service and buried Dmitrii in the church to which his body was conveyed after his fateful outing. Since the commission would not allow the boy's clothing to be changed he was still attired in what he had worn on the walk—caftan with a belt, undershirt, and red boots. Tradition holds that his mother never left his side the entire eight days his body lay in the church.

20. HHS, Folios 74-78.

21. *Uchenye zapiski instituta istorii RANION,* 4 (1929), p. 70.

22. TsGADA, Fond 79, Book 21, leaves 206-206 ob.; Book 22, leaf 28.

CHAPTER 7

1. PMR, pp. 286-287, 294, 327.

2. *Pamiatniki diplomaticheskikh snoshenii drevnei Rossii s derzhavami inostrannymi,* 1 (1854), p. 1228.

3. G. Anpilogov, *Novye dokumenty o Rossii kontsa XVI-nachala XVII v.* (hereafter NDR) (Moscow, 1967), pp. 77-78.

4. HHS, Kart. 3, Folio 36.

5. VIT, p. 73.

6. *Pamiatniki diplomaticheskikh i torgovykh snoshenii Moskovskoi Rusi s Persiei,* 1 (1890), p. 296.

7. *Gosudarstvennaia biblioteka im. V.I. Lenina* (hereafter GBL), sobr. Gorsk., No. 16, leaf 434.

CHAPTER 8

1. Charles Langlois (1863-1929), author of numerous scholarly works in the field of French history, was professor of paleography and medieval history at the Sorbonne and director of the national archives. As such, he was well qualified to comment on the issue at hand (ed.).

2. For further detail see Skrynnikov, *op. cit.,* pp. 178-180.

3. D.Ya. Samokvasov, *Arkhivnyi material. Novoootkrytye dokumenty pomestno-votchinnykh uchrezhdenii Moskovskogo gosudarstva,* Vol. II, Part II (Moscow, 1909), p. 450.

4. TsGADA, pomestnyi prikaz, Fond 1209, Book 959, leaf 199.

5. Simeon Bekbulatovich was khan of the Kasimov Tatars, a group that had come under Moscow's control in the fifteenth century. He proved a faithful and uncritical servitor of Ivan, who rewarded him with advancement. He was subsequently baptized and became related to the royal house by marriage. This was the reason why Bogdan Belskii later offered him as a candidate for the throne as a counterpoise to Boris, as Professor Skrynnikov notes in Chapter 9. In 1575, feeling menaced by a new boyar conspiracy, Ivan adopted the ingenious expedient of abdicating a second time and making Simeon grand prince. Occupying this equivocal office Simeon carried out Ivan's orders, which were couched in the form of petitions "Little Ivan of Moscow" submitted to the new grand prince. Well aware that the notion of a Tatar khan ruling Russia was

anathema to his subjects, Ivan knew he could remove Simeon whenever he wished. He did so in 1576 after he concluded the danger to his person had passed. He designated Simeon grand prince of Tver (thereby creating another large appanage), where the latter remained undisturbed during the remainder of Ivan's reign (ed.).

6. V.N. Tatishchev, *Istoriia rossisskaia*, Vol. VII (Leningrad, 1968), p. 373.

7. *Arkheograficheskii ezhegodnik za 1966 g.* (Moscow, 1968), p. 313.

8. ChIOIDR, 2 (1902), p. 359.

9. An inclusive term comprehending the natural disasters that overtook Russia in the late 1560s and early 1570s, causing crop failure, famine and general destitution. The situation was further complicated by Tatar depredations and the activity of the oprichnina. These factors, plus the losses incurred during the final phases of the Livonian war, had weakened Russia seriously by the time Tsar Fedor and Boris Godunov came to power. They influenced the policies analyzed in this chapter (ed.).

10. RIB, 14 (1894), Col. 137.

11. NDR, pp. 307-373.

12. *Arkheograficheskii ezhegodnik za 1966 g.*, p. 318.

CHAPTER 9

1. A more detailed version of the material covered in this chapter is found in R.G. Skrynnikov, "Boris Godunov's Struggle for the Throne," translated and edited by Hugh F. Graham, *Canadian-American Slavic Studies*, 11:3 (1977), pp. 325-353 (ed.).

2. Russian dates at this time were given *anno mundi*. They are obtained by adding 5508 years (the time churchmen calculated God created the earth) to the year *anno domini* (ed.).

3. *Drevniaia rossiiskaia vivliofika* (hereafter DRV), 7 (1788), pp. 111, 116, 118.

4. *Ibid.*, pp. 94, 103.

5. *Ibid.*, p. 38.

6. *Akty, sobrannye v bibliotekakh i arkhivakh rossiiskoi Imperii arkheograficheskoi ekspeditsiei* (hereafter AAE), 2 (1832), p. 19.

7. GPB, sobr. Solovetsk., No. 1184/1294, leaves 4-4 ob. The patriarch and Queen Irina earnestly strove to have the dying Fedor name Godunov his successor (*Cf. Zapiski otdela rukopisei*, GBL, 32 (1971), p. 159, and K. Bussow, *Moskovskaia khronika 1584-1613* (Moscow, 1961), pp. 80-81).

8. *Polnoe sobranie russkikh letopisei* (hereafter PSRL), 14 (1965), p. 49; *Zap.* ORGBL, 19 (1957), p. 174; *Voprosy istorii*, 5 (1971), p. 139.

9. M.N. Tikhomirov, *Rossiiskoe gosudarstvo XV-XVII vv.* (Moscow, 1973), p. 83.

10. ChIOIDR, 1 (1893), pp. 298-299.

11. MIS, p. 108.

12. VIT, p. 24.

13. PSRL, p. 50.

14. ChIOIDR, 1 (1893), pp. 298-299.

15. I. Massa, *Kratkoe izvestie o Moskovii v nachale XVII v.* (Moscow, 1937), p. 47.

16. *Donesenie M. Shilia o poezdke v Moskvu (1598 g.)* (Moscow, 1875), p. 12.

17. PSRL, p. 50.

18. *Russkii arkhiv* (hereafter RA), 11 (1910), pp. 341, 344.

19. *Ibid.*

20. SGGD, Part II, p. 181.

21. Bussow, p. 82; RIB, p. 12.

22. VIT, p. 218.

23. DRV, p. 52; AAE, p. 24.

24. The well-informed secretary described the convocation: "In the morning, just as day was breaking and the sun was beaming his rays on the world, all his (Boris—R.S.) strong-voiced partisans enthusiastically met together . . . carefully inscribed the charter with their signatures . . . and hurried the archpriest himself (Iov—R.S.) to the palace and handed it up," etc. (VIT, pp. 52-53).

25. Donesenie . . . Shilia, pp. 12-13.

26. *Elementa ad fontium editiones,* Vol. IV (Rome, 1961), p. 217.

27. *Zap.* ORGBL, 32 (1971), p. 160.

28. RIB, pp. 14-15. Such well-informed contemporaries as the Trinity-St. Sergius cellarer Avraamii Palitsyn and the author of the *New Chronicle* do not mention pressure brought to bear on the crowd. *Cf.* SAP, p. 103, and PSRL, p. 50.

29. VIT, p. 53.

30. DRV, p. 8.

31. AAE, p. 15.

32. DRV, p. 95.

33. GPB, sobranie Ermitazhnoe, d. 390, leaf 873; GBL, sobr. Gorsk., No. 16, leaf 479.

34. DRV, pp. 107-108.

35. Oblique allusions are found to the fact that the patriarchal chancellery was considering the possibility of carrying out the coronation without participation by leading boyars. The Solovetskii monastery collection has preserved a whole group of documents composed in the patriarch's residence at that time. One of them is a draft variant of a *Procedure for Crowning Boris* that omits any reference to boyars taking part in the ceremony; their tasks would be performed by the patriarch and his bishops (GPB, sobr. Solovetsk., No. 1184/ 1294, leaves 1-9).

36. RA, p. 345.

37. *Razriadnye knigi 1598-1638 gg.* (Moscow, 1974), p. 44.

38. The *Stepennaia kniga,* or Book of Degrees, was an early native attempt to inquire systematically into Russia's past. Compiled between 1560 and 1563 at the initiative of Metropolitan Makarii, it surveyed Russia's history from the time of Vladimir to the end of Ivan IV's reign, glorifying the Muscovite rulers

and emphasizing the divine origin of their autocratic power. The Book of Degrees claimed these monarchs were descended from the Roman emperor Augustus, an idea popular at the time, and stressed their piety so strongly that their portraits sound like saints' lives. The work was influential in the sixteenth and seventeenth centuries (ed.).

39. DRV, p. 116.

40. *Ibid.,* p. 117.

41. AAE, pp. 58-59.

42. *Arkhiv Leningradskogo otdeleniia instituta istorii AN SSSR,* koll. 114, No. III/127, leaf 13.

43. These humbler figures present at the final ratificatory assembly were members of urban complexes composed of merchants, traders, artisan manufacturers, and other elements that had formed around the fortified administrative centers in Russian cities and towns which were known as Kremlins. They were organized along corporate lines, discharging tax responsibilities and fulfilling other government obligations jointly, on a collective, communal rather than an individual basis. This called into existence offices such as those of hundredmen, who were charged with seeing to it that the system functioned properly and the complex they supervised carried out its tasks. Anomalies that had developed in the structure of these entities (known as *posady*) by the late sixteenth century led to Boris' somewhat obscure experiment, the "town edifice" Professor Skrynnikov explores in Chapter 11 (ed.).

CHAPTER 10

1. AAE, pp. 58-59.

2. *Ibid.,* p. 38.

3. GPB, Fond F. Adelunga, Fond 7, No. 193, leaf 37.

4. AAE, p. 38.

5. *Cf. Boris Godunov,* p. 363. This translation is by the editor.

6. AAE, p. 38.

CHAPTER 11

1. The reference to the "quiet Don" will remind Russian readers of Mikhail Sholokov's masterful tale, *Tikhii Don,* in which, significantly, the story tells of opposition cossacks in a later period offered another central government (ed.).

2. The contrast between the names of Boris' new fortress—*Tsarev Borisov*—and the adjacent cossack center—*Razdory,* meaning "quarrels" or "differences"—was provocatively deliberate (ed.).

3. *Letopis zaniatii arkheograficheskoi komissii,* 9 (1893), p. 57.

4. NDR, p. 432.

5. AAE, p. 20.

6. *Ibid.,* p. 23.

7. PSRL, p. 58.

CHAPTER 12

1. RA, p. 41.

2. In this chapter Otrepev has several names. They are: Yurii Bogdanovich (his secular forename and patronymic); Yushka (a diminutive of his secular forename); Grigorii (the name he assumed when he became a monk); Grishka (a diminutive of Grigorii), and finally, of course, Dmitrii (ed.).

3. *Sbornik Imperatorskogo russkogo istoricheskogo obshchestva* (hereafter SIRIO), 137 (1912), p. 176.

4. TsGADA, 3/A, 28, Austria.

5. AAE, pp. 78-79.

6. SIRIO, pp. 247, 319.

7. ChIOIDR, 9 (1847), pp. 3-4.

8. RIB, p. 638.

9. SIRIO, p. 247.

10. RIB, p. 19.

11. SIRIO, pp. 193-194.

12. AAE, p. 143.

13. *Vestnik zapadnoi Rossii,* Vol. II, Book 6 (1866), p. 96 (published in Vilna).

CHAPTER 13

1. *Skazaniia sovremennikov o Dmitrii Samozvantse,* Part I (Spb., 1868), p. 282. (Captain Jacques Margeret's report on his experiences in Russia, *Estate de l'Empire Russe et Grande Duché de Muscovie,* 3rd. ed., Paris, 1821, an authoritative, sober eyewitness account, deserves greater recognition than it has received heretofore [ed.].)

2. GPB, sobranie Ermitazhnoe, d. 390, leaf 999 ob.

3. I. Massa, *op. cit.,* p. 105.

4. S. Belokurov, *Razriadnye zapiski za smutnoe vremia* (Moscow, 1907), p. 5.

Notes are presented approximately as Professor Skrynnikov has given them; certain supplementary material is by the editor.

AUTHOR'S BIBLIOGRAPHY

K.V. Bazilevich, "Boris Godunov v izobrazhenii A.S. Pushkina," *Istoricheskie zapiski*, 1 (1937).

B.D. Grekov, *Krest'iane na Rusi*, Vol. II, Moscow, 1954.

B.N. Floria, *Russko-pol'skie otnosheniia i baltiiskii vopros v kontse XVI-nachale XVII v.*, Moscow, 1973.

V.O. Kliuchevskii, *Kurs lektsii po russkoi istorii: Sochineniia*, Vol. III, Moscow, 1975.

V.I. Koretskii, *Formirovanie krepostnogo prava i pervaia krest'ianskaia voina v Rossii*, Moscow, 1975.

N.I. Kostomarov, *Smutnoe vremia v Moskovskom gosudarstve*, Vol. III, Spb., 1883.

D.S. Likhachev, *Chelovek v literature Drevnei Rusi*, Moscow, 1970.

S.P. Mordovina, "Kharakter dvorianskogo predstavitelstva na zemskom sobore 1598 g.," *Voprosy istorii*, 2 (1971).

P. Pirling, *Dmitrii Samozvanets*, Moscow, 1912.

S.F. Platonov, *Lektsii po russkoi istorii*, Prague, 1915.

– –, *Boris Godunov*, Prague, 1921.

– –, *Ocherki po istorii Smuta v Moskovskom gosudarstve XVI-XVII vv.*, Moscow, 1937.

I.I. Polosin, *Sotsial'no-politicheskaia istoriia Rossii XVI-nachala XVII v.*, Moscow, 1963.

A.M. Sakharov, *Obrazovanie i razvitie edinogo rossiiskogo gosudarstva v XIV-XVII vv.*, Moscow, 1969.

R.G. Skrynnikov, *Rossiia posle oprichniny*, Leningrad, 1975.

– –, "Politicheskaia borba v nachale pravleniia Borisa Godunova," *Istoriia SSSR*, 2 (1975).

– –, "Boris Godunov i tsarevich Dmitrii," in *Issledovaniia po sotsial'no-politicheskoi istorii Rossii*, Leningrad, 1971.

N.A. Smirnov, *Rossiia i Turtsiia v XVI-XVII vv.*, Vol. I, Moscow, 1946.

P.P. Smirnov, *Posadskie liudi i ikh klassovaia bor'ba do serediny XVII v.*, Part I, Moscow and Leningrad, 1947.

S.M. Soloviev, *Istoriia Rossii s drevneishikh vremen* Book IV, Parts 7-8, Moscow, 1960.

M.N. Tikhomirov, *Istoriia Rossii v XVI veke*, Moscow, 1962.

– –, *Rossiiskoe gosudarstvo XV-XVII vv.*, Moscow, 1973.

S.B. Veselovskii, *Issledovaniia po istorii klassa sluzhilykh zemlevladel'tsev*, Moscow, 1969.

INDEX

THE AUTHOR

Ruslan Grigorevich Skrynnikov was born in 1931 in Kutais. His parents, natives of a small Cossack village in the Kuban region of southern Russia and schoolmates there, attended professional schools, his father becoming an hydrological engineer and his mother a chemistry instructor. Lovers of music and literature, the parents named their three children after characters in Pushkin's tales—Liudmila, Ruslan and Ratmir. In the 1930s the family moved to North Russia to help build an electrical plant on the Svir river. The construction crew erected for themselves a large building in Leningrad where Professor Skrynnikov met his future wife and where he lives today.

Returning to Leningrad from the Urals after World War II, he was drawn to physics and mathematics but, to everyone's surprise, began to study history at Leningrad State University where he worked with the noted historians D.S. Likhachev and B.A. Romanov. With their help he found his greatest interest, success and satisfaction in applying new analytical methods to old sources in search of new information of significance for the history of his country. Professor Skrynnikov's most recent success has been the reconstruction of the records of Ermak's sixteenth-century expedition which opened Siberia to Russian influence. Meanwhile, he has continued his portrayal of Old Russian life through a series of scholarly-popular biographies of the leading personalities of that time.

A teacher for practically all of his life and now professor of history at Leningrad State University, where students flock to his lectures, Professor Skrynnikov continues to make many appearances before large public audiences fascinated by the heroes and villains of Old Russia. All these activities leave him little time for his violin, which he played for fifteen years in the university symphonic orchestra, although he still finds time for music with his family and for his film and stamp interests. With his son and daughter, aged twelve and nine, he and his family enjoy the theater and concerts, and frequent visits to historical sites throughout his country.

ACADEMIC INTERNATIONAL PRESS

THE RUSSIAN SERIES

1 S.F. Platonov *History of Russia* Out of print
2 *The Nicky-Sunny Letters, Correspondence of Nicholas and Alexandra, 1914-1917*
3 Ken Shen Weigh *Russo-Chinese Diplomacy, 1689-1914* Out of print
4 Gaston Cahen *Relations of Russia with China . . . 1689-1730* Out of print
5 M.N. Pokrovsky *Brief History of Russia* 2 Volumes
6 M.N. Pokrovsky *History of Russia from Earliest Times . . .* Out of print
7 Robert J. Kerner *Bohemia in the Eighteenth Century*
8 *Memoirs of Prince Adam Czartoryski and His Correspondence with Alexander I* 2v
9 S.F. Platonov *Moscow and the West*
10 S.F. Platonov *Boris Godunov*
11 Boris Nikolajewsky *Aseff the Spy*
12 Francis Dvornik *Les Legendes de Constantin et de Methode vues de Byzance*
13 Francis Dvornik *Les Slaves, Byzance et Rome au XIe Siecle*
14 A. Leroy-Beaulieu *Un Homme d'Etat Russe (Nicolas Miliutine) . . .*
15 Nicholas Berdyaev *Leontiev* (In English)
16 V.O. Kliuchevskii *Istoriia soslovii v Rossii*
17 *Tehran Yalta Potsdam. The Soviet Protocols*
18 *The Chronicle of Novgorod*
19 Paul N. Miliukov *Outlines of Russian Culture* Vol. III (3 vols.)
20 P.A. Zaionchkovskii *The Abolition of Serfdom in Russia*
21 V.V. Vinogradov *Russkii iazyk. Grammaticheskoe uchenie o slove*
22 P.A. Zaionchkovsky *The Russian Autocracy under Alexander III*
23 A.E. Presniakov *Emperor Nicholas I of Russia. The Apogee of Autocracy*
24 V.I. Semevskii *Krestianskii vopros v Rossii v XVIII i pervoi polovine XIX veka*
25 S.S. Oldenburg *Last Tsar! Nicholas II, His Reign and His Russia* 4 volumes
26 Carl von Clausewitz *The Campaign of 1812 in Russia*
27 M.K. Liubavskii *Obrazovanie osnovnoi gosudarstvennoi territorii velikorusskoi narodnosti. Zaselenie i obedinenie tsentra*
28 S.F. Platonov *Ivan the Terrible* Out of print
29 Paul N. Miliukov *Iz istorii russkoi intelligentsii. Sbornik statei i etiudov*
30 A.E. Presniakov *The Tsardom of Muscovy*
31 M. Gorky, J. Stalin et al., *History of the Civil War in Russia* (Revolution) 2 vols.
32 R.G. Skrynnikov *Ivan the Terrible*
33 P.A. Zaionchkovsky *The Russian Autocracy in Crisis, 1878-1882*
34 Joseph T. Fuhrmann *Tsar Alexis. His Reign and His Russia.*
35 R.G. Skrynnikov *Boris Godunov*
43 Nicholas Zernov *Three Russian Prophets: Khomiakov, Dostoevsky, Soloviev*
44 Paul N. Miliukov *The Russian Revolution* 3 vols.
45 Anton I. Denikin *The White Army*
55 M.V. Rodzianko *The Reign of Rasputin—An Empire's Collapse. Memoirs*
56 *The Memoirs of Alexander Iswolsky*

THE CENTRAL AND EAST EUROPEAN SERIES

1 Louis Eisenmann *Le Compromis Austro-Hongrois de 1867*
3 Francis Dvornik *The Making of Central and Eastern Europe* 2nd edition
4 Feodor F. Zigel *Lectures on Slavonic Law*
10 Doros Alastos *Venizelos—Patriot, Statesman, Revolutionary*
20 Paul Teleki *The Evolution of Hungary and its Place in European History*

FORUM ASIATICA

1 M.I. Sladkovsky *China and Japan—Past and Present*

THE ACADEMIC INTERNATIONAL REFERENCE SERIES

The Modern Encyclopedia of Russian and Soviet History 50 vols.
The Modern Encyclopedia of Russian and Soviet Literatures 50 vols.
Soviet Armed Forces Review Annual
USSR Facts & Figures Annual
Military-Naval Encyclopedia of Russia and the Soviet Union 50 vols.
China Facts & Figures Annual

SPECIAL WORKS

S.M. Soloviev *History of Russia* 50 vols.